TRAJECTORY

★★★★★

"If the Tribulation is near, the Rapture of the Church is even closer.
This book is a storm warning!"

– Jan Markell, Founder/Director, Olive Tree Ministries

TRAJECTORY

TRACKING THE APPROACHING

TRIBULATION STORM

TERRY JAMES, GENERAL EDITOR

WITH CONTRIBUTORS

Tim Moore, Alan Franklin, Dr. Thomas R. Horn, Pete Garcia, Dr. David R. Reagan,
Nathan Jones, Jim Fletcher, Thomas J. Hughes, Todd Strandberg, Jeff Kinley, Wilfred J. Hahn,
Jonathan C. Brentner, Mike Gendron, Daymond Duck, Matt Ward, Gary W. Ritter, Bill Salus

DEFENDER

CRANE, MO

TRAJECTORY: Tracking the Approaching Tribulation Storm

Editor: Terry James

Defender Publishing
Crane, MO 65633
© 2021 Thomas Horn

All Rights Reserved. Published 2021.

ISBN: 9781948014588

A CIP catalog record of this book is available from the Library of Congress.

Cover design by Jeffrey Mardis.

All Scripture quoted is from the King James Version unless otherwise noted.

Dedication

This book is dedicated to the memory of Scott Curtis, who was devoted to doing his Lord's work like few others I know—and who was devoted to his friends to the same degree.

He genuinely helped the blind to "see," as I can fully attest.

—Terry James, General Editor

Acknowledgments

My profound thanks to each of the authors of these chapters. I am blessed by their brotherly friendship. Their words are Holy Spirit-influenced, with insightful examination and presentation that light up for readers the clearly defined trajectory for end-times prophetic fulfillment.

To Tom Horn and Defender Publishing, my thanks for seeing in this book a volume that is needed at this prophetic moment so near the time of Christ's return.

My love and gratitude to my daughter in my heart, Angie Peters, and all she means to me personally and in the business of writing and editing books.

To daughter, Dana Neel, my love and appreciation for all she does in keeping me on track in so many ways.

To my loving and extremely patient wife, Margaret, without whom my life would lack the inner light that brightens the darkness—all my love and devotion.

My love to Terry, Jr., Nathan, Kerry, and Jeanie, for being at the heart of my family joy and life's fulfillment.

To Todd Strandberg, my thanks and love for being family-close as well as founder of and partner in our Rapture Ready website.

To our Lord Jesus Christ belongs all love, worship, and devotion. There is no way, truth, or life apart from Him.

—Terry James

I'm afraid this new trajectory in our nation is more than just a trend. It is a seismic shift toward the socialist agenda. If you look closely you can draw the connection.... This is a concerted effort to erase the past. The first step in liquidating a people is to erase its memory, destroy its books, its culture, its history. Then have someone write new books, manufacture a new culture, and before long the nation will forget what it is, and what it was....

The world has been getting smaller with each passing era. Its interconnectedness is greater and its inhabitants more vulnerable to one-world government, given the right conditions. The events of recent years, including the COVID-19 pandemic, have only accelerated the discussion and increased the trajectory of globalism.

—Dr. David Jeremiah
Turning Point Television, 2021

CONTENTS

FOREWORD

WHERE ARE YOU HEADED?

By Tim Moore

Enter through the narrow gate; for the gate is wide and the way
is broad that leads to destruction, and there are many who enter
through it. For the gate is narrow and the way is constricted that
leads to life, and there are few who find it.

MATTHEW 7:13–14[1]

WHERE IS OUR WORLD HEADED? For that matter, where are you headed?

The first question is important to all of us living through this moment
in history and to the generations that will follow us if the Lord stays His
coming. But the second question has eternal ramifications to you personally. The path you are on—leading you inevitably toward a particular
destination—is your trajectory.

This book offers an overview of a number of facets that will describe
our world's condition and the direction we're headed. The signs of the
times it describes provide glaring evidence that we are living in the season
of the Lord's return.

Pathway to an Inevitable Destination

Any expert in ballistics can tell you that analyzing an object's exact trajectory can be challenging under the best of conditions. After an initial impetus propels the object, atmospheric conditions, crosswinds, and unexpected perturbations can cause it to veer off path. Yet, rifle marksmen, artillery soldiers, and rocket scientists alike have long understood that an object's destination can be accurately predicted based on its trajectory.

Similarly, an analysis of the spiritual conditions of a society (or an individual) will reveal where their trajectory will inevitably lead.

Every Christian aspires to progress along the straight and narrow path toward eternal life and our heavenly home. In this life we will encounter headwinds of resistance, crosswinds of cultural confusion, and fiery darts that Satan hurls at us in an attempt to knock us off that path. But the power of Christ and the indwelling presence of the Holy Spirit assure our inevitable destination.

Those who have rejected Jesus Christ as God's Messiah—"the Way, the Truth, and the Life" who embodies His only provision for salvation—have chosen a course that will inevitably lead them to the wide gate and destruction (Matthew 7:13–14).

The World is Hurtling Toward Its Destiny

For many years, prophetic signs foretold in the Word of God have been converging. They bear testimony to the imminence of Jesus' return for His Church. Just as falling barometric pressure readings portend the approach of a hurricane, these signs also warn of the approaching Tribulation storm.

Even secular observers recognize that something is amiss in the world. Our society seems to be coming apart at the seams, and our ordered liberty is quickly giving way to chaos.

What is most shocking is that we have allowed our own culture to be undermined. Slowly at first, but with increasing speed, America's Christian foundations have been willfully rejected. Like a building whose main pillars are blasted away in a controlled implosion, the edifice may remain standing for a few agonizing seconds, but collapse will come suddenly and inevitably.

Until our Bridegroom comes, we are called to serve faithfully wherever we are—and whatever our circumstances.

May this book serve as a "storm warning" to followers of Jesus that strong cultural forces threaten our children and grandchildren. And may it motivate unbelievers to "flee from the wrath to come," and into the loving arms of our Savior.

Godspeed!

Tim Moore

CEO and Senior Evangelist

Lamb & Lion Ministries

SECTION I

PROPHECY'S GREATEST FORECASTER

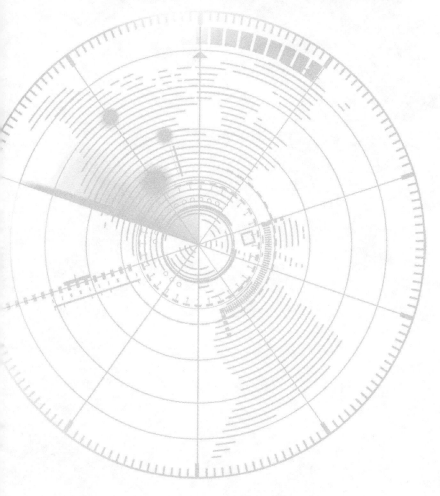

CHAPTER 1

THE REAGAN REPORT: TRIBULATION THRESHOLD SIGNS

by Dr. David R. Reagan

I WAS HAVING LUNCH WITH A FRIEND, and we were discussing the First Coming of Jesus and His fulfillment of Bible prophecy. As we concluded the discussion, my friend leaned forward and said, "Wouldn't it have been great to live in Bible times?"

My response: "Brother, we are living in Bible times! We are being blessed to witness the fulfillment of manifold prophecies made over two thousand years ago concerning the time when Jesus will return to this earth to inaugurate His millennial reign."

I went on to point out that, just as the Church Age began with an overlap period of seventy years during which the nation of Israel existed alongside the Church, we have been in a similar overlap period ever since the reestablishment of Israel in 1948. That first overlap period ended in AD 70 when the Romans destroyed Jerusalem and the Jewish people were taken from their land and dispersed worldwide. Likewise, this second period will end when the Church is taken from this world in the Rapture, which could occur any moment.

I further pointed out something to him that I had gleaned from the writings of Mike Gendron:

The first two thousand years of human history ended when the wrath of God was poured out on sin in the Flood. The second two thousand years ended when the wrath of God was poured out on sin at the Cross. And the third two thousand years will end with God pouring out His wrath on sin during the Tribulation.[2]

We are at the end of the six thousand years referred to in this quote. We are on the very threshold of the Tribulation. We are living on borrowed time.

I concluded the discussion with my friend by pointing him to a prophecy in Hosea that substantiates what is known as the "Millennial Day Theory." This is an ancient theory that dates back to the earliest days of Judaism and was endorsed by several of the earliest Christian writers.[3] The theory states that the Creation narrative of six days of work followed by one day of rest is a pattern for human history and will be manifested in six thousand years of toil and warfare followed by one thousand years of rest and peace.

The passage that seems to confirm this is found in Hosea 5:15–6:3:[4]

I will go away and return to My place until they acknowledge their guilt and seek My face; in their affliction they will earnestly seek Me....

Come, let us return to the LORD. For He has torn us, but He will heal us; He has wounded us, but He will bandage us.

He will revive us after two days; He will raise us up on the third day, that we may live before Him.

This passage indicates that the Messiah will return to Heaven and stay there until the Jewish people begin to seek Him in the midst of their affliction (the Tribulation). This will occur after "two days" (two thousand years), and in response, the Messiah will return to save the Jewish remnant. Then, they will "live before Him" (the Millennium) for a "third day" (one thousand years). This is the exact sequence that is revealed in the book of Revelation and in Zechariah 14.

Knowing the Season

The Bible says we cannot know the *time* of the Lord's return (Matthew 25:13). But, the Scriptures make it equally clear that we can know the *season* of the Lord's return. Consider, for example, this passage from 1 Thessalonians 5:2–6:

> You yourselves know full well that the day of the Lord will come just like a thief in the night.... But you brethren, are not in darkness, that the day should overtake you like a thief; for you are all sons of light and sons of day. We are not of night or darkness; so then let us not sleep as others do, but let us be alert and sober.

This passage asserts that Jesus is coming like "a thief in the night." But then it proceeds to state that this will be true only for the pagan world and not for believers. His return should be no surprise to those who know Him and His Word, for they have the indwelling of the Holy Spirit to give them understanding of what the Bible says about the nature of the times when Jesus will return.

Furthermore, the Scriptures give us signs to watch for that will indicate Jesus is ready to return. The writer of the Hebrew letter referred to these when he proclaimed believers should encourage one another when they *see* the day of judgment drawing near (Hebrews 10:25–27). Jesus also referred to the end-time signs in His Olivet Discourse, given during the last week of His life (Matthew 24 and Luke 21). Speaking of a whole series of indicators He had given His disciples, He said, "When you see all these things, recognize that He [the Son of Man—that is, Jesus] is near, right at the door" (Matthew 24:33).

A Personal Experience

Every time I think of "signs of the times," I am reminded of a great man of God named Elbert Peak. I had the privilege of participating with him in a Bible prophecy conference in Orlando, Florida, in the early 1990s. Mr. Peak was about eighty years old at the time.

He had been assigned the topic, "The Signs of the Times." He began his presentation by observing, "Sixty years ago when I first started preaching, you had to scratch around like a chicken to find one sign of the Lord's soon return." He paused for a moment, then added, "But today there are so many signs I'm no longer looking for them. Instead, I'm listening for a sound—the sound of a trumpet!"

I shouted, "Maranatha!"

The First Sign

At the beginning of the twentieth century, there was not one tangible, measurable sign that indicated we were living in the season of the Lord's return. The first to appear was the Balfour Declaration issued by the British government on November 2, 1917. This was prompted by the fact that, during World War I, the Turks sided with the Germans. Thus, when Germany lost the war, so did the Turks, and the victorious Allies decided to divide up both the German and Turkish empires. The Turkish territories, called the Ottoman Empire, contained the ancient homeland of the Jewish people—an area the Romans had named "Palestine" after the last Jewish revolt in AD 132–135.

In 1917, Palestine included all of modern-day Israel and Jordan. In the scheme the Allies concocted for dividing up German and Turkish territories, Britain was allotted Palestine, and this is what prompted the Balfour Declaration. In that document, Lord Balfour, the British foreign secretary, declared that it was the intention of the British government to establish in Palestine "a national home for the Jewish people."

Evangelical Response to the First Sign

The leading evangelical in England at the time was F. B. Meyer. He immediately recognized the prophetic significance of the Balfour Declaration, for he was well aware the Scriptures prophesy that the Jewish people will be regathered to their homeland in unbelief right before the return of the Messiah (Isaiah 11:11–12).

Meyer sent a letter to the evangelical leaders of England asking them to gather in London in mid-December to discuss the prophetic implications of the Balfour Declaration. In that letter, he stated, "The signs of the times point toward the close of the time of the Gentiles…and the return of Jesus can be expected any moment."[5]

Before Meyer's meeting could be convened, another momentous event occurred on December 11, 1917. On that day, General Edmund Allenby liberated the city of Jerusalem from four hundred years of Turkish rule.

There is no doubt that these events in 1917 marked the beginning of the end of the Church Age, because they led to the worldwide regathering of the Jewish people to their homeland and the reestablishment of their state.

Since 1917

Since the time of the Balfour Declaration, we have witnessed throughout the twentieth century, and continuing to this day, sign after sign pointing to the Lord's soon return. There are so many of these signals today, in fact, that one would have to be either biblically illiterate or spiritually blind not to realize we are living on borrowed time.

I've been searching the Bible for years in an effort to identify all the signs, and it hasn't been an easy task, because there are so many—both in the Old and New Testaments. I've found that the best way to deal with them is to put them in categories, and in doing that, I came up with six categories of end-time signs.

1) Signs of Nature

>...and there will be great earthquakes, and in various places
>plagues and famines; and there will be terrors and great signs from
>heaven. (Luke 21:11)

This category of signs has always been the least respected, even among believers. The mere mention of it usually evokes a sneer accompanied by the words, "Come on, what else is new? There have always been earthquakes and tornados and hurricanes." But those who have this attitude forget that Jesus said the signs would be like "birth pangs" (Matthew 24:8). That means they will increase in frequency and intensity the closer we get to the Lord's return. In other words, there will be more frequent natural disasters as well as more intense ones.

And that is exactly what has been happening worldwide. Natural calamities increased in frequency and intensity throughout the twentieth century and are continuing to occur exponentially, as evidenced by the COVID pandemic.[6]

God is literally shouting from the heavens that our time is short. This is happening because He is about to pour out His wrath in the Tribulation, and He doesn't want anyone to perish. Accordingly, He is issuing a worldwide call for repentance.

2) Signs of Society

>Realize this, that in the last days difficult times will come. For men
>will be lovers of self, lovers of money, boastful, arrogant, revil-
>ers, disobedient to parents, ungrateful, irreconcilable, malicious
>gossips, without selfcontrol, brutal, haters of good, treacherous,
>reckless, conceited, lovers of pleasure rather than lovers of God.
>(2 Timothy 3:1–4)

This passage sounds like a typical evening newscast today! Notice the three things it says people will love in the end times: self, money, and pleasure.

The love of self is humanism, the belief that man can accomplish anything on his own. **The love of money is materialism.** When humanism is your religion, your god will always be money. **The love of pleasure is hedonism,** the lifestyle that is always produced by humanism and materialism.

But God cannot be mocked (Galatians 6:7). He therefore sees to it that when people choose humanism, materialism, and hedonism, the payoff is always nihilism, which is a fancy, philosophical word for "despair."

Need I emphasize that our world is wallowing in despair today? We live in a society plagued by abortion, sexual perversion, domestic violence, child molestation, blasphemy, pornography, alcoholism, drug abuse, and gambling.

Like the days of the judges in the Old Testament, people are doing what is right in their own eyes, and the result is that people are calling evil "good" and good "evil" (Isaiah 5:20).

3) Spiritual Signs

There are more signs in this category than in any other. Many are evil in nature, but there are also some very positive ones.

Negative Spiritual Signs: Concerning the negative signs, a typical passage is the following one found in 2 Timothy 4:3–4:

> The time will come when they [professing Christians] will not endure sound doctrine, but wanting to have their ears tickled, they will accumulate for themselves teachers in accordance to their own desires; and will turn away their ears from the truth, and will turn aside to myths.

Some of the negative spiritual signs specifically prophesied include false christs, cultic groups, heresies, apostasy, skepticism, deception, occultism, and persecution.

The one Jesus mentioned most frequently was false christs and their cultic groups (Matthew 24:5, 11, 24). In fulfillment of these prophecies, we have experienced an explosion of cults since 1850.

Positive Spiritual Signs: Praise God, we're told there will be some very positive spiritual signs in the end times.

- **A great outpouring of the Holy Spirit** (Joel 2:28–29) is the most important positive spiritual sign; it is prophesied in many places. This outpouring began at the dawn of the twentieth century and proved to be one of the greatest spiritual surprises—and blessings—of the century. You see, when that century began, the prevailing viewpoint among both Catholics and Protestants regarding the Holy Spirit was cessationism. This view held that the gifts of the Spirit ceased when the last apostle died. In effect, it was a belief that the Holy Spirit had "retired" in the first century.
- The twentieth century had hardly gotten started when a Holy Spirit revival broke out at a small Bible college in Topeka, Kansas, in 1901. Three years later, a similar Holy Spirit revival swept Wales and began to spread worldwide. Then, in 1906, the Spirit fell with great power on a humble Black preacher in Los Angeles named William J. Seymour. The Azuza Street Revival, as it came to be called, continued for four years and gave birth to the Pentecostal Movement.[7]
- The Bible prophesies two great outpourings of the Spirit and symbolically pictures them as the "early and latter rains" (Joel 2:23), based on the two rainy seasons of Israel. The early rain occurred at Pentecost in the first century when the Church was established. The latter rain was prophesied to occur after the Jewish people had been reestablished in their homeland (Joel 2:18–26).
- The latter rain began with the Pentecostal movement, just as God began to regather the Jews to their homeland in the early 1900s under the visionary leadership of Theodore Herzl. But the rain did not become a downpour until after the reestablishment of the state of Israel in May of 1948, just as prophesied by Joel.

- First came the anointing of Billy Graham's ministry in 1949, followed by the charismatic movement of the 1960s. Today, most of Christianity—whether Pentecostal, charismatic, or traditional—fully recognizes that the ministry of the Holy Spirit is alive and well in Spirit-led worship, the continuing validity of spiritual gifts, the reality of spiritual warfare, and the importance of a Spirit-filled life in winning that warfare.

- **Additional Positive Spiritual Signs:** In addition to the rediscovery of the Holy Spirit, other positive spiritual prophecies are being fulfilled today, like the preaching of the gospel worldwide (Matthew 24:14), the revival of Davidic praise worship (Amos 9:11), and the emergence of Messianic Judaism (Romans 9:27).[8]

Another remarkable positive sign is the understanding of Bible prophecy. You see, the Hebrew prophets often didn't understand the end-time prophecies the Lord gave them. A good example can be found in Daniel 12:8–9, where the prophet complains to the Lord that he doesn't understand the prophecies entrusted to him. The Lord's response is, "Don't worry about it. Just write the prophecies. They have been sealed up until the end times.

In other words, the Bible teaches that many of the end-time prophecies will not be understood until the time comes for them to be fulfilled. That's exactly what's been happening in the past hundred years. Historical developments and scientific inventions are now making it possible for us to understand end-time prophecies that have never been understood before.

Take Israel, for example. All end-time prophecy revolves around that nation. But how could those prophecies be understood when Israel did not exist and there was no prospect that it would ever exist again?

This is the reason Hal Lindsey's book, *The Late Great Planet Earth*, became such a phenomenal bestseller in the 1970s. For the first time, it explained the events prophesied in the book of Revelation in natural terms that people could easily understand.

4) Signs of World Politics

You will be hearing of wars and rumors of wars…for nation will rise against nation, and kingdom against kingdom. (Matthew 24:6–7)

I taught international politics for twenty years before entering full-time ministry, so this area is particularly fascinating to me. The Bible prophesies a specific end-time configuration of world politics. Israel is pictured as being reestablished (Ezekiel 37:21–22) and surrounded by hostile Arab neighbors intent on its destruction (Ezekiel 35:1; 36:7). This, of course, has been the situation in the Middle East since the Israeli Declaration of Independence in May of 1948.

Daniel prophesied that the Roman Empire would be revived (Daniel 2:36–41), something many men—like Charlemagne, Napoleon, and Hitler—tried to do through force. But the prophecy had to await God's timing for its fulfillment, and that came after World War II, with the formation of the European Common Market that has since morphed into the superpower called the European Union.

The Bible pictures a great power located in the land of Magog in the "remote parts of the north." This nation will menace Israel in the end times and will ultimately lead an invasion of Israel together with specified allies, all of which are modern-day Muslim states (Ezekiel 38:1–39:16). Russia, with all its Muslim republics and its Muslim allies, fits this description precisely.

All the nations of the world are prophesied to come together against Israel over the issue of the control of Jerusalem (Zechariah 12:2–3)—a prophecy being fulfilled today.

The magnitude of warfare in the twentieth century is another fulfillment of end-time prophecy related to world politics. The twentieth century was one of unparalleled war. Like birth pangs, the frequency and intensity of war increased exponentially. It is now estimated that more people died in wars during the twentieth century than in all the previous wars throughout recorded human history.

5) Signs of Technology

Men will faint from fear over the expectation of the things that are coming upon the world, for the powers of the heavens will be shaken (Luke 21:26). The development of nuclear weapons seems to be foreshadowed by this prophecy in Luke 21 that speaks of people "fainting from fear" due to the "powers of the heavens being shaken."

The incredible carnage of the seal and trumpet judgments portrayed in chapters 6 and 8 in the book of Revelation indicates the Antichrist will conquer the world through the use of nuclear weapons. We are told a third of the earth will be burned and half of humanity will be killed. Further evidence that this is a nuclear holocaust is found in Revelation 16, where we are told that, at the end of the Tribulation, the survivors will be covered with sores that will not heal (Revelation 16:11).[9]

As I pointed out earlier, many end-time prophecies simply cannot be understood apart from modern technological developments. Consider the prophecy in Revelation 11 about the two witnesses who will call the world to repentance during the first half of the Tribulation. When they are killed by the Antichrist, we are told their bodies will lie in the streets of Jerusalem for three and a half days, and the whole world will look upon them (Revelation 11:9). How could anyone understand such a prophecy before the development of satellite television in the 1960s?

Likewise, how could the Antichrist control all buying and selling worldwide (Revelation 13) without the aid of computer technology? How could the False Prophet create the illusion of giving life to a statue (Revelation 13) without the technology of holograms, virtual reality, and robotics? How could an army of two hundred million come out of the Far East (Revelation 9) before the population explosion that was produced by modern medical technology? How could the gospel be proclaimed to all the world (Matthew 24) before the invention of motion pictures, radio, television, and the Internet? The list goes on and on.[10]

6) Signs of Israel

And it shall come about in that day that I will make Jerusalem a heavy stone for all the peoples; all who lift it will be severely injured. And all the nations of the earth will be gathered against it. (Zechariah 12:3)

The signs that relate to Israel are the most important group of all, because the Jews are God's prophetic clock. What I mean by this is that the Scriptures often tie a prophesied future event with something that will happen to the Jews. We are told to watch the Jews, and when the prophecy concerning them occurs, we can be sure the other prophesied event will also occur.

An example can be found in Luke 21:24, where we read that Jesus prophesied that the Jews would be dispersed from Jerusalem and be led captive among the nations. But then He added that one day they would return to reoccupy Jerusalem, and when this happens, the end-time events will occur that will lead to His return.

There are many prophecies concerning the Jews in the end times, many of which began to be fulfilled in the twentieth century, but there are four key ones. The first is their **worldwide regathering in unbelief** (Isaiah 11:11–12). In 1900, there were only forty thousand Jews in Palestine. By the end of World War II, that number had risen to six hundred thousand. Today, there are more than seven million who have come from all over the world—more than the number of people who died in the Holocaust.

The prophet Jeremiah says twice that when history is completed, the Jewish people will look back and conclude that their worldwide regathering was a greater miracle than their deliverance from Egyptian captivity (Jeremiah 16:14–15 and 23:7–8). We are truly living in momentous times!

The second key prophecy concerning the Jews is a natural consequence of their regathering. It is **the reestablishment of their state**, which occurred on May 14, 1948 (Isaiah 66:7–8).

The third key prophecy is the **reoccupation of Jerusalem**, which occurred on June 7, 1967, during the miraculous Six Day War (Zechariah 8:4–8).

The fourth key prophecy is the one whose fulfillment we are witnessing today—**the refocusing of world politics upon the nation of Israel** (Zechariah 12:2–3). All the nations of the world, including the United States, are coming against Israel over the issue of the control of the nation's capital—the city of Jerusalem. The Vatican wants the city put under its control. The United Nations wants it to be internationalized. The European Union and the United States are demanding it be divided between the Arabs and the Jews. The Arabs want all of it.

Other Prophecies Concerning Israel

In addition to these four key prophecies, there are other prophetic fulfillments in Israel today, such as the reclamation of the land, the revival of the language, the resurgence of the military, and the restoration of biblical Judaism.[11]

Regarding the land, it was prophesied by Moses that a time would come when the Jews would be scattered from their land because of their disobedience to God, and when that happened, the land would become a desolation (Deuteronomy 29:22–28). This became a reality after the Jews were dispersed from their land by the Romans. But Ezekiel prophesied that when the Jews returned, the land would become like the Garden of Eden (Ezekiel 36:34–35)—and it has.

The revival of the language refers to the fact that when the Jews were dispersed worldwide, they stopped speaking Hebrew. The Jews in Europe mixed Hebrew with German and came up with a language called Yiddish. Those in the Mediterranean Basin combined Hebrew with Spanish to produce a language called Ladino. But the prophets of Israel had foretold that, in the end times, the Hebrew language would be revived (Jeremiah 31:23 and Zephaniah 3:9), and it was—by a man named Eliezer Ben Yehuda. That is the language of Israel today.[12]

The resurgence of military strength when the Jews were reestablished in their land was prophesied several times. For example, Zechariah said their military power would be overwhelming—like "a flaming torch among sheaves"—and they would "consume" all the peoples around them (Zechariah 12:6). Need anything be said about the fulfillment of this prophecy? Despite its small size, the nation of Israel is consistently ranked among the top ten military powers in the world.[13]

Another consequence of the worldwide dispersion of the Jews was the replacement of biblical Judaism with rabbinical Judaism. This occurred in response to the destruction of the Temple and the cessation of the biblical sacrifice system. But the prophets affirmed that in the end times a Temple would be rebuilt and the system of sacrifices resumed (Isaiah 2:2–3; Daniel 9:27; 2 Thessalonians 2:4; and Revelation 11:1–2). Today, the Orthodox Jews of Israel have made all the preparations for the resumption of biblical Judaism. The Sanhedrin Council has been reconstituted, the Temple furniture and implements have been constructed, and the priests are being trained. When the opportunity presents itself, the Jews will be able to erect a tent Temple overnight, like the Tabernacle of Moses in the wilderness. They will then proceed to build a permanent Temple over and around the tabernacle.[14]

Summary: CONVERGENCE

And so you have it—six categories of signs, each containing many prophecies concerning the end times, all of which are being fulfilled before our very eyes. Yet, I still haven't identified the most important sign of all. It is an overarching one that applies to all six categories.

What I have in mind is the sign of CONVERGENCE.[15] It refers to the fact that, for the first time in history, ALL the signs have come together. None is missing. We are standing on the threshold of the Tribulation.

Jesus is about to appear in the heavens for His Church. Will you be taken, or will you be left behind to face the Antichrist? The decision is yours. If you want to be prepared, "call on the name of the Lord" by placing your faith in Jesus as your Lord and Savior (Joel 2:32 and Acts 2:21).

Maranatha! (1 Corinthians 16:22)

CHAPTER 2

DELUGE OF DECEPTION

By Terry James

THIS GENERATION IS LIKELY FACING, if not enduring, the last-days flood predicted through the prophet Daniel. Here is the prophecy the angel Gabriel brought to Daniel from the very throne of God:

> And after threescore and two weeks shall Messiah be cut off, but not for himself: and the people of the prince that shall come shall destroy the city and the sanctuary; and the end thereof shall be with a flood, and unto the end of the war desolations are determined. (Daniel 9:26)[16]

That deluge of evil cannot be missed by the Christian who is spiritually attuned to things transpiring minute by minute in our world today. We can already see the flood of Daniel's seventieth week developing. The gush rages through the conduits of our daily lives. Society washes toward the sewer that these end times have created. Culture is becoming more debased and debauched, as is provable by the surge of news assaulting our eyes and ears in a nation-destroying tsunami of wickedness.

Is this all simply imagery I've created to inflame the readers' fear? Or can the issues and events of the moment be sustained as validation of the charge made—that we're on a trajectory for final prophetic fulfillment and we're now seeing the "book of the end" Daniel was told about being opened?

> But thou, O Daniel, shut up the words, and seal the book, even to the time of the end: many shall run to and fro, and knowledge shall be increased. (Daniel 12:4)

Bible prophecy students who believe the pre-Tribulation view of things to come see all that is going on at this moment as setting the stage for the end of the Age of Grace. That is, it all means we're at the very close of the Church Age.

The book given Daniel that was closed up and sealed until the end has now been opened. This generation is experiencing a tremendous increase of knowledge. People are literally running "to and fro" because technological advances make it possible.

Knowledge flowing from that end-times book now opened also enlightens us as to what all this madness occurring around the world means *prophetically*. While many churches in America and around the world have been egregiously silent on Bible prophecy, keeping the people filling the pews ignorant, Heaven seems to have circumvented this great neglect. Here is the way one excellent Bible prophecy teacher put it:

> On August 24, 2020, the president of the Barna Research Group said one in five churches could permanently close within the next eighteen months because of the coronavirus crisis. Church attendance and giving are down, and many pastors will lose their pulpits. My sympathy goes out to these churches and pastors.
>
> But God's Word cannot be silenced. The good news is that some of those pulpits were silent on prophetic matters, and large numbers of their members are tuning in on TV and the Internet

to hear what some of the prophetic preachers of our day are saying. If a pastor does not want to preach the whole Word, God can
close the pastor's church and feed the members through another
venue.[17]

Of course that writer—also a contributor to this book—continues
to be proven right. Many churches closed their doors and haven't opened
fully as of this writing. Thankfully, Internet and satellite broadcast venues
have enabled numerous Bible prophecy teachers to get the true message
out that we're in the last of the last days, and Jesus Christ is preparing to
return to put an end to the insanity taking place in this fallen world of
rebelliousness.

It is obvious that satanic forces are in a rage to shut down many of the
venues that allow the truth about things to come. As a matter of fact, I'm
convinced the cancel culture we observe and hear so much about is the
direct assault upon America aimed at bringing this nation into compliance with the developing globalist blueprint. It is a blueprint drawn up
by hellish forces, and if not for the Restrainer's supernatural influence,
America and the world would have already succumbed to the "wickedness
in high places" forewarned about by the Apostle Paul (Ephesians 6:12).

Jesus Himself, while sitting with His disciples atop the Mount of Olives,
said that the generation immediately preceding His Second Advent would
be plagued by deceivers and great deception. He had earlier expressed
His displeasure with the Judaizers—the pious religionists of the day. He
confronted them directly about their inability to discern that their Messiah was even at that moment confronting their self-deception—denial
that the time of Israel's visitation was upon them. These were, therefore,
deceiving all those who listened to their false teachings.

I wrote the following in our book, *Discerners: Analyzing Converging
Prophetic Signs for the End of Days*:

Jesus looked directly and deeply into the eyes of the pious religionists and elitist-legalists (the Pharisees and Sadducees). His

omniscient, penetrating, piercing, eyes saw into their very souls. These religious zealots and lawyers sought to disprove the claims by His followers that He was sent from God. They wanted Him to immediately perform a private miracle for them, thinking, no doubt, that He would fail, giving them fodder for their attacks against Him.

Jesus, in answer to their probing demands that He show them a sign to prove His Commission from Heaven, said: "When it is evening, ye say, It will be fair weather: for the sky is red. And in the morning, It will be foul weather to day: for the sky is red and lowring. O ye hypocrites, ye can discern the face of the sky; but can ye not discern the signs of the times?" (Matthew 16:2–3).

Jesus then said: "A wicked and adulterous generation seeketh after a sign; and there shall no sign be given unto it, but the sign of the prophet Jonas." And he left them, and departed. (Matthew 16:4).

Today's self-deception—which actually is nothing more or less than unbelief—is as evil in its wicked denial of Jesus Christ as that practiced by the Jewish religious overlords of the people of Israel. The deception seems almost as prevalent within so-called religious circles as it is within every other facet of life.

And the deception is indeed profound.

Economy

For nearly two decades, we've watched the globalists elite take over the most powerful nation ever to exist. Chief among their conquest has been the undoing of America's economic position.

The human minions in the high places who constitute, at least in part, the powers and principalities according to Ephesians 6:12 continue to contrive scams and schemes in order to bring United States monetary matters into their orbit of control. They have the Federal Reserve system firmly in their insidious grip. They control members of Congress in ways that can't be understood, because they control those who are supposed to be the guardians of the public treasury. The minions direct those supposed guardians to never truly investigate the larceny those in the wicked high places perpetrate.

Trillions upon trillions of dollars are printed upon their command, while the nation's taxpayers are told lie after lie about the reasons and methods being employed on the American people's behalf. America must be brought to heel at the feet of the powers that be. The dollar must be manipulated to conform to the globalists' evil purposes. That, wittingly or unwittingly on the human minions' parts, is to bring Satan's Antichrist to power.

COVID-19 is the instrumentality many prophecy observers believe is the purposefully manufactured disease to bring America's economic hegemony into compliance with the globalist blueprint in order to begin the Great Reset that is more and more being front and center as a term that frames what will help soon produce the New World Order. Many are convinced the COVID crisis and all it entails is one of the most heinous deceptions of history. It is poised to bring down the most powerful, materially blessed nation-state to ever exist.

Government

Powers and principalities in high places have to achieve one major accomplishment in order to bring the American economy into compliance with their blueprint: They have to get total control of the American government. Can there be any doubt that this is in process at an astounding level?

The process of dismantling the American way of life is well underway, and was greatly fast-tracked with the presidential election of 2020. It was, in my mind, the greatest example of prophesied deception of our time. The election was stolen, and it took the master of deception at its heart to pull it off.

Every element needed to make it happen was at work—the minions, both human and supernatural (demonic), doing their parts to carry out the luciferian, globalist blueprint.

Government Deep-State operatives at many levels within the State Department, intelligence services, and other bureaucratic enclaves have continued to be complicit in this devilish assault. The mainstream media, at most every level of news and entertainment, has been orchestrated by the maestro of evil in joining the governmental minions to bring about the fraud that was the election of November 3, 2020.

Marxist principles/lies are being employed to once again deceive the masses. Social democracy is the evil being foisted upon we the people. "Social justice" is the masterfully wicked term used to foment racial upheaval—the prophesied ethnic last-days warfare Jesus foretold as recorded in Luke 21:10. America's founding is undergoing a historical rewrite to fit the satanic blueprint narrative that will construct Antichrist's tyrannical government. America, the luciferian lie goes, is an evil empire built upon the murderous enslavement of indigenous people and other nations. The founding fathers were, in this deception narrative, white, tyrannical individuals with hatred of the darker races at their hearts.

Social media adds to the mainstream-media cancel culture to destroy all forms of resistance to the blueprint. Even the most recent former president of the United States was cancelled by Twitter, eliminating his many millions of followers.

Tremendous advances in technology, especially in communications, have made life better in many ways. But that progress has also made it possible to enslave a world of people who are fallen in nature and gullible, thus susceptible, to the wiles of the one who stalks about like a roaring lion seeking to destroy them. The following brings to light the dangers presented by exponentially developing technological advancements.

Consider if we still lived in any of the previous "ages" such as the Industrial Age or even the Computer Age. How could the masses be deceived? Logistically speaking, mankind ability to be deceived was limited to newspapers, the radio, the telegraph, and decade's later limited television and movies. Think about how H. G. Wells' 1938 dramatized *War of the Worlds* broadcast and how people tuning in late actually thought an alien invasion was happening. Think about how everything today is connected to the Internet, from laptops and smart devices to appliances, vehicles, accessories, and even clothes. We live in the Information Age, and we are quickly entering an even greater extension of that with the Internet of Things (IoT).

So, in light of the fact that none of us can definitively see into the future, we have to trust God's Word and heed the various warnings issued by Jesus, Peter, Paul, James, and John as given to them by the Holy Spirit. Therefore, we go with what we know and make the best reasonable explanations that we can. Seeing the world events play out is simply confirmation of what the Bible has already stated as fact.

One thing to consider, though, is that prior to the age of global communications and instant newsfeeds, the whole world could not be deceived. Too many people were disconnected from other parts of the world, so the majority of people would not know what deception was going on regardless of where it happened unless it specifically happened to them. We know (to the best of our ability) that the Beast is the governmental/political system headed by the Antichrist that takes control during the Tribulation (the Seventieth Week of Daniel). We currently live in the "Age of Information" and believe this to be the same age in which our Lord will return for a whole host of reasons.

The Information Age (and the rapidity with which knowledge doubles), is almost entirely reliant upon the ability to process said information through computers and the Internet. However, considering how the then Obama administration's agenda (and now the Democrat platform), along with Silicon Valley technocrats (who control the major media platforms) seem to want to do three things:

1. Blanket the entire US with free 5G Wi-Fi
2. Cement governmental control over who uses it, what they can see
3. and silence, shut down, shadow-ban, block, and deny usage of the Internet for dissenting voices.

This has moved beyond what even honest liberals will concede as free speech. Leftists (globalists/socialists/communists) seek to place the entire planet on the electronic grid for the sole purpose of controlling it with an iron fist. With the use of low-orbiting satellites and taking advantage of the newly freed-up "white space" from television's frequency waves (since we've gone digital), this is a very achievable agenda. The initial plan was called WIMAX, but that fell through to Lightsquared (now Ligado). Regardless of what plan actually succeeds, the plans are in the works to get everyone on board and "on the grid."

Remember a simple idea here, in that no matter what freebies are offered or what promised legislation will fix, increased control is the outcome of whatever plan they put forward. Wi-fi may be offered free, but it will come at the cost of your anonymity.[18]

Power of the Air

The great deception deluging the nation and world shouldn't be surprising. Neither should it surprise that Satan, who is bringing prophecy to fulfillment in these strange times, is at the heart of that delusion and deception.

Let's suppose a fictional, though very possible, scene taking place somewhere in a bar open only for the elite, because everyone else has to be masked and have a vaccination passport—which neither of our fictional characters has:

A couple of elderly former television network news anchors are engaging in ever-recurring conversations while sipping their favorite evening libations.

"Remember how we once ruled the airwaves?" might be one such conversation starter.

"Yeah," the commiserating drinking partner might say. "In the old days, we could say it on the evening news, and by noon the next day, public opinion would begin to come around."

I can imagine a Dan Rather type and some other no-longer-relevant propagandist lamenting as the tonic and gin or bourbon on the rocks burns a liquid trail down their once-golden throats.

"Those were the good old days," one of them shakes his head, blinks, and calls to the bartender for a refill.

"There's no leadership to ever bring those days back," I can imagine the other saying. "Now they all go their separate ways…there are far too many of them to ever come together."

"It almost makes you see the need for the power of dictatorship…for the good of the republic," the Dan Rather type says, taking the first sip from his newly refreshed beverage.

"Yeah. We used to at least have that kind of influence over public opinion…for the good of the republic," the other aging broadcaster puts in.

They must dream happily of when they and their network colleagues had the three-network monopoly. Now, it must be a nightmare that they live through daily. Their personal influence is no more—the power of their profession significantly diminished.

That this is the case is plainly presented in polls taken about how America's people feel about that profession. Always, news media, as being trustworthy in the eyes of the public, ranks very near the bottom of those polls. If there ever was a question about why that ranking is so low, we need only think on the recent past and where we are at present.

It would almost seem that our two aging former anchors need not worry for a second about the ability of the news conglomerate to speak with the power of one. The mainstream news media has coalesced in a way that ABC, CBS, and NBC never could have done when they had, collectively, nearly sole power of the air.

It is true that today's now-fractionalized mainstream news media, as individual news forums, draws infinitesimally small numbers of viewers in comparison to the numbers attracted by the big three networks during the "good old days." But the power exerted by the new collective—the fractionalized mainstream media—is even stronger than that wielded by the big three those years earlier.

The proof is the fanatical cohesion this new media collective has cemented. Before the months leading up to Donald J. Trump's election to the presidency, the new, collective news conglomerate at least presented the pretense of being independent from one another. Following Trump becoming the Republican candidate and up to now, with him long out of office, that agglomeration of news forums has melded as one to destroy Donald Trump and his presidency.

They have, in the process, infected about half of the adult citizenry of America with an insane rage that I've characterized a number of times as a "reprobate mind," the mindset described by the Apostle Paul as recorded in Romans 1:28.

In this sense, the new mainstream news media is far more effective than the big three that pretended to be independent of each other in trying to shape public opinion. The media today is as driven in insane rage as are the left-wing, anti-God public they possess. And possession is what it amounts to, in my estimation.

I can say this because at the black heart of this propagandist cabal is the chief minion of the underworld. This is provable biblically.

Broadcasts—at least as originally conceived and implemented—projected over the airwaves. They were received by antennae of those who tuned in to the news, entertainment programs, and commercials. So, as the broadcast industry was foundational, that method—over the air—was progenitor of this new mainstream media.

This evil cabal—although fractionalized as being individual entities—is totally conjoined in delivering messages their master director wants delivered. That master director is indeed the maestro, who for the time being is allowed to be the infernal minister of propaganda to seduce and delude the rebellious among earth's inhabitants. He is undertaking to do that with massive effort.

Scriptural proof of his temporary right to his position as master of deluding all who will watch and listen follows:

Wherein in time past ye walked according to the course of this world, according to the prince of the power of the air, the spirit that now worketh in the children of disobedience. (Ephesians 2:2)

Be sober, be vigilant; because your adversary the devil, as a roaring lion, walketh about, seeking whom he may devour. (1 Peter 5:8)

Satan is the prince of the power of the air, and he's using that power in a literal way to seek and devour as many as he can. He has, during the last three and a half years, managed to bring into his insane rage nearly half of the adult population of the United States of America, it appears.

But the God of Heaven hasn't left us without defense against this evil prince and his media minions. God's Word tells of this protection for Christians:

Ye are of God, little children, and have overcome them: because greater is he that is in you, than he that is in the world. (1 John 4:4)

So the impression strikes as the depression deepens in thinking on these matters: "You have left out one ingredient to all this seeming madness afflicting the nation and world." Indeed, I've almost left out the most important ingredient when thinking on the insanity raging within our nation and beyond: God's staying hand.

My thinking is America-centric because it is the last bastion of freedom during this fleeting age. Israel is God-guaranteed to be His nation and people forever, so I dwell on the one nation that presently still stands, although precariously, as target for the prince of the power of the air and his minions. America, although it shows every indicator of precipitous decline from which there seems no escape, remains the freest nation on earth. Its economy, already untenable because of debt extrapolated into hundreds of trillions of dollars for future generations, remains intact, despite suffering a complete shutdown due to a largely contrived virus threat. Most of the nation's heartland continues to function and show progress toward a return to a degree of normalcy, despite the most vicious attempts imaginable by globalist diabolists in DC and other capitals of the world to rip American sovereignty and autonomy to shreds.

God continues to restrain the raging efforts to bring down this supernaturally inspired experiment in liberty. America will be here, I'm believing, until that restraint is withdrawn when Christ calls all born-again believers to Himself.

Meantime, it is incumbent to pray fervently that He who sits in Heaven—and obviously has the rebels of planet earth in derision, as in Psalm 2—continues to restrain the satanically enraged evil with His omnipotent, staying hand.

CHAPTER 3

WINDS OF WAR, RUMORS, AND ETHNIC ANARCHY

By Tim Moore

SATAN HAS ALWAYS ENDEAVORED to foil God's plan for mankind.

In the Garden of Eden, he planted seeds of doubt when he asked Eve, "Did God really say?" The resulting Fall left humanity evicted from the Garden, scattered over the earth, and separated from God.

In the millennia since, Satan has sought to undermine all of God's good gifts, morphing them into twisted and unholy facsimiles laced with wickedness and sin. God gave men and women the gift of sex; Satan incited perversion and pornography. God gave men and women relationships with family and friends; Satan convinced humanity to elevate those temporal relationships above our relationship with Him.

In general, Satan's *modus operandi* is to lie, steal, and murder (John 8:44). He does this through deception, often contradicting God and His plan for humanity. Echoing Satan's own desire to be like God, mankind was enticed to assert its own godlikeness. That sinful inclination toward unfettered autonomy from God has caused untold human suffering.

In the end times, Satan will once again deceive humanity to embrace a world leader who controls a one-world government and commands universal worship of himself. We see efforts to promote such a system even now. But until the Antichrist arrives on the scene, Satan will sow discord, leading to increasing wars, rumors of war, and ethnic anarchy.

Wars

War is as old as mankind.

In only the fourth chapter of Genesis, Cain rose up and murdered Abel because he became resentful of Abel's relationship with God. In all the generations that have followed, jealousy, resentment, mistrust, and a never-ending struggle for power have led to almost continual human conflict between individuals and between nations.

That conflict often builds in the shadows of men's hearts, but from time to time it manifests itself in open conflict. For most of human history, the ramifications of such conflict were limited to the destruction individuals or collective armies could inflict with crude weapons and physical strength. That is not to minimize the horror of war in the ancient world. Scores of people died, including combatants and noncombatants alike. Famine and pestilence often followed after wars, and human suffering was widespread. But recent generations have faced the grim prospect of cataclysmic war that is capable of annihilating millions.

From the beginning, most wars resulted as tribes, city-states, and nations clashed. Economic interests were often at the forefront of motivations leading to war. One empire sought to protect its interests or expand its influence; in doing so, it disrupted the status quo relative to another nation and hostilities ensued.

Some wars have been fought for matters of principle. The Trojan War supposedly began over an insult inflicted on the beautiful Helen. Abram went to battle in order to free his kidnapped nephew Lot (Genesis 14:1–16). Wars were fought in the Middle Ages between Catholic and Protestant kings due to their different interpretations of Scripture and their determination to expand their empires. The American Revolutionary War was fought to secure liberty, although exorbitant taxation and an out-of-touch monarch in England were prime instigators as well.

The twentieth century witnessed two world wars. The first began as a clash of empires, and the second started when a resurgent Germany and militaristic Japan began pursuing expansionist aspirations. The latter involved a clash of ideologies—pitting the free Allied nations of the West against the militaristic and maniacal Axis dictators in Germany, Italy, and Japan. The Cold War that raged from 1945 into the early 1990s pitted two great superpowers—and the ideologies they espoused—against one another.

Lately, ideological and religious wars are once again in the fore. Although America is too naïve to acknowledge the truth, Islamic fanatics in places like Afghanistan, Iraq, Iran, Syria, and Africa are behind the conflicts the United States has actively engaged in since 2020. Even the looming threats from China and North Korea are just as ideological as economic in nature.

An Old New Threat

An era of tribal conflict seems to be descending upon the world once again. The tribes are not identified by geographic or familial connectivity, but are based on racial and ethnic identity. The seeds of that kind of conflict are taking root in America as well.

The United States was unusual among nations, because from its founding it included people from disparate national and ethnic backgrounds who simply demonstrated a "yearning to breathe free" (to cite Emma Lazarus' famous poem inscribed on the Statue of Liberty in New York Harbor). Although not always as inclusive as our national psyche would like to think (consider the treatment of Native Americans and various waves of immigrants), we have nonetheless been a melting pot of people from many tribes and nations. That is why German-Americans and Japanese-Americans fought with great distinction during World War II.

Now, well into the twenty-first century, our national motto (*E pluribus unum*—"out of many, one") is under attack as never before. Division threatens to tear our civil society apart at the seams.

Proponents of division have taken a page from Karl Marx and applied his call for revolution in a new and diabolical way. Whereas Marx sought to divide along socioeconomic and class distinctions, the new social warriors want to divide people along racial, ethnic, and sexual identities. Seeking to drive wedges between everyone, they even invent new hierarchies of intersectionality—where an individual's right to be respected or even heard is determined by their claim to a variety of identity markers.

The inevitable offspring of such warped thinking is ever-increasing polarization of people. Sadly, that term is insufficient to describe the chaos that is ensuing. It suggests two extremes of thought, whereas the identity revolutionaries see an unending list of necessary divisions. The multiplicity of gender identities exemplifies this rising entropy.[19] For example, although the Bible clearly speaks of male and female, modern revolutionaries insist that there are hundreds of stops along an ever-expanding spectrum of human genders. Culture drivers like government, Hollywood, and mass media have all jumped on board this crazy train.[20] Some churches and entire denominations are succumbing to this false narrative.

Foretold Dissolution of Society

What is causing such a rapid disintegration of our society? Why is the American experiment in ordered liberty breaking down so quickly? The explanation is more spiritual than cultural.

In Romans 1, the Apostle Paul describes the trajectory of mankind throughout the ages. His observations have become pointedly descriptive of our own day and age. He says that although they know God, unrighteous men do not honor God or give Him thanks. Instead, they engage in futile speculations and their foolish hearts are darkened (Romans 1:21).

As a result, God gives them over to lust and impurity. The explosion of pornography around the world, and in the United States in particular, testifies to the truth of that prophetic word. The sexual revolution began in the 1960s here in America with a call for free love, no-fault divorce, sexual debauchery, and abortion. It has only metastasized into a tidal wave of moral degeneracy. To quote David Reagan, it's as if God said, "You want to live in that kind of filth, I'll let it multiply."[21]

In a further slide into depravity, men deny the truth of God as our Creator—embracing lies and worshiping mere creatures (or themselves). Once again, the just penalty for such foolishness is another "giving over" as God lowers His hedge of protection and allows rampant homosexuality to overwhelm a society. That scourge accelerated in 2003 when the US Supreme Court struck down all sodomy laws and kicked into high gear with its Obergefell decision legalizing same-sex marriage in 2015. And still the sexual revolutionaries were not satisfied, as demonstrated by the gleeful San Francisco Gay Men's Chorus video (released online in the summer of 2021) proclaiming "We're Coming for Your Children!"[22]

In the end, men do not even acknowledge God, so He turns them over to a depraved mind. Solomon's wisdom expressed in Proverbs 29:18 holds true today: "Where there is no vision, the people are unrestrained."[23] In other words, where people do not see truth with clarity and do not have a God-inspired eternal perspective, they are unrestrained. Some translations say they "run amok." We are witnessing the tragedy of an entire society running amok before our very eyes.

Paul and Solomon offer wisdom to those who revere God and His Word. But they also offer prophetic warning to those who reject God and flaunt their rebellion against His declared order. Heeding that wisdom, the pilgrims who settled in America aspired to establish a city on a hill where they could worship the living God freely. Ignoring that warning, our nation has since devolved to not only practice abomination but to promote its practice around the world.

President Barack Obama infamously traveled to Africa and literally wagged his finger at African leaders, telling them to adapt to twenty-first-century sexual mores and specifically embrace homosexuality.[24] President Biden has pledged that abortion will be celebrated at home and funded abroad. Homosexuality, gay marriage, and transgenderism are not just tolerated at home, they are celebrated; soon those abominations will be supported with taxpayer dollars and propagated around the world. And, lest we think it can't get any worse, the extremists who have advocated for unfettered sexual contact between adults and children are pushing to provide children the "autonomy" to engage in illicit sexual relationships.[25]

The demand for unfettered personal autonomy amounts to rebellion against God and His Anointed. The same people who want to cast off the perceived shackles of Western society (which they recognize is based on Judeo-Christian values) direct their greatest resentment at the God who dared to set boundaries on their individual liberty. Harkening to Satan's lie that they can become their own gods, they have no use for the God who actually created the universe and gave them life.

In the midst of our society's great moral confusion, other voices are stirring the pot by promoting conflicts based on race and ethnicity. The advocates of social chaos actually encourage wanton destruction of society because they are determined to reject order and embrace anarchy.

The Ultimate Rejection of Order

A new old threat is emerging—in America and the West in general. Amidst all the other chaos, a growing number of misguided souls have become disciples of Marxism and are propagating its destructive dogmas. To understand the satanic underpinnings of Marxism, consider the man who popularized this ideology and became the hero of socialists around the world.

Karl Marx was a German Jew who came from a family of converted Roman Catholics and Lutherans. Upon his arrival at a public university, Marx came under the tutelage of a theology professor who was an avowed atheist. They soon joined forces to promote atheism through a newly published academic journal and designed various stunts to shock and offend the devote citizens of Trier, Germany.

In short order, Marx developed a fascination with the occult, specifically idolizing Satan himself. He wrote extensively about rejecting Heaven and embracing Hell. Determined to reject all of society's conventions, he became a vile and repulsive character, refusing to bathe or work even to support his own family.

As author Paul Kengor documents in his book, *The Devil and Karl Marx*, Marx's own friends and family feared that he was possessed. His hatred of society in general, religion in particular, and Christianity most of all consumed him. Even Marx alluded to the presence inside him that seemed to control his thoughts and actions.[26]

Marx's stated goal was to tear down the pillars of civilized society. He sought to incite revolution by convincing the proletariat (the working-class people) to rise up against the bourgeoisie (the middle class who support conventional values and control the means of production in a capitalist society). Marx theorized a socialist utopia would emerge from the ensuing anarchy. Clearly, that has not happened in any of the countries where his ideology has been embraced and imposed—always by force.

At its core, Marxist philosophy was built upon critical theory—but the "criticism" he offered was not meant to improve upon the status quo. Marx repeatedly expressed his hatred for his own family and humanity in general. He demanded total annihilation of every social structure, including capital and property, marriage and family, and religion—particularly Christianity. As ideologies go, Marxism seeks to purposely steal, kill, and destroy,[27] demonstrating its satanic origins.

Critical theory taken to its logical extreme still advocates for the destruction of every human institution. Whether something better rises up to replace that which is destroyed is irrelevant. Modern-day anarchists seek to tear down and obliterate simply as a matter of course. And they are multiplying in our midst.

The riots that sprang up in 2020 as racial tensions were fanned into flames by self-serving race-baiters too often gave way to waves of lawlessness and destruction. In many instances, the advocates of anarchy flew in for the occasion. Places like Portland, Oregon, and Minneapolis, Minnesota, had to contend with scores of homegrown and imported anarchists torching property, looting businesses, threatening safety, and flaunting their contempt for the law and its enforcers.

Yet liberal politicians at the national level could not bring themselves to condemn even that level of anarchy and violence. Although the US

Constitution offers guarantees for legal process and equal protection *under the law*, too many of those sworn to uphold that Constitution remained silent, calculating that this domestic crisis could be turned to their own political advantage.

The tragic result of pitting a favored group, ethnicity, or tribe against another has been demonstrated through the Ottoman Turkish slaughter of Armenian Christians, the Nazi Holocaust, the Rwandan genocide, and the Chinese decimation of the Uyghur people. Sadly, those who do not learn from history are prone to repeat the mistakes of the past. Throughout 2020, many American cultural influencers were actually adding fuel to the flames of racial division.

Metastasized Threat

Like a cancer that grows more malignant and life-threatening when left untreated, the coddling of demonic, anarchist ideologies is undermining civil order in our society. Antifa, a group that claims moral superiority as "anti-fascists," regularly incites violence and unrest in major American cities. It is merely one manifestation of this propensity toward lawlessness and destruction. Another Marxist organization that has exploded on the national scene is BLM—Black Lives Matter.

Every Christian should affirm that all lives matter. As the children's Sunday school song rightfully teaches, Jesus loves us all—red and yellow, black and white. We are all precious in His sight. Too often that reality has been lost on those who have suffered injustice. Followers of Christ should always advocate for justice and reject the ungodliness of racism.

Groups such as BLM emerged following highly publicized shootings over the past several years, taking advantage of the emotion and outrage. BLM organizers are avowed Marxists—and they make no apologies about their desire to tear down every institution of society. They express particular animosity toward the traditional family—a vestige of what they consider a racist, Western or "White," Christian patriarchal system.

As Mike Gonzalez and Andrew Olivastro of the Heritage Foundation wrote, BLM's "radical Marxist agenda would supplant the basic building block of society—the family—with the state and destroy the economic system that has lifted more people from poverty than any other. Black lives, and all lives, would be harmed. Theirs is a blueprint for misery, not justice."[28]

BLM's Marxist roots are also evident in the way it embraces critical theory and seeks to tear down and destroy. Supposedly organized to oppose police violence against Blacks (without commenting on the epidemic of Black-on-Black crime), BLM actively supports the most radical aspects of the sexual revolution. With two of its three founding members identifying as "queer," BLM has made promotion of LGBTQ ideologies central to its advocacy.[29] Finally, true to its satanically inspired Marxist roots, BLM consistently condemns Israel but shamelessly defends Palestinian terrorism. In 2021, BLM leaders vocally supported Hamas even as that Palestinian terrorist organization was raining rockets down on Israel.[30]

BLM is by no means the only organized threat emerging within the United States and abroad. What has been unprecedented is the rush by America's social institutions—government, media, corporations, academia (from universities down to the secondary level), and even Christian denominations—to embrace this group and its radical agenda, including critical race theory (CRT).

Although CRT seeks to divide Americans along racial lines, many leading US corporations now pay critical theory advocates to indoctrinate their employees to reject offensive "whiteness." Even my own alma mater, the United States Air Force Academy, recently required its incoming freshmen to undergo training that promotes the Marxist BLM group and its divisive agenda.[31]

Organizations like BLM and agendas like CRT are not healing racial tensions in America; they are multiplying them. As far back as 1996, one reporter referenced the rising racial tension as "short fuses burning on a thousand powder kegs."[32] A generation later, even more fuses have been lit by foolish political and media figures who sow the wind with abandon.

Once again, the determination to oppose racism and right societal wrongs is valid and praiseworthy. But no rational society turns itself over to those who want to tear it down. Perhaps saddest of all, the riots and violence that BLM and Antifa fomented in 2020 destroyed urban neighborhoods that need jobs and investment the most. And still, elected officials, CEOs, and military leaders who ought to know better declared their solidarity with these advocates of mindless destruction.

Impact Overseas

This dithering in the face of lawlessness has real and tragic consequences, both at home and abroad. Far from preserving the peace, it enables the forces of lawlessness. Lacking the vision cited by Solomon or the backbone to respond with authority, American leaders have also failed to promote the rule of law around the world.

For many generations, the United States could call on nations around the world to adhere to the rule of law. It rallied allied nations to condemn Nazi atrocities under the heading of "crimes against humanity." America invested itself in righting wrongs and improving societies around the world. But now, allies and adversaries alike realize that America does not enforce the rule of law at home and is morally bankrupt abroad.

On that note, the 2021 debacle in Afghanistan demonstrated American weakness once again to a watching world. The tragic state of affairs following the Biden administration's disastrous exit from Afghanistan validates renowned Middle East scholar and historian Bernard Lewis' sad observation: "America is harmless as an enemy but treacherous as a friend."

Given the incompetence of the US pullout, much of the world perceived that radical Islam (even the semi-literate Taliban in Afghanistan) is ascending in power. America and the West—ostensibly Christian nations—are seen as declining. Indeed, China immediately began crowing that message around the world.[33]

There is another spiritual dynamic pitting much of the Christian world against America and the West. In several Protestant denominations, Christians in Africa and the Far East are holding the line on biblical orthodoxy against "woke" American advocates of the sexual revolution. The Methodist church would have already pitched over into complete advocacy of homosexual and transgender agendas except for the stalwart resistance of Christians in Africa and elsewhere who still stand on the authority of Scripture. How sad it is that American Christians are abandoning the truths that they once championed.

The Greatest Ethnic Animosity

In spite of rising tribal and ethnic strife, the greatest animosity in the world today is the satanically inspired hatred that has plagued the people of God for four thousand years.

Christians will immediately respond, "But we've only been on the scene for two thousand years." That is true. Yet before men and women responded to the gospel of Jesus Christ and placed their trust in Him, God had set aside a group of people as His own. He chose the Jews, not because they were deserving or special in any worldly sense, but to become both a reservoir for and a conduit of His blessing.

Because God chose the Jews, Satan hated them. In fact, Satan's driving impulse has been to eradicate the Jews—in hopes of preventing God from fulfilling His promises and proving Him to be a liar. So, beginning in Genesis, Satan instigated a series of manipulations and pogroms to undermine and destroy the Jewish people.

That satanic agenda is supported by many allies. Following the establishment of the Church, woefully misguided Christians (or those who thought they were doing the bidding of God) sought to punish the Jews for their rejection of Christ. In recent years, militant Muslims have seen Jews as the intolerable stain on Islamic honor. So, instead of addressing rampant challenges at home and blessing the people in Arab nations with respectable economies and governments, radical Muslim leaders stoke hatred toward the Jews.

Hamas is a perfect example of this sad impact of Satan's manipulation. Hamas has been given millions of dollars to raise the standard of living in

Gaza. Instead of pouring resources into lifting the people of Gaza out of abject poverty, it launches rockets toward Israeli cities and builds tunnels to sneak terrorists into Israeli territory. In May of 2021, Hamas sowed the wind once again with a barrage of rocket attacks on Israel. The inevitable result was another round of destruction and suffering as Israel rightfully defended itself.

What kind of irrationality drives a person or a whole people to act in such a self-destructive manner? Ethnic hatred that spews from the mind of Satan and infects the hearts of those who embrace darkness themselves.

God's-Eye View

It would be easy to become distraught by such a recounting of the trends evident in our world today. Indeed, many people are discouraged, if not despairing. And, to be quite frank, the Bible is clear that the situation will only grow worse.

Jesus said, "Nation will rise up against nation, and kingdom against kingdom" (Matthew 24:7). Greek scholars tell us that the word translated as "nation" in our English versions is actually *ethnos*—meaning "race, tribe, or pagan group."[34] As such, what the Lord warned about is not an increase in warfare between modern nation-states so much as a breakdown of civil order among racial and ethnic groups. We are witnessing that today. Where our nation once shared a common ideology and cultural consensus, there is no center that will hold. This reality was beautifully captured in a poem by William Butler Yeats:

The Second Coming

Turning and turning in the widening gyre
The falcon cannot hear the falconer;
Things fall apart; the centre cannot hold;
Mere anarchy is loosed upon the world,
The blood-dimmed tide is loosed, and everywhere
The ceremony of innocence is drowned;

The best lack all conviction, while the worst
Are full of passionate intensity.
Surely some revelation is at hand;
Surely the Second Coming is at hand.
The Second Coming! Hardly are those words out
When a vast image out of *Spiritus Mundi*
Troubles my sight: somewhere in sands of the desert
A shape with lion body and the head of a man,
A gaze blank and pitiless as the sun,
Is moving its slow thighs, while all about it
Reel shadows of the indignant desert birds.
The darkness drops again; but now I know
That twenty centuries of stony sleep
Were vexed to nightmare by a rocking cradle,
And what rough beast, its hour come round at last,
Slouches towards Bethlehem to be born?[35]

William Butler Yeats wrote those words in 1919. He recognized that anarchy would soon be unleashed upon the world, and that the Antichrist was ready to be revealed—slouching toward Bethlehem in his poetic description.

One hundred years later, things are "falling apart" faster than ever before. But from a God's-eye view, as Jan Markell, director of Olive Tree Ministries, says, "Things are not merely falling apart; they are falling into place." By that, she means that God foretold that all these things must come to pass; then the end will come. Jesus is at the very gates of Heaven and we are living on borrowed time.

Our Blessed Hope

So, should Christians be concerned? Yes and no.

The "yes" regards our determination to be salt and light in a world gone awry. Christians should discern what is happening in the world around us from a biblical worldview. As darkness descends, our light should shine. We must be ambassadors of Jesus Christ and advocates of rationality and truth.

For example, over the past 120 years, Marxist ideology has created more human suffering and led to the worst human genocides in history. Yet, today, our country is being overrun by progressives who proclaim their allegiance to Marxism. Bernie Sanders, a self-described democratic socialist, was once a leading candidate for the Democratic Party's nomination to president of the United States. And other prominent national leaders avidly embrace the policies of Marxist socialism today.

Russia, Cambodia, Venezuela, and every other nation that has attempted to impose Marxist socialism demonstrate that this demonically inspired ideology is contrary to God's plan for mankind. But where Christians are silent, evil creeps in. Right now, it is not just creeping into our society. It is being shoveled into young minds in public schools and universities. It is being pumped into unsuspecting brains plugged in to devices and absorbing whatever entertainment Hollywood cooks up. It is even showing up in the attitudes and thinking of too many who still darken the doors of American churches on a regular basis.

Christians need to push back whenever these godless ideologies are advocated. Prophetic voices from Al Mohler (president of Southern Baptist Theological Seminary) to Moody Church Pastor Erwin Lutzer have recognized: We cannot be silent.[36] We need to identify the rotten fruit of a philosophy that criticizes everything and aims to destroy every institution given to humanity by God Himself. Make no mistake, the proponents of critical theory—whether in theology, humanities, race relations, or politics—are unashamed of their insistence on tearing down Judeo-Christian norms. And the leaders of BLM are avowed Marxists with an LGBTQ and anti-Israel agenda.

But even as we advocate passionately, we must do so lovingly. Indeed, as disciples of the Prince of Peace, we should be known as people of peace. So, following Paul's admonition, "If possible, so far as it depends on you, be at peace with all people" (Romans 12:18). That is why the answer to the question of whether we should be concerned is also, "No." Even as the world inevitably falls into darkness and chaos swirls around us, Christians should never give in to despair or allow the love of Christ to waver in our hearts.

A Personal Challenge to Love

This point was driven home to me in 2020. As I witnessed the anarchy and violence being tolerated and even celebrated in American cities, I became angry. I could claim that my indignation was righteous, but truthfully, I was just mad. I was disappointed in fellow citizens and disgusted by elected leaders who fomented unrest instead of standing in opposition to it.

During that season I turned to Matthew 24 and the Lord challenged me anew. In Matthew 24:12, Jesus warned: "Because of an increase in lawlessness, most people's love will grow cold." Many Christians have interpreted that verse to address the cold-heartedness demonstrated by a world gone awry. But, as Christians witness the rise of lawlessness in our own land—manifested by unprecedented political turmoil, racial tension, unrest, and riots—it is easy for our love to ebb away.

I had long thought that verse applied to the world. As it descends into lawlessness in the end times, I figured that most people's love would grow cold. But the Holy Spirit opened my eyes to realize that the world does not have Christ's love in the first place. While not immune from frustration and deep sadness, only Christians have a wellspring of love that can overcome unprecedented political turmoil, racial tension, unrest, and riots. For the first time, Jesus' words struck me personally.

Do I have the love of Christ for the very people perpetrating violence and acting out their pagan ideology? Does my heart break for them in a way that motivates me to share the gospel of Jesus Christ with them? In other words, do I love them as much as God does? The Bible says He sent His only begotten Son for them—and for undeserving sinners just like me.

Do I love my brothers and sisters in Christ enough to offer them grace if they disagree with me on an issue like COVID precautions and vaccine acceptance? Or, am I so agitated that any digression from my personal opinions elicits a spirit of condemnation and division? Is my faith in Jesus Christ strong enough to overcome the daily discouragement of discerning the world as it is? Finally, will those who observe my actions and attitudes testify as Jesus foretold when He said, "By this all men will know that you are My disciples, if you have love for one another" (John 13:35)?

Looking for the Blessed Hope

In his letter to Titus, Paul cited "the grace of God that has appeared, bringing salvation to all men, instructing us to deny ungodliness and worldly desires and to live sensibly, righteously and godly in the present age, looking for the blessed hope and the appearing of our great God and Savior, Christ Jesus" (Titus 2:11–13).

Paul's encouragement is for all Christians waiting and watching for Jesus Christ. If we are united in watching for Him, the aggravations of this world grow strangely dim (Psalm 123:1). With that perspective, Christian discernment will make us neither an optimist or a pessimist. What do I mean by that?

I believe that Al Mohler, the earlier-mentioned president of Southern Baptist Theological Seminary, captured the right sentiment. In an interview aired on Lamb & Lion Ministries' television program, *Christ in Prophecy*, Dr. Mohler said:

> People will often ask me, "Are you optimistic or pessimistic?" And I say, "Neither. A Christian cannot be either." We know too much about the world to be optimistic, too much about sin. And we know too much about God's purposes to be pessimistic. The Christian mode is not optimism or pessimism, that can wax and wane with our mood. It's hope, and that hope is Christ. Hope has a name: Jesus Christ.
>
> We actually can go to sleep at night with all these concerns so real, and we're not ignoring them, we're not denying them.

We sleep at night because Jesus Christ is Lord, and because He is coming. And because the coming thing is His Kingdom, and the going thing is the kingdoms of this world.

We just need to remind ourselves of that. And yet, Christ has not yet come to claim His Church and to inaugurate His Kingdom in full. So, we are here right now for a purpose. And that purpose is to do what Jesus commanded us to do until He comes.

I pray that you have the assurance of knowing our Blessed Hope and that sense of purpose.

Final Thoughts

It is important to recognize the threats gathering in the rising darkness. Evil forces are swirling around us and tearing our society apart. But we cannot succumb to the wicked spirit of the age that incites war, spreads rumors, stokes ethnic and racial hatred, and even sows division among followers of Jesus Christ. Instead, we must fix our eyes upon Jesus, the author and perfector of our faith (Hebrews 12:2).

As we do so, through the power of the Holy Spirit, the light of Christ will shine in our lives in such a time as this. We have this assurance regarding the One who called us to follow Him: "Greater is He who is in you than he who is in the world" (1 John 4:4).

CHAPTER 4

STELLAR STORM WARNING

By Dr. Thomas R. Horn

AS MOST READERS PROBABLY KNOW, both Old and New Testament prophets foresaw unusual heavenly activity connected with arrival of the Great Tribulation period and Second Coming of Jesus Christ.

In Luke 21:25, Jesus Himself prophesied: "There shall be signs in the sun, and in the moon, and in the stars." The Great Tribulation period actually begins with the opening of seals immediately accompanied by signs and wonders in the heavens. For example, Revelation 6:12–14[37] says:

> And I beheld when he had opened the sixth seal, and lo, there was a great earthquake; and the sun became black as sackcloth of hair, and the moon became as blood; and the stars of heaven fell unto the earth, even as a fig tree casts her untimely figs, when she is shaken of a mighty wind. And the heaven departed as a scroll when it is rolled together; and every mountain and island were move out of their places.

In the Old Testament, Joel prophesied similarly:

And I will show wonders in the heavens and in the earth, blood and fire, and pillars of smoke. The sun shall be turned into darkness, and the moon into blood, before the great and terrible day of the LORD come. (Joel 2:30–31)

These prophecies were on my mind back in April of 2019 when one night I had gone to bed, not anticipating anything unusual, when, at around 2 o'clock the next morning, I "awoke" in a hyperdimensional reality and saw in the heavens above me what looked like a horned, fiery serpent, hundreds of feet wide, plunging past the stars toward earth at an incomprehensible speed. This terrifying monster seemed to be swimming across the sky, past the planets, as it descended toward earth.

Then, suddenly, my point of view shifted, and I was lifted above the massive object only to realize it wasn't a dragon after all, but rather a very large rock, and the way it was rolling through space, it caused the light of the sun to glide over its contours, giving it the appearance of something undulating like a living thing.

The next thing I knew, I was on a tall hill or mountain somewhere, surrounded by thousands of people. We were running, terrified, and people were screaming for God to deliver us from the menace barreling through the sky toward this planet.

Moments later, I heard a deafening sound. It was as if the earth was splitting apart, the ground beneath our feet jerking violently, knocking us to the soil where we bounced viciously against the rocks, desperately reaching out for anything we could cling to for stability.

Somehow, I knew an asteroid had plunged into the Pacific Ocean, its massive form sending a sequence of tsunamis hundreds of feet into the air.

As I glanced over my shoulder, I could see an overwhelming wall of water coming up over the hillside behind us. I perceived we wouldn't be able to escape.

But then, it was as if two very large hands slid under my arms, lifting me high into the sky, where, looking down, I watched in shock as people everywhere were swept away by astonishingly large waves slamming into coastal terrains as far as I could see. The atmosphere was simultaneously infused with scorched particles of aerosol and vapor as a blistering culmination of moisture and extreme heat subsequently combusted into a series of high-velocity hurricanes. Tornadoes, volcanoes, and earthquakes seemed to be going off like fireworks with what were likely some of the eleven deadliest volcanoes on earth—those of the Cascadia region of the United States—being triggered like dominos, releasing so much debris into the sky that, for about a week, darkness covered the heavens worldwide as the entire landscape was pounded by hurricanes and atmospheric annihilation circulating within the jet stream. By the time days later when the waters finally settled, storms subsided, and the sky grew clear, much of life on earth was dead.

When I awoke, I nearly fell out of bed.

Grabbing for pen and paper to record what I had seen, I was interrupted by what seemed like an audible voice. It could have just been in my head, but it seemed spoken to me. The voice uttered a single word—"Apophis."

Now, I knew there was an ancient Egyptian god of chaos and enemy of light known by that name.

I also knew that NASA (National Aeronautics and Space Administration) had named an asteroid Apophis, but I didn't know any details about it.

When I got out of bed and headed for my computer to begin research on this particular space rock, I didn't anticipate that a year-long investigation would ensue that ultimately would lead me to uncover evidence of a cover-up by NASA, ESA (European Space Agency), and other space organizations involving the likelihood of Apophis impacting the earth in less than nine years—Friday, April 13, 2029.

Now, you may have seen recently that NASA is saying Apophis will likely not impact earth on that date, but will instead barely skim safely past the world while knocking out some of the satellites in orbit around our planet. That said, just one of many scientists is warning that NASA's trajectory calculation of Apophis is off by as much as six hundred thousand miles, which mathematician Harry Lear implies could very well send it crashing into earth in just eight years. Lear sent an open letter to the president of the United States and US government scientists begging them to cross check these calculations immediately, even though he ends his dispatch with an ominous admonition that we may already be out of time.[38]

Besides Lear, top-100 scientist Nathan Myhrvold, in a recent peer-reviewed paper, "An Empirical Examination of WISE/NEOWISE Asteroid Analysis and Results," also refutes much of the data from NASA, and in fact charges the organization with deliberately misreporting threats by near-earth objects and of behaving "extremely deceptively" with deliberate "scientific misconduct" in a cover-up of very real and potentially imminent space threats.[39]

Even famous planetary scientist and astrophysicist Neil deGrasse Tyson admits that, on April 13, 2029:

Apophis will come so close to Earth that it will dip below our orbiting communication satellites. It will be the largest closest thing we have ever observed to come by earth…the orbit we now have for it is UNCERTAIN…because these things are hard to measure and hard to get an exact distance for—WE CANNOT TELL YOU EXACTLY WHERE THAT TRAJECTORY WILL BE.[40] (Emphasis added)

But the mystery of these revelations involving Apophis—and my contention that it could very well be the Wormwood asteroid of Revelation chapter 8—has gotten deeper since I wrote the books *The Wormwood Prophecy* and subsequent *The Messenger*. In fact, it wasn't until after those books were in print and I was doing media interviews on their claims that the biggest insights involving Apophis came to light.

From Revelation to Revelation

It was 2 o'clock a.m. when suddenly I sat straight up in bed. A moment earlier, during what was perhaps REM sleep (that mysterious mechanism created by God called "rapid eye movement") when most dreams or "night visions" occur, glimpses of Wormwood impacting earth and the aftermath following it had startled my subconscious mind, shaking me from slumber.

I had been wrestling inside that spectacular vision moments before, trying to make sense of what was happening around me and what I was watching play out across the world. But not until I awoke did I hear the word "Apophis" whispered across the room, and something deeper—indistinguishable—troubled me. It was as if the ominous voice had only paused to follow later with more revelations from the beyond. What had been concealed in plain sight would suddenly and unexpectedly be exposed live in studio—and right as we were recording the first SkyWatch TV broadcast programs (which aired November–December 2019) regarding my Wormwood vision and supernatural experience. It happened when I was describing how evangelical dispensationalists (and some Catholic prophecy believers) might find the timing of the Apophis-Wormwood impact date (April 13, 2029) ominous regarding a possible Rapture of the Church as being soon to occur. (The Rapture is the eschatological, or end-times, event when all true Christians who are alive will be transformed into glorious bodies in an instant and joined by the resurrection of dead believers who ascend with them into Heaven). During that program recording, as I was making the case that, depending on one's position, the asteroid's impact date as first set by NASA could place the last possible timing of a pre-Tribulation Rapture happening around October 13, 2025, Derek Gilbert—the host for that show—was studying something on his MacBook. Unknown to me, while I was talking, he was searching a Hebrew calendar and checking whether anything interesting would be happening three and a half years before the date I was talking about involving when Apophis will strike earth. He was doing that because prophecy scholars say Wormwood will fall to earth in the middle of the seven-year Great Tribulation period, thus pre-Tribulation Rapture believers place the "catching away" of the saints three and a half years before then.

What Derek discovered raised the hair on our necks.

His eyes had fallen on a prominent timeline. Exactly three and a half years to the day before the original date set by NASA for Apophis to come crashing down on this planet, the high holy days of the Feast of Tabernacles will be unfolding on earth. Just a few days before that will be the Feast of Trumpets. Both festivals are strongly tied by eschatologists to the Rapture of the Church.

For example, Jesus said:

In my Father's house are many [rooms-tents]: if it were not so, I would have told you. I go to prepare a place for you. And if I go and prepare a place for you, I will come again, and receive you unto myself; that where I am, there ye may be also. (John 14:2–3)

When He spoke those words, His Hebrew followers would have immediately caught the connection between the Feast of Tabernacles and His Second Coming (or the Rapture), for this annual feast was one of the occasions requiring the Israelites to make a pilgrimage to the wilderness tabernacle and, later, the Temple in Jerusalem to appear before God where they would set up temporary tents/rooms at "the Father's house." This is the event that will be transpiring on earth exactly three and a half years before Apophis-Wormwood crashes into this planet. Is this mere coincidence, or does it point to an imminent pre-Tribulation Rapture?

The Feast of Trumpets is likewise connected to the Rapture and/or Second Coming because the Apostle Paul said in 1 Corinthians 15:51–52:

Behold, I tell you a mystery; we will not all sleep, but we will all be changed, in a moment, in the twinkling of an eye, at the last trumpet; for the trumpet will sound, and the dead will be raised imperishable, and we will be changed.

During the Feast of Trumpets, a series of shofars are sounded until "the last trumpet" is blown.

However, exactly 120 days before the start of the Feast of Tabernacles in 2025 is Pentecost. And the number 120 in the Bible represents "the end of all flesh" (for example, Genesis 6:3 says, "And the LORD said, My spirit shall not always strive with man, for that he also is flesh: yet his days shall be an hundred and twenty years." Moses is another example. He was 120 years old when he died [Deuteronomy 34:7]).

The number 120 is also tied to the Feast of Pentecost:

And in those days Peter stood up in the midst of the disciples, and said, (the number of names together were about an hundred and twenty), Men and brethren, this scripture must needs have been fulfilled. (Acts 1:15–16)

Pentecost is likewise connected to the Rapture as, to this day, Orthodox Jews believe sometime during this feast a window is opened in Heaven, allowing entry for a very brief time.

These connections continue, but when Derek pointed that out during the show, you could have knocked me over with a feather, as they say. How had I not seen this before sending *The Wormwood Prophecy* to the printer?

Even then, things were about to get profusely more enlightening. We had but scratched the surface of a much larger revelation tying Apophis-Wormwood with prophecy, Jewish feasts, and the ancient idea that asteroids and comets are "messengers" of the gods and omens of important coming events. For example, when the magi in Matthew 2:2 saw the "star" (Greek *aster*, from which the English word "asteroid" is derived), they interpreted it as a "messenger" saying that the "King of the Jews" was born; they had seen "his star [*aster*] in the east, and were come to worship him" (Matthew 2:1–2). Similarly, the Apophis-Wormwood-feasts connection could imply that a countdown clock is ticking now—a countdown that the world and the organized church are unaware of—and just as an asteroid heralded the First Coming of Christ, Apophis could be set to herald the Second Coming of Jesus and may even be connected to Matthew 24:30, which states:

The world will mourn when they see the sign of the son of man coming in the heavens.

Of course, it is just my opinion, but given all of the above, I thus have a strong intuition (which has been very accurate before; for example, I publicly predicted the exact moment Pope Benedict would resign over a year in advance)—that mankind has likely entered the last decade of history as it has been known—what prophecy teachers call the Church Age. In my newest book, *Zeitgeist 2025*, I examine how even the Essenes of Dead Sea Scrolls fame (astonishingly accurate Hebrew prophets) predicted over two thousand years ago that mankind would enter its final age (Jubilee cycle) in 2025, three and a half years before Apophis likely fulfills the Wormwood prophecy of Revelation chapter 8.

Obviously, the Rapture could happen at any time, but these facts intrigue when also compared to the prophecy-infused Jewish feasts connected with the Wormwood prophecy and the date of the asteroid's arrival in 2029.

So...wrap your mind around what I am saying: Exactly three and a half years before Apophis-Wormwood is set to smash into this planet, the Feast of Tabernacles will be happening on earth following the Feast of Trumpets a few days before, and 120 days earlier the feast of Pentecost. These will unfold all in the same year the Essenes predicted mankind will enter its final age—2025.

Why should we care what the Essenes predicted? Because of their accuracy to date. For example, they correctly prophesied hundreds of years ahead of time (among many other things I outline in *Zeitgeist 2025*):

- That a man named Herod would be king but would turn bad.
- That the Messiah would arrive exactly when Jesus did.
- That the Messiah would raise the dead, which is not found in the Old Testament.
- That the Messiah would die in AD 32, exactly the correct date.
- That the Messiah would be for Gentiles as well as for Jews.

- That the Messiah would begin an Age of Grace.
- That a Benjamite would explain everything about this Messiah to the Gentiles, and his knowledge would be in the synagogues, which is obviously Paul and the New Testament.

The list goes on and raises the serious point: Assuming for the moment I am right, and all these heavenly signs, prophecies, and feasts insinuate that the asteroid Apophis is biblical Wormwood and therefore 2029 represents a time around the middle of the Great Tribulation period when the trumpet judgments begin, Monday, October 13, 2025 (April 13, 2029, minus three and a half years), would be the approximate start date of the seven years of Tribulation foreseen in Scripture (see Matthew 24:21; Revelation 7:14; and Daniel 12:1)—the very time the Essenes predicted the final age of man.

It's not just ancient prophets and Jewish feasts that seem to be strangely connected to the year 2025.

The same period is also the one envisioned ten years ago in a series of studies co-organized by the Atlantic Council and government organizations from Europe, the US, Beijing, Tokyo, Dubai, and other partnering nations that led the US National Intelligence Council and the EU Institute of Security Studies to produce a report titled *Global Governance 2025: At A Critical Juncture*. In that document, the highest-level intelligence agencies in the world determined a global government could emerge around 2025 from "an unprecedented threat" that would materialize, requiring all nations to lay down their differences and come together in mutual defense of one another against a "menace." In particular, they foresaw an incoming asteroid, a new pandemic (which I believe Apophis is bringing with it via an extremophile microorganism with a virus), as well as a biotech-created "new form of human" representing existential threats.

But the list doesn't stop there. In addition to these prophets and intelligence agencies, in 1997, a work describing itself as a thesis "that turns history into prophecy" by professors William Strauss and Neil Howe was released. It was titled *The Fourth Turning*, and examined Western historical paradigms over the past five centuries. It unveiled cycles of life and generational archetypes that reveal an astoundingly prescient pattern of incidents that ultimately lead to chaos and a so-called Fourth Turning.

The authors describe these "Turnings" as "an era with a characteristic social mood (a zeitgeist), a new twist on how people feel about themselves and their nation. It results from the aging of the generation [before it]."[41] A society enters a Turning once every twenty years or so, when all living generations begin to penetrate their next phases of life. The living generations, or *saeculae*, comprise four cyclical Turnings, characterized as:

- **The First Turning (THE HIGH)**: An era of enthusiastic collective strengthening and civic development, having burned the brush and swept the ashes of preceding structure.

- **The Second Turning (THE AWAKENING)**: Built on the energies and accomplishments of the High, but finds increasing yearning for introspection with a high tolerance for spiritual expression outside the parameters of predetermined standards.

- **The Third Turning (THE UNRAVELING)**: Begins as the "society-wide embrace of the liberating cultural forces" loosed by the Awakening shows signs of civic disorder and decay, a heightened sense of self-reliance, and an increasing withdrawal of public trust. This builds to a near crisis of downcast pessimism and a palpable pall that can only be remedied by yielding to the next.

- **The Fourth Turning (THE CRISES and the era we have now entered)**: By far, the most perilous, as societies pass through the greatest and most dangerous gates of history. As desperate solutions are sought for "sudden threats" on multiple cultural fronts, confrontation is passionate and decisions are often reactive, aggressive. "Government governs, community obstacles are removed, and laws and customs that resisted change for decades are swiftly shunted aside. A grim preoccupation with civic peril causes spiritual curiosity to decline.... Public order tightens, private risk-taking abates, and...child-rearing reaches a smothering degree of protection and structure. The young focus their energy on worldly achievements, leaving values in the hands of the old. Wars are fought with fury and for maximum result."[42]

Through the examination of an enormous amount of political and cultural history, Strauss and Howe processed more than five hundred years of such Anglo-American cultural Turnings into remarkable, well-organized, and predictable cycles, and from this reservoir they finally staked an uncanny claim about America and the future of the world (keep in mind they made these predictions nearly twenty-five years ago, long before the September 11, 2001, attacks on America, the pandemic of today, or the January 6, 2021, riots at the US Capitol and subsequent prosecution of Donald Trump). Among the scenarios they foresaw were:

- A terrorist attack involving an airliner, a military response, authorization for house-to-house searches, and false-flag accusations against the administration.
- An eco-environmental malaise with the Centers for Disease Control announcing the spread of a new communicable virus (COVID-19) with quarantines and relocations.
- Growing anarchy throughout the world largely generated along racial divisions leading to unprecedented government suppression of personal freedoms.

In describing these insightful scenarios, Strauss and Howe felt a catalyst would unfold as a result of a specific dynamic, and "an initial spark will trigger a chain reaction of unyielding responses and further emergencies."[43] They further foresaw:

Just after the millennium, America will enter a new era that will culminate with a crisis comparable to the American Revolution, the Civil War, the Great Depression, and World War II. The very survival of the nation will almost certainly be at stake.[44]

Strauss and Howe determined the United States of that time (1997) was in a Third Turning, "midway through an Unraveling":

America feels like it's unraveling. Although we live in an era of relative peace and comfort, we have settled into a mood of pessimism about the long-term future, fearful that our superpower nation is somehow rotting from within.

The next Fourth Turning is due to begin shortly after the new millennium. Real hardship will beset the land, with severe distress that could involve questions of class, race, nation, and empire....

The very survival of the nation will feel at stake.

Sometime before the year 2025, America will pass through a great gate in history, commensurate with the American Revolution, Civil War, and twin emergencies of the Great Depression and World War II.

The risk of catastrophe will be very high. The nation could erupt into insurrection or civil violence, crack up geographically, or succumb to authoritarian rule.[45] (Emphasis added)

Although the authors of *The Fourth Turning* note that the events described in their thesis are not absolute, they also insist the cycles, these Turnings, cannot be interrupted. As summer follows spring, an Unraveling precedes a crisis of Faustian proportions:

It will require us to lend a new seasonal interpretation to our revered American Dream. And it will require us to admit that our faith in linear progress has often amounted to a Faustian bargain with our children.

Faust always ups the ante, and every bet is double-or-nothing. Through much of the Third Turning, we have managed to postpone the reckoning. But history warns that we can't defer it beyond the next bend in time.[46]

In Strauss and Howe's vision, Faust's "deal with the devil" ultimately includes the arrival of an unexpected national leader who would emerge during this current Fourth Turning from an older generation and lead the globe into a New World Order, which they envisioned developing by 2025. This commander—whom they call the "Grey Champion" (and whom some of us might worry could be—or could pave the way for—Antichrist)—would come to power as a result of the nation losing faith in existing government and desperate for a political savior to arrive and "calm" nerves by offering to "Build Back Better" a socialist governance with welfare for the masses. This leadership would seize what can only be described as a cancel-culture crusade warm to promulgating suppression of unapproved dialogue in order to rein in any and all challenges to the new social construct.

By the end of his term, America and the world would embrace arrival of a totalitarian leader and world government.

Is this starting to sound familiar?

CHAPTER 5

PANDEMIC TIDAL WAVE:
MASKING PERDITION'S PLAN FOR HUMANKIND

By Jonathan C. Brentner

IN HIS 1933 BOOK, *Lost Horizon*, British author James Hilton gave the name "Shangri-La" to a mystical, harmonious valley that rests secluded far away from the known world. "In the novel, the people who live at Shangri-La are almost immortal, living hundreds of years beyond the normal lifespan and only very slowly aging in appearance."[47]

If you listen to the globalists of our day, one might think they envision just such a utopia. They promise a pristine environment, health protocols that will someday significantly lengthen our lives, and superhuman abilities through the combining of people with machines.

In recent years, the World Economic Forum (WEF) has risen to the forefront of those telling us they know the way to just such a paradise. What they call the "Great Reset" comprises their economic vision of a blissful one-world government. One can spend hours on the WEF website surveying their plans for a happy populace where the government guarantees all its basic needs.

Their not-so-secret sinister agenda lies in the control they seek to exert over everyone on the planet in return for their hollow acts of benevolence.

The Great Reset is nothing less than a communist state where people become slaves of the state. The future these globalists envision for humanity resembles a prison where the warden ensures that inmates receive all their basic necessities, but freedom doesn't exist in any form.

The environment alarmists' panic over too much CO_2 in the atmosphere failed to bring about the radical changes desired by the elite of our day. In order to achieve their goal of worldwide governance, they needed a fear-generating, worldwide crisis, a plausible catalyst that would cause people to willingly surrender their rights and freedoms for the sake of personal safety.

COVID-19, with the aid of an amenable media that eagerly reported greatly inflated numbers of cases and deaths, provided these power brokers with precisely what they desired to create the needed public alarm. The carefully orchestrated and timed worldwide outbreak of the coronavirus resulted from years of concentrated planning so as to open the door for the globalists to proceed with their mission of ruling over all the nations, which they disguise as a Shangri-La existence.

COVID-19: The Pestilence of Luke 21:11?

In Luke 21:11,[48] Jesus said:

And there will be great earthquakes in various places, and famines and pestilences; and there will be fearful sights and great signs from heaven.

The Got Questions website defines the Lord's reference to "pestilences" here in this way:

Pestilence is a deadly disaster, usually a disease, that affects an entire community. Pestilence is contagious, virulent, and devastating. For example, the Black Plague in Europe that killed over thirty percent of the population during the late Middle Ages was a pestilence.[49]

Though not yet nearly as deadly as the Black Plague, COVID-19 certainly qualifies as "the beginning of sorrows" Jesus predicts will become astronomically worse during the time of Tribulation leading up to His Second Coming (Matthew 24:8).

In the last half or Revelation 6:8, John says this about the fourth rider of the apocalypse (accompanied by "death and hades"):

And power was given to them over a fourth of the earth, to kill with sword, with hunger, with death, and by the beasts of the earth.

The word "death" is translated "pestilence" in other versions of the Bible, because in this context it refers to disease as the cause of death. John MacArthur, pastor and Bible commentator, added that the word "death" in this verse "could also refer to the effects of biological and chemical weapons."[50] Those words, written twenty-two years ago, fit with what many doctors and health experts today claim about the virus and its vaccines.

Is the coronavirus a key part of Satan's plan to enslave the world under the Antichrist's future reign of terror? I believe it is.

COVID-19 and its accompanying mRNA injections are leading people toward the world order of the seven-year Tribulation at an ever-accelerating pace. Though this time of God's wrath on the earth has not yet begun and cannot start until after the Rapture, the virus and future jabs may very well become the pestilence Jesus warned about in Luke 21:11.

How can I make such a radical claim? Please allow me to make my case.

All Paths Lead to the Great Reset

Klaus Schwab, head and founder of the WEF, unveiled the Great Reset in May of 2020 as a way for governing powers to build back the world's economies destroyed by the anticipated COVID-19 devastation. A couple of months later, he said, "The pandemic represents a rare but narrow window of opportunity to reflect, reimagine, and reset our world."[51] Here, "reimagine" equals the adding of superpowers to humans via injections, and "reset" refers to the Marxist regime the WEF promotes via its Great Reset.

Lest one thinks the WEF is some obscure fringe group, please know it has the full support of most government leaders throughout the world.

President Joe Biden's 2020 campaign slogan of "Build Back Better" came directly from the WEF and accurately reflects his administration's plan to submit the United States to its Great Reset. John Kerry, whom Biden named as his special presidential envoy for climate, strongly affirmed Biden's unshakable allegiance to the Marxist agenda of the WEF. Just before Biden took office, Kerry assured these elites that a Joe Biden presidency will quickly advance the globalist Great Reset agenda "with greater speed and greater intensity than many might imagine."[52] That explains a lot of what we see today.

Has the world experienced the severe degree of financial turmoil the WEF hoped the virus lockdowns would create from which they intend to "build back better?" I don't believe it has. However, Revelation 6:5–6 tells of an economic catastrophe that will occur early in the Tribulation period. Such a disaster will create an intense fervor among the nations for the seeming economic security of the Great Reset, or for something identical to it.

The Role of COVID-19 Injections

The widespread panic generated by highly inflated numbers of cases and deaths has enabled the globalists to take the next step in their plan: COVID-19 injections. What does this have to do with the Great Reset? It's an essential aspect of the plan to first monitor people and then control them so they will accept the rigid confines of their still-future, communist-like solution to the coming fiscal catastrophe.

The evidence suggests these shots existed long before December of 2019 when the virus first appeared. It's impossible that the concept of an mRNA vaccine to deliver a "spike protein" to every cell in the human body materialized and became a reality less than a year after the first case of the illness. At a minimum, they were far along in their development, just waiting for the "right" virus to come along.

From its beginning as a company in 2010, Moderna grew to employ hundreds of scientists and engineers working on the mRNA injections.[53] Where did they get the massive funding for this? How did they know they would eventually make billions of dollars from their vaccines for a yet unknown virus, which would require their precise spike protein technology?

Moderna is now "anticipated to make $13.2 billion in COVID-19 vaccine revenue in 2021." The Moderna CEO, Stéphane Bancel, became a billionaire with a net worth that rapidly jumped all the way up to $4 billion.[54] *Not a bad payoff for a company's first-ever medication to reach the market.*

As further evidence of the long-term planning behind what we see happening today, consider this quote from Aldous Huxley, an English author and philosopher, at the California Medical School in 1961:

There will be, in the next generation or so, a pharmacological method of making people love their servitude, and producing dictatorship without tears, so to speak, producing a kind of painless concentration camp for entire societies, so that people will in fact have their liberties taken away from them, but will rather enjoy it, because they will be distracted from any desire to rebel by propaganda or brainwashing, or brainwashing enhanced by pharmacological methods. And this seems to be the final revolution.[55]

What Huxley talked about in 1961 is quickly becoming a reality sixty years later. For decades, the globalists have planned to brainwash people through "pharmacological methods," which are now becoming the means for the elite to change humanity and thereby control the masses for their own purposes.

To fully understand how this fits with the elite's craving for power, we must explore their scheme to combine people with machines and what it means for the future. It brings the words of Huxley into the moment in which we live.

The mRNA Injections and Transhumanism

Many of the rich and powerful of our day propose to fundamentally change humanity by altering our DNA (something they call "nano-technology"). The result of what the WEF calls the "Fourth Industrial Revolution"—"transhumanism" by any other name—will be something far different than what God created and Jesus died to redeem.

Dr. Carrie Madej, an internal medicine specialist from Forest Park, Georgia, warned in an April 19, 2021, video of the many dire consequences for our future as the elite of the world seek to control our behavior through transhumanism. The altered beings that will result from merging people with mechanical devices through a series of injections will no longer possess the basic qualities of what makes us human.[56]

Consider this quote from the WEF website regarding their transhumanism plans for our world. It appears under the heading of "Fourth Industrial Revolution" and confirms Dr. Madej's warnings:

The Fourth Industrial Revolution represents a fundamental change in the way we live, work and relate to one another. It is a new chapter in human development, enabled by extraordinary technology advances commensurate with those of the first, second and third industrial revolutions. These advances are merging the physical, digital and biological worlds in ways that create both huge promise and potential peril. The speed, breadth and depth of this revolution is forcing us to rethink how countries develop, how organisations create value and even what it means to be human.[57]

Again, could the plans of the globalists be any more obvious? The WEF calls this a "new chapter in human development" as though this is something we really need. The group states that merging humans with machines will cause people to "rethink…even what it means to be human."

Do we have further confirmation of the link between the mRNA vaccines and transhumanism? Yes, we do.

In November of 2017, a telling article appeared on the *Forbes* website with this title: "Transhumanism and the Future of Humanity: 7 Ways the World Will Change By 2030." Here is a quote from the introduction of this article:

> This transformation will be messy, complex, and sometimes scary, but signals already point to a future of humanity that will blur our identities into "transhumanism."[58]

Several disturbing statements emerge here. The assertion of the author that transhumanism will "blur our identities," however, shocks me the most. The article in this respected magazine confirms that the intent of the planet's powerbrokers is to forever change what it means to be a human being—and to do so in the near future.

An additional quote from this insightful article ties mRNA injections to the merging of people with machines. The words below appear under the subheading, "Our Bodies Will Be Augmented."

> The coming years will usher in a number of body augmentation capabilities that will enable humans to be smarter, stronger, and more capable than we are today. Wearables will be one form of body augmentation, but they will far surpass the fitness trackers of today…. We will also see increased use of implants ranging from brain microchips and neural lace to mind-controlled prosthesis and subdermal RFID chips that allow users to unlock doors or

computer passwords with the wave of a hand. However, the most powerful body augmentation will come from biological augmentation as a result of increased insight into our genomes, advances in IVF technology that may allow us to select the most intelligent embryos, and powerful CRISPR gene-editing technology which may one day give us the ability to eliminate all heritable diseases.

These body augmentation capabilities will give rise to humans that are more resilient, optimized and **continually monitored.**[59] (Emphasis added)

This report in *Forbes* reveals three important factors related to the push for transhuman technologies. First, the author envisions that the merging of humans with machines will happen by 2030, the same year the UN plans to have its one-world government in place. *This is not a coincidence.*

Second, the "CRISPR gene-editing technology" they say will augment our bodies is precisely what appeared three years later in the form of the current mRNA jabs. What the *Forbes* article predicted in 2017 that would open the door to transhumanism became a reality in 2020–21 with the emergence of the COVID-19 vaccines.

Third, is it really anyone's desire to be "continually monitored?" The article mentions this aspect of the shots almost as an afterthought when it's a key puzzle piece of the globalists' agenda that will lead to their control of all those under their jurisdiction.

Although the WEF website paints the end of its "Fourth Industrial Revolution" as a paradise, it's anything but. It's the vehicle through which they, along with globalists at the United Nations and in America, intend to use to force people into accepting a tyrannical government that will enslave the earth's population.

The trajectory is clear. Despite the claims of the elite that they have a magnificent future in mind for humanity, a Shangri-La, the plans of the globalists will ultimately lead a system whereby they will monitor and later subjugate people of every nation on earth. It will become a hell on earth for those living under the Antichrist's reign of terror during the seven-year Tribulation.

The Path to the Mark of the Beast

The late spring and summer months of 2021 brought a brief respite from the lockdowns and mask restrictions in much of the US. Where I live, people flocked to restaurants and for the most part abandoned wearing masks in stores.

However, dramatic changes were in the not-too-distant future. As newsfeeds began to fill with increased cases of the Delta variant of the virus, more people returned to wearing masks. Dr. Anthony Fauci, the current US infectious disease expert, ramped up fear through repeated appearances on the mainstream media warning of the new virus strains, which were supposedly becoming more contagious and deadly than the original coronavirus.

The new forms of the bug, along with the increasing loss of efficiency of the vaccines, led to calls for booster shots. The *Wall Street Journal* reported the Biden administration was pushing for a third jab among the most vulnerable and those who received the initial injection in the late December 2020 to January 2021 timeframe.[60]

Do you see the pattern? New strains of COVID-19 will continue to arrive along with nonstop calls for booster jabs or altogether new mRNA injections. Perhaps adding to the fervor for ongoing injections, on August 19, 2021, the CDC announced that fully vaccinated people can spread the virus to other people.

Dr. Richard M. Fleming, an esteemed scientist and a nuclear and preventive cardiologist, claims COVID-19 came from a lab, created as a "bioweapon," and "is now mutating and spreading new variants **because of the vaccines**." Fleming believes that Fauci and others "are already working on the next bioweapon that will contain stronger HIV-like properties designed to suppress human immunity"[61] (emphasis added).

Do you recall that, according to Dr. John MacArthur, the reference to deaths from "pestilences" in Revelation 6:8 could include "bioweapons and chemicals?" Are today's untold thousands of deaths due to the virus *and* its related injections merely a prelude to the widespread deaths from them during the Tribulation?

The persistent need for more vaccines, which we already see, aligns perfectly with the Fourth Industrial Revolution of the WEF, does it not? With each successive dose of the mRNA injections, people will receive more changes along the path to transhumanism. Motivated by fear and driven by the elusive dream of normalcy, people will continue lining up for future jabs until the final one, which I believe is the mark of the Beast, fundamentally changes them into what the WEF states will cause people to "rethink what it means to be human."

Please understand that what we see today is *not* the mark of the Beast; it cannot arrive until the Antichrist comes to power during the seven-year Tribulation. And it's not until the halfway point that he enforces it with the penalty of death. Those secure in Christ, however, will be in Heaven with Jesus *before* this time of God's wrath starts.

Technology Leading to the Mark of the Beast

Today we see three emerging technologies related to vaccines that speak to the fulfillment of Revelation 13:16–17.

> He causes all, both small and great, rich and poor, free and slave, to receive a mark on their right hand or on their foreheads, and that no one may buy or sell except one who has the mark or the name of the beast, or the number of his name.

By themselves, the following three initiatives might not set off alarm bells in our minds, but together they provide a path for the future fulfillment of the verses quoted above.

1. Patent WO2020060606: Controlling the Buying and Selling

Microsoft, along with Bill Gates, obtained this international patent in 2020: Patent WO2020060606 – Cryptocurrency System Using Body Activity Data. Yes, this patent is real as is its number.

Here is the legal description of the patent:

> Human body activity associated with a task provided to a user may be used in a mining process of a cryptocurrency system. A server may provide a task to a device of a user which is communicatively coupled to the server. A sensor communicatively coupled to or comprised in the device of the user may sense body activity of the user. Body activity data may be generated based on the sensed body activity of the user. The cryptocurrency system communicatively coupled to the device of the user may verify if the body activity data satisfies one or more conditions set by the cryptocurrency system, and award cryptocurrency to the user whose body activity data is verified.[62]

This patent envisions the use of a sensor that detects "the body activity of the user" and reports it to an outside digital computing source. The system will rely on outward sensors initially, but people will learn how to manipulate them. That will lead to a device injected into the human body.

The behavior of the individual will become the basis for his or her award of "cryptocurrency." The reward or lack thereof results from what the sensor reports regarding the person's conduct.

Imagine a world where all currency exists digitally (that day is rapidly approaching) and your receipt of it doesn't come solely from the fruit of your labor, but from behaving according to the mandates of a distant governing body that sets the parameters by which the computing source rewards you with the means to buy and sell.

We don't know whether the Antichrist will employ this exact system to control the world's commerce. However, this patent provides a clear picture of how he will accomplish it and tells us the technology for his control of all the buying and selling on earth already exists.

2. ID2020: The Inclusion of the "Great and Small" in the Mark

What about people in the remote parts of the earth? Does Bill Gates have a plan to include them in his futuristic world of reward and punishment? Yes, he does.

ID2020 is another Bill Gates and Microsoft scheme that seeks to provide the 1.1 billion people who live in remote parts of the world with the "legal identification" they currently lack; he plans to give them this digital ID in the form of a vaccine, of course.

Here is a description of ID2020 from the official Microsoft blog, dated January 22, 2018:

> As discussions begin this week at the World Economic Forum, creating universal access to identity is an issue at the top of Microsoft's agenda, and we think technology can be a powerful tool to tackle this challenge. It was last summer that Microsoft took a first step, collaborating with Accenture and Avanade on a blockchain-based identity prototype on Microsoft Azure. Together, we pursued this work in support of the ID2020 Alliance—a global public-private partnership dedicated to aiding the 1.1 billion people around the world who lack any legal form of identity. To say that we were encouraged by its mission would be an understatement.[63]

Notice the players include the WEF that vigorously promotes both the Great Reset and transhumanism. ID2020 is not an isolated initiative that doesn't relate to the COVID-19 injections or the Great Reset; it's all about identifying everyone on earth so the globalists can include them in their scheme for a world government, vaccinate them, and thereby monitor and control them. It's all about fulfilling the "great and small" of Revelation 13:16.

3. "Quantum Dot" Technology: Marking the Right Hand or Forehead

When the Antichrist comes to power, how will he mark everyone on the planet on the forehead or hand?

"Quantum dot" technology answers that question, and I believe this will someday become the means for the Antichrist to deliver his infamous mark and accompanying vaccine to the world's population.

Bill Gates, in March of 2020, referred to quantum dot technology as the means for implantable *vaccine* "digital certificates," thus joining this emerging technology with his ID2020 initiative. The technology leading to the mark of the Beast is all about injecting people with something to identify them and control them.

The "digital certificates" Gates was referring to are human-implantable "QUANTUM-DOT TATTOOS" that researchers at MIT and Rice University are working on as a way to hold vaccination records….

The quantum-dot tattoos involve applying dissolvable sugar-based microneedles that contain a vaccine and fluorescent copper-based "quantum dots" embedded inside biocompatible, micron-scale capsules. After the microneedles dissolve under the skin, they leave the encapsulated quantum dots whose patterns can be read to identify the vaccine that was administered.

The quantum-dot tattoos will likely be supplemented with Bill Gates' other undertaking called ID2020, which is an ambitious project by Microsoft to solve the problem of over 1 billion people who live without an officially recognized identity…. Currently, the most feasible way of implementing digital identity is either through smartphones or RFID [radio frequency identification] microchip implants.[64]

The quantum dot delivery of a future vaccine will connect the recipient to an external digital source via the ID2020 technology to verify the vaccination and of course, ensure the recipient has a viable identity.

While this might sound benign at first, it fits perfectly with the plans of globalists for world domination under the Great Reset of the WEF (or the UN's Agenda 2030). And, like with all the other technologies related to injecting something into our bodies, we see the name of Bill Gates, the founder of Microsoft and vaccine mogul. Does not his stated goal to reduce the world's population make us wonder about all these advancements related to vaccinating people make us wonder about his true aim in all these things?

The Road to Perdition

Revelation 14:9–11 depicts the tragic end of all those who receive the mark of the Beast during the Tribulation period:

> Then a third angel followed them, saying with a loud voice, "If anyone worships the beast and his image, and receives his mark on his forehead or on his hand, he himself shall also drink of the wine of the wrath of God, which is poured out full strength into the cup of His indignation. He shall be tormented with fire and brimstone in the presence of the holy angels and in the presence of the Lamb. And the smoke of their torment ascends forever and ever; and they have no rest day or night, who worship the beast and his image, and whoever receives the mark of his name."

What is there about this mark that will make those who receive it unredeemable in God's sight? I have read stories of Satan worshipers who have repented and turned to Jesus. What makes is impossible for those who receive the mark of the Beast to do so as well?

If the final combining of humans with machines comes as the result of the mark of the Beast, I believe that explains it. Jesus died for Adam's helpless race (Romans 5:19), not for a gene-edited and mechanically modified version that bears no resemblance to what God created.

Another possibility for the unredeemable nature of those who receive the mark is that the final injection will change human beings in such a way that they will be incapable of placing their faith in Jesus. The transhumanists of our day openly talk about removing the "God gene" from humans in order to make them incapable of worshiping the Lord.

Whatever the cause, the warning is dire for those who will seek to save their lives by taking the mark of the Beast. It will lead to unimaginable suffering in Hell.

We Are So Close

We are so close to the Lord's appearing to take His Church back to the place He's preparing for us (John 14:2–3). The trajectory of COVID-19 and future injections will take an unsuspecting world straight to the mark of the Beast.

The globalists have grabbed hold of the virus, which many believe they created, and they will not let go. Variant strains requiring subsequent injections lie ahead for a populace eager for a return to normalcy. The elusive goalpost will keep moving as the powerbrokers of our day achieve additional monitoring capabilities to control those they govern.

Outwardly, they dangle the carrot of a Shangri-La existence in front of people. Behind the scenes, however, they carry out deadly schemes through what Jesus called a "pestilence," a bioweapon that may very well lead to the huge number of deaths that will occur after the Rapture.

Are you ready for what lies ahead? If you know Jesus as your Savior, the road between now and the Rapture may be daunting and quite hazardous, but you will miss all of God's wrath upon the world during the coming seven-year Tribulation. *You will not see the final path to the mark of the Beast.*

If you have yet not called upon the Lord in faith for the forgiveness of your sins, please do so today. *The time is exceedingly short.* Jesus assures us all through the New Testament that belief in Him, and in Him alone, leads to eternal life. I love the words of 1 John 5:11–12 in this regard:

And this is the testimony: that God has given us eternal life, and this life is in His Son. He who has the Son has life; he who does not have the Son of God does not have life.

No one else paid the great debt for your sins, only Jesus. You will not find life in any other name; your goodness is of no account. Christ alone saves, and we abide in Him only because of His grace, mercy, and steadfast love.

People will still come to the Savior during the Tribulation, but how much better to trust Him today and miss what lies ahead for the world.

SECTION II

DANIEL'S SEVENTY-WEEKS FORECAST

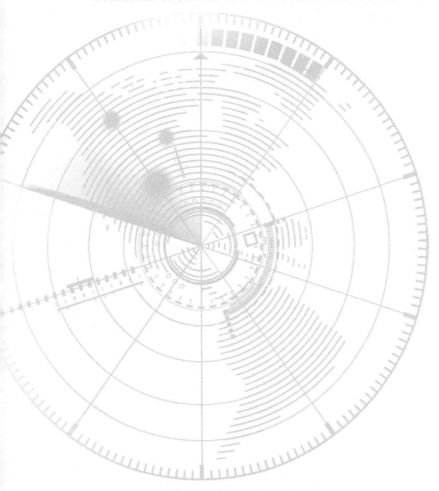

CHAPTER 6

PEACE AND SAFETY: THE SEDUCTIVE STORM SHELTER

By Thomas J. Hughes

For when they say, "Peace and safety!" then sudden destruction comes upon them, as labor pains upon a pregnant woman. And they shall not escape. (1 Thessalonians 5:3)[65]

GOD PROMISES MANY THINGS. His promises bring assurance and encouragement. Ultimately, followers of Christ will be comforted by all of them. But right now, looking at the world around us and the time before us, it can be jarring to remember His promises include judgment and wrath.

First Thessalonians 5:3 refers to a time when much of humanity will believe it has found peace even as it rejects the Prince of Peace. Just as they see themselves stepping into the dawn of a new utopian age, sudden destruction will fall.

That moment will take place during the seven years of Tribulation. God promises He will take those who are in Christ out of harm's way before that occurs. Christians will not be here for the final fulfillment of the verse. But we can see the groundwork for that time already being laid.

Universal Longing

Human beings have a fundamental desire for peace and safety. This is even more obvious when we examine the words as used in the Bible. Most people know that *shalom* means "peace." But in Hebrew, the definition of *shalom* goes beyond the English word "peace." It carries the connotation of "total well-being."

The *Bible Exposition Commentary* explains:

Shalom…is a precious word to the Jewish people. It means much more than just the absence of war or distress. *Shalom* means wholeness, completeness, health, security, even prosperity in the best sense.[66]

Because the New Testament was written in Greek, 1 Thessalonians 5:3 uses the Greek word for "peace"—*eirene*. According to the *NAS New Testament Greek Lexicon, eirene* means "a state of national tranquility, exemption from the rage and havoc of war, peace between individuals, i.e., harmony, concord." Then, like *shalom*, it goes further. It also means "security, safety, prosperity, felicity." As you can see, *eirene* does a good job of expressing the Hebrew concept of *shalom*.

The definitions of "peace" and "safety" have a large area of overlap. But there are also differences. The Greek word used here for "safety" is *asphaleia*. It includes many kinds of safety. It carries the connotation of "stability and certainty" as well as "security from enemies and other dangers."

Combine the definitions of *eirene* and *asphaleia*—peace and safety—and you get national tranquility, exemption from the horrors of war, peace between individuals, harmony, concord, security, safety, prosperity, contentment, and stability, as well as security from enemies and other dangers. That's a lot!

Consider how much work, money, energy, and thought goes into the quest for those conditions. Think about your own life. Consider the amount of money you spend on them—and don't forget to include the tax dollars you send to every level of government. Also, think about how much energy and time you put into your pursuit of those things. Then multiply that by the more than seven and a half billion people now alive on earth. The combination of peace and safety is big deal!

"Peace and Safety" vs. Freedom and Common Sense

Humans have always desired peace and safety. But in the end times, as the world spirals in on itself, human hunger for peace will take on increasing urgency. Coupled with the continued rejection of Christ, this will ultimately lead to the Antichrist and judgment.

In today's world system, peace and safety trump everything. The longing for safety overpowers the desire for freedom. The desire for peace overcomes ideals, principles, and even common sense.

The world's COVID response has given us a powerful preview. No matter how we feel about COVID vaccines, we have to wonder about pushing the least-tested publicly available vaccine in modern history into every human body on earth—no matter what.

Do you have a medical condition that makes the vaccine especially dangerous for you? Individual differences don't matter to public health officials. To them, it is a game of percentages, and a few losses are just collateral damage. Does your doctor say that, in your case, it would be better not to take the vaccine? Officials don't allow for exceptions: "For the sake of your health, you must do what your doctor says not to do."

On August 27, 2021, the peer-reviewed academic journal *Science Magazine* reported:

> The natural immune protection that develops after a SARS-CoV-2 infection offers considerably more of a shield against the Delta variant of the pandemic coronavirus than two doses of the Pfizer-BioNTech vaccine, according to a large Israeli study that some scientists wish came with a "Don't try this at home" label. The newly released data show people who once had a SARS-CoV-2 infection

were much less likely than never-infected, vaccinated people to get Delta, develop symptoms from it, or become hospitalized with serious COVID-19.

That study should have been part of the COVID discussion. But just try to bring it up on social media and see what happens. The powers that be do not want such things discussed. That's why *Science Magazine* added the caveat that "some scientists wish" the study had come "with a 'Don't try this at home' label."

Fear in the populace—combined with the desire of some to manipulate said populace—has resulted in millions of people being essentially forced to take a powerful, potentially deadly medicine into their bodies… *medicine that they may not have needed.* That's what fear does. It steals principles and common sense.

It is remarkably similar to the kind of thinking that will one day lead to the mark of the Beast and the worldwide totalitarian regime described in Revelation 13 and elsewhere.

Fear Amplified

Jesus warned that the last days will be a time when men's hearts fail them for fear. That level of desperation will make peace and safety paramount in people's lives, and it will grow more acute as they go farther into the end times.

To see why people will become more and more desperate for peace and safety, look at some of the disquieting things the Bible states about the time leading up to Christ's return. It speaks of an increase in natural disasters, including earthquakes, volcanoes, and extreme weather. It foretells intrusive and oppressive government using power over money to gain control of people's lives. It describes chaos, confusion, and an era of deception.

Control of the media will help make such deception possible. That includes censorship of social media. This is easy to imagine because we already see it beginning. What the military calls "information operations" have become a normal part of civilian life. Television, video games, music, theater, books, films, education, news, and even the human resources departments of many multinational corporations have all joined in the operation.

Bible prophecy says the last days will be a time of lawlessness, with violent gangs controlling the streets. It tells of an era when police lose control, then gain it back with vengeance.

Right now, we see a major purge of police departments across the country. Good cops are being driven out by bad policy imposed by corrupt politicians. But that situation will not last. Lawlessness invariably leads to greater state control. That means future police will have more power than ever. Rap artist and social media star Zuby posted on Twitter "20 Things I've Learned (or Had Confirmed) about Humanity During the 'Pandemic.'" They were all insightful, but one especially caught my eye: "When sufficiently frightened, most people will not only accept authoritarianism, but demand it."

The reasons to crave peace and safety go beyond local lawlessness. Jesus spoke of wars and rumors of war. We're already getting a strong taste of that with major nations such as China and Russia openly threatening their neighbors with nuclear annihilation.

To make it worse, the United States military is going through a purge very much like the one experienced by police departments. The military seems intent on getting rid of anyone with a biblical worldview. They're expelling able warriors in favor, for instance, of men who think they are women. Gender dysphoria is a real thing. But it is folly to encourage it, especially in the military.

Meanwhile, much of the church looks on and applauds. Churches are less and less Bible centered. Many have rejected the Bible altogether. Some parishioners in those anti-Bible churches may still be holding on to faith, but with every sermon, that faith becomes more diluted and polluted. As followers of Jesus, they should be walking in Holy Spirit power, but instead they find themselves sickly and weak.

The Bible says there will come a time of falling away from the true faith. It says people will not endure sound doctrine, "giving heed to deceiving spirits and doctrines of demons." It says people will have "itching ears," and they will find churches with teachers to scratch them.

This may sound like an ecclesiastical crisis rather than something that will induce fear in the secular populace. But God made the church to be a preserving agent in the world. Christendom's retreat will trigger some of the most fearful events of all time. Even now, it is undermining societal stability. It's making evil stronger and danger ubiquitous.

Jesus warned of last-days plagues, pestilence, and disease. Recent experiences have given us a taste of that. But Jesus didn't just warn about one "pestilence." He spoke of "pestilences"—plural. There are more to come.

In September of 2021, officials from the White House Office of Science and Technology issued a report warning that, at present, the United States is "not adequately prepared" to handle future pandemics. They expect serious biological threats to occur with "increasing frequency." They also pointed out that the technology to make biological weapons has become more potent and more widespread, increasing the "disturbing possibility that a malign actor could develop and use a biological weapon."

This is one of many cases where signs overlap; it is pestilence combined with rumors of war. And, as time progresses, it will cause people to crave peace and safety more and more.

Brain Damage

Romans 1:18–32 describes a society turning away from God, then falling apart. Those verses describe the human attitudes, beliefs, and actions that trigger ruin and judgment on a given civilization.

But what if those attitudes, beliefs, and actions are not confined to a single society? What if they have spread across the whole world? In that case, it has to mean the whole world is charging headlong toward judgment and ruin. When is the whole world judged and brought to ruin? The end times. With that, Romans 1:18–32 becomes an end-times passage. It depicts what previous generations of Americans would have seen as a nightmarish world of moral, emotional, and mental breakdown across the populace. Verse 28 stands out in particular:

And even as they did not like to retain God in their knowledge, God gave them over to a debased mind.

The King James Version ends that verse with the words "reprobate mind." My friend, Hal Lindsey, defines a "reprobate mind" as "a mind that is so perverted it cannot think in its own best interest." When widespread, that kind of mental handicap makes the world radically unstable and dangerous.

The Bible talks about other scary issues that will affect people's thinking—like increases in brutality, selfishness, and racial strife. People will become more abusive in the last days, as well as more arrogant and heartless. They will desire sensual things like sex, food, and violence—cravings that will not be satisfied. Their behaviors will be out of control.

Morality will break down. People will call evil "good" and good "evil." They will not only tolerate evil, they will encourage it, celebrate it, and eventually apply all their ingenuity to creating darker and uglier expressions of it.

The Apostle Paul, in 2 Timothy 3:1, wasn't kidding when he called the last days "perilous times." So, naturally, people will want and need well-being, stability, and all the other conditions that peace and safety stand for. Peace and safety will be among the most precious and sought-after commodities in the world. The promise of them will be more enticing than ever.

Famine and Upheaval

Jesus said there would be famines in the last days. Here again, COVID has given us a preview. We have seen the breakdown of supply lines on everything from chicken to computer chips. Even in the wealthiest countries, food insecurity suddenly became a major issue after the onset of COVID.

In Genesis, we read that Joseph advised Pharaoh to build up food supplies in times of plenty in order to survive the lean years. America once took that pattern to heart. We had massive warehouses of food all over the country. But today's computerized supply lines have us balanced on a razor's edge of supply versus demand.

A lean system that just meets demand is far more profitable than warehousing. But after years of this mentality, we are now working without a net. We have no margin for safety. Even small disruptions can turn catastrophic.

Dark Religion

Perhaps most unsettling of all, the Bible describes the rise of a new political/religious orthodoxy. We can already see it forming. Notice, for instance, how "science" isn't science anymore. A new, politicized science has arisen—one that goes against the "scientific method" by disallowing questions and criticism.

The old field we once called science has been captured and subverted for use by the political/religious orthodoxy. The new faith demands that its adherents hold establishment thinking as sacred, no matter how absurd. For instance, we are now supposed to believe men can have babies. *People* magazine has been reporting on the phenomenon since 2008. But the basic idea is as dumb as a bag of hammers!

In a reply to criticism of the idea that men can have babies, on September 2, 2021, an article in *Newsweek* proclaimed, "Transgender men are capable of becoming pregnant."[67] Does this prove men can have babies? No. It proves "transgender men" are women and not men, because women can have babies and men cannot. That, my friends, may be politically incorrect, but it is biology 101.

The bizarre belief in male pregnancies also illustrates the Bible's warning about "reprobate minds." Talking about the ancient Christian School of Antioch and its more literal style of biblical interpretation, Frederic

Farrar once said it was "crushed by the iron hand of a dominant ortho-doxy." Today, we also have a dominant orthodoxy with an iron hand. It, too, crushes that which does not adhere to its agenda.

Despair

In 1865, life expectancy in the United States stood at its all-time low—thirty-five years. By 1900, life expectancy for men had risen to forty-six. Women lived two years longer. By 2015, it had risen to an average of sev-enty-nine. We don't yet know the full effect of COVID on life expectancy, but after 2015, the needle started turning the wrong direction. Starting in 2016, three years *before* the pandemic, life expectancy began to go down.

Before we examine why, think about how extraordinary that is. The USA—the wealthiest nation in the history of the world—spends almost 18 percent of its gross domestic product on healthcare. That's a lot of money. Research institutions make great strides all the time in the areas of medicine and medical technology. Yet, even with all that money and all those breakthroughs, life expectancy has been falling since 2015.

How is that even possible? The Centers for Disease Control (CDC) blames it on what Professor Anne Case of Princeton University calls "deaths of despair."[68] The CDC says longevity numbers are going down for three reasons—increases in the number of suicides, drug overdoses, and liver disease due to alcoholism. These are not the results of a boda-cious party. They are symptoms of despair.

People need peace. They need security and stability. They need to feel safe. And, as the last days proceed, those needs will become increasingly intense.

The Seductive Shelter

Mankind's manipulators have long recognized that the universal human desire for peace and safety can be highly useful as either a carrot or a stick. They promise peace and safety every election—safety from crime, peace with foreign powers, and now even safety from viruses. On the other hand, they warn of grave danger if their policies are not enacted. Sometimes they're telling the truth, but often they lie.

When the peace and safety of 1 Thessalonians 5:3 arrives, it will be another iteration of that theme. It will be a sham—the end game of a long, elaborate illusion. The people who believe the illusion will be "in darkness." Obviously, they will have been fooled—obvious because, just as "safety" arrives, so does "destruction."

In the Tribulation, most of the world will be ready to accept all propaganda regarding peace and safety. That's easy to believe, because we're already well on our way. At every turn, our "scientific" generation willingly believes obvious nonsense. Such vulnerability to propaganda lays the groundwork for the Tribulation with its mark of the Beast and worship of Antichrist.

Sadly, this is nowhere truer than in our churches. Many pastors scoff at Bible prophecy and disdain fellow ministers who stand as watchmen on the wall, pointing to the Lord's own signs of His return. They seem unaware of Matthew 16:2–3, where we read that Jesus said the following:

When it is evening you say, "It will be fair weather, for the sky is red"; and in the morning, "It will be foul weather today, for the sky is red and threatening." Hypocrites! You know how to discern the face of the sky, but you cannot discern the signs of the times.

His point is obvious. We are to be just as aware of the signs of the times as we are of signs in the weather. Today, we use computers to analyze data from earth-observation satellites and ground-based meteorological stations across the world. Most people rely on weather apps or TV reporters to tell us what that data means. But whether we use our own eyes or the reports, we still do what the ancient mariners did. We look at the signs and decipher the weather.

Jesus used strong language to describe people who discern the weather, but ignore the signs of the times. He called them, "Hypocrites"! And they are paying a price. First Thessalonians 4:13–17 gives a glorious picture of the Rapture of the Church. Verse 18 then says, "Comfort one another with these words."

The Christians most upset by the signs of the times are those who don't understand their context. To these folks, what should be comforting is terrifying. Many churches today are miles wide and inches deep. They replace the rich Word of God with banal platitudes. They place people's focus squarely on their navels—giving them affirmations of self instead of affirmations of God. The result? In times of trial, members of such churches fall apart with fear, they hide, or they self-medicate.

The "Peace and Safety" Delusion

First Thessalonians 5:1–11 tells God's people how the Lord's imminent return should affect their lives. Verse 2 says:

The day of the Lord so comes as a thief in the night.

Verses 4–6 say:

But you, brethren, are not in darkness, so that this day should overtake you as a thief. You are all sons of light and sons of the day. We are not of the night nor of darkness. Therefore let us not sleep, as others do, but let us watch and be sober.

These are important instructions. But verse 3 is somewhat different. It contains a specific prophecy to be fulfilled at a specific time.

According to Daniel 9:27, the seven years we call the Tribulation will begin when the Antichrist confirms a treaty bringing "peace" in the Middle East. It will be a seemingly miraculous achievement. The world will marvel at Antichrist—even worship him. The vast propaganda machines of modern media will sell the Antichrist to the world as a miracle worker, convincing almost every one of the peace-and-safety message.

Because it happens in the Tribulation, what's described in 1 Thessalonians 5:3 will take place *after* the Rapture. In fact, the chaos left by the Rapture will cause a significant increase in the desperation for peace and safety. But despite the chaos of so many disappearances, the event will seem to have a couple of happy side effects. First, the world will be rid of people they saw as obstructing the New World Order of peace and safety. And with them gone, a superman will arise promising to create that New World Order.

When Jesus gave a discourse on the time leading up to His return, He began with a warning against deception. He then repeated that admonition three more times. Each of the warnings deals with false Christs and false prophets. These can apply to *the* Antichrist and *the* False Prophet. But Lord's wording makes it clear He was also giving a general caution against anyone who claims deity for himself or who claims to speak for God while contradicting His Word.

The Long-Game Hoax

When Franklin Roosevelt gave his 1941 State of the Union message, America had not yet entered World War II. But President Roosevelt was already looking forward to a new, post-war world. He called for four universal freedoms—the freedoms of speech and worship and freedom from want and fear. Most of us would agree those are worthy goals.

Then he said, "That is no vision of a distant millennium. It is a definite basis for a kind of world attainable in our own time and generation."

FDR was fluent in the phraseology of the Bible. By "distant millennium," he meant the future millennium to be led by Christ. We can applaud those who work toward the four freedoms he articulated. But use of the term "millennium" put his dream in another category. He proposed a "millennium" to be built with human hands—a tower to Heaven.

President Roosevelt hoped to build his humanist millennium through a reconstituted League of Nations—this one to be called the United

Nations. Every subsequent US presidential administration saw the UN as an instrument for moderating military conflict, increasing human rights, and diminishing global poverty.

But in recent years, the dream changed. It morphed into something more utopian in societal terms, while less centered on the rights of individuals. World elites now speak of a global entity that will end income disparity (except among the very rich—i.e., themselves), end racial injustice, and protect humanity against the coming horrors they expect from "climate change."

Along the way, something happened that American liberals of earlier generations did not expect. The globalists dropped two of the four freedoms—worship and speech.

Meanwhile, freedom from want and fear dominate the plans of governments, universities, think tanks, and even popular entertainment. I think the shift would have stunned Franklin Roosevelt, but it was entirely predictable in light of Bible prophecy. They shifted away from active freedoms for individuals and toward the passive desire for...*peace and safety*.

Freedom of speech and religion impede elitist control of the world. That's why the suppression of those freedoms has become a global priority for those who want to impose their version of utopia on everyone else.

Giving in to Get By

History shows the willingness of people to trade in their rights and freedoms for perceived increases in peace and safety. We see it in the War on Terror and in the COVID crisis. Increasingly, we see it in the battle against climate change.

Peace and safety make for great propaganda. Practically the whole world will follow Antichrist. The masses will believe that, because they have conformed to his will, they will have finally arrived at the gates of Eden. The media will tell them they have arrived. Antichrist and the False Prophet will tell them they have arrived.

They will believe it…until sudden destruction proves the absurdity of that belief. It will have been a delusion—a delusion they chose.

The Bible likens the arrival of destruction to the arrival of birth pangs. Though labor begins suddenly, it rarely comes as a surprise. Most women have been expecting labor for months. Except with C-sections, labor pains are inevitable just before childbirth.

For a sin-soaked world, judgment is inevitable.

Working for peace and safety is good. We're supposed to work for such things, and sometimes we're even meant to fight for them. It is our job to take care of our families, communities, churches, and nations. But we must understand that, until Jesus returns, achieving peace and safety will remain an ongoing struggle. Today's happy endings inevitably melt away into tomorrow's new challenges.

Real Peace

In the New Testament, Jesus promised His followers a special kind of peace. In John 14:27, He said:

Peace I leave with you, My peace I give to you; not as the world gives do I give to you. Let not your heart be troubled, neither let it be afraid.

The peace Jesus gives is not limited to happy circumstances. It abides with us during sickness, battle, and storm. Jesus offers a better kind of *shalom*—not built on the narrow efforts of humanity, but on the power and faithfulness of God. His kind of peace abides. It lasts beyond death and into life everlasting. It will not change, because He does not change.

One key to experiencing the fullness of God's peace is to look at life from His perspective. We don't know everything about His point of view, but His Word communicates important parts of it. For instance, God views time in the context of eternity. He sees our earthly lives in the context of Heaven. We need to see our lives that way, too.

In Acts 20:24, Paul was speaking to his Ephesian friends about the pain and imprisonment that awaited him in Jerusalem. Then he said:

> But none of these things move me; nor do I count my life dear to myself, so that I may finish my race with joy, and the ministry which I received from the Lord Jesus, to testify to the gospel of the grace of God.

Shouldn't he have been moved with terror knowing what was ahead? No. Because he did not count his life dear to himself. Neither should we. To finish our lives life with joy, we must not hold it too tight. In Mark 8:35, Jesus said:

> Whoever desires to save his life will lose it, but whoever loses his life for My sake and the gospel's will save it.

Jesus said we should give up our lives for Him and for the gospel. Paul spoke of finishing his course with joy and continuing the ministry he "received from the Lord Jesus, to testify to the gospel of the grace of God."

Isaiah 9:6 calls Jesus the "Prince of Peace." Ephesians 2:14 says something similar in a more personal way. "He Himself is our peace."

Real Safety

In English, the words "saved" and "safety" are related—"save," "saved," "safe." It's the same in Greek. For real safety, we need the salvation found only in Jesus.

Romans 10:13 says "whoever calls on the name of the Lord shall be saved." The very next verse points out something obvious—we don't call on someone we don't believe in. That's why in John 6:29, Jesus said, "This is the work of God, that you believe in Him whom He sent."

Whom did He send? Jesus said in John 3:16–17 that God sent His Son into the world. John 3:15 says, "Whoever believes in Him should not perish but have eternal life."

Another Bible word for "saved" is "justified." Romans 5:1 says, "Therefore, having been justified by faith, we have peace with God through our Lord Jesus Christ."

And there they are—*peace and safety*—but not like the world's version. God's peace and safety are better in every way.

CHAPTER 7

BABEL TROPICAL DEPRESSION FULLY FORMED

By Gary W. Ritter

THE DEEPLY DEPRAVED globalist system flexing its power and authority throughout the world has roots that go far beyond what most people realize. Not
only is it Babylonian, arising from the empires Daniel foresaw in the
image of Nebuchadnezzar's dream, but its origins go much farther back
into antiquity. It is a cabal ruled by a few. Their goals are intimately linked
with hatred of God; this fuels their ambitions and will cause them to bring
the world to the brink of annihilation.

Mankind's rebellion against God is intimately connected with insurrection in the spiritual realm. In order to understand this, we must explore
the biblical history of rebellion up to the present. With this context, we
can gain a deeper perspective of the evil that pervades today's world.

We only have to consider the Genesis account of Adam and Eve to
see how the spiritual and human realms intersect and how the wickedness in the heavenlies causes depravity on the earth. Scripture provides the
evidence.

The question we have to initially ask is: Would the first humans, made
in God's image, have considered eating from the tree of the knowledge of
good and evil if left to their own devices?

Why would they? Yahweh told them not to, and they had no reason for disobeying Him. Everything around them was perfect; all they had was good, and they were sinless. In this state, they had no concept of doing anything contrary to God's will.

The first part of this discussion summarizes a combination of various biblical scholarly efforts, reading Scripture from the perspective of ancient Israel, extrabiblical material, and some conjecture that comes from reading between the lines in God's Word. God doesn't spell everything out for us. He enjoys watching man use the mind and skills He gave us to discover His deeper mysteries. As Proverbs 25:2[69] indicates:

> It is the glory of God to conceal things, but the glory of kings is to search things out.

Scripture declares that we are kings and priests (Revelation 1:6), so this encouragement to investigate that which is hidden is for us. One of the revelations we glean by examining the Bible from a broader perspective is that sin isn't the only problem that causes our undoing. In fact, the ancient Israelite view is that sin is only the first of three rebellions against God that have brought misery to the world.

Rebellion #1: The Garden Incident

We don't think of this often, but the Garden of Eden wasn't just humanity's first home; it was also a favored place that God—as the Second Person of the Trinity, God manifesting in human form—walked in the cool of the day. Another consideration we typically avoid is the lack of surprise on Eve's part when confronted by the serpent.

The reality is Eden was where Heaven, the spiritual realm, overlapped with earth, the physical realm. Sometime in the past before God made the heavens and the earth as recounted in Genesis, He also made the heavenly host—i.e., the spiritual inhabitants of Heaven. How do we know? Job 38:4–7 tells us in God's questioning Job's lack of omniscience:

Where were you when I laid the foundation of the earth?
Tell me, if you have understanding.
Who determined its measurements—surely you know!
Or who stretched the line upon it?
On what were its bases sunk,
or who laid its cornerstone,
when the morning stars sang together
and all the sons of God shouted for joy?

The morning stars and sons of God celebrated along with Him upon completion of this incredible act of creation.

Because Eden was this intersecting location, it shouldn't surprise us that many of these spiritual entities likely spent time in the Garden. True, we don't have biblical text that explicitly details this, but Eve's conversation with the serpent indicates she (and Adam) may have had numerous discussions with beings like him. An intriguing aspect about the serpent is that its Hebrew word, *nachash*, has the less-recognized meaning of "shining one." (Dr. Michael Heiser discusses this in his book, *The Unseen Realm*, pp. 87–88.). The heavenly host is often referred to as appearing with a shining intensity. It's not even necessarily a given that the *nachash* had a serpent form at the time he spoke with Eve. The point is a spiritual being had a not-out-of-the-ordinary conversation with Eve that took a turn for the worse for her and Adam. If, previously, Eve's discussions with these entities had been harmless, why would she think otherwise in this instance?

The critical issue for us is that sin began because it first occurred in the heavenlies. Sometime before the serpent tempted Eve with God-like abilities, he had rebelled. He simply parroted to Eve what he had already thought and decided. In the human realm, we call it "projection" when someone attributes his own negative traits to others.

I hinted above that this incident in the Garden wasn't the only rebellion, either with man or in the spiritual realm. When we consider Scripture from the perspective of an ancient Israelite rather than in light of our typical Western thinking, we see that Adam and Eve participated in only the first of three major rebellions that have set the course of mankind.

Rebellion #2: Trespassing Divine Boundaries

During the Intertestamental Period, also known as the Second Temple period, from roughly 500 BC to AD 100, many in Israel pondered the ways of God during His extended silence after Malachi. The book of 1 Enoch was written during this time. Although not canonical, Enoch correlates with the account in Genesis 6:1–4 that details another step in the spiritual decline of humanity and those in the heavenly realm. The sons of God (*bene Elohim*) trespassed their divine boundaries, came to earth, and procreated with human women. What or who stirred them up to take this leap across the red line that God had drawn? Regardless, their presence on earth caused great chaos. They fathered the hybrid Nephilim—part divine, part human—which created extreme violence. More importantly, their subsequent breeding with mankind increased the corruption of human DNA so that man, as God had created him, ceased to exist with the exception of righteous Noah and his family.

It is presumed that the world's mythologies of gods and titans come originally from the reality of what occurred. As an aside, note there is also belief that the tales of hybrid beasts, such as the minotaur, satyr, centaur, and cyclops, inevitably arose from the interbreeding of the fallen entities and their offspring with the animal kingdom.

This depravity throughout the earth was so extreme God had no alternative but to destroy the world with the Flood and effectively begin again with Noah. Two important spiritual events occurred as a result:

1. The sons of God who committed this atrocity paid dearly for their insurrection. Both Jude 6 and 2 Peter 2:4 refer to their penalty. God cast them into the lowest pit of Hell known as Tartarus, a place of gloomy darkness where these once-exalted princes have

spent millennia in chains until the day they will be judged and ultimately relegated to the Lake of Fire for eternity. One would think this example would be sufficient to prevent further mutiny. As we'll see momentarily, that's not been the case.

2. All flesh—humans and beasts—perished in the Flood. All corrupted humanity died and descended to Sheol. The fate of the hybrids created from the mating of spiritual entities and humans differed. The physical bodies of the Nephilim drowned, but that fleshly death released their spirit essence. Have you ever questioned how demons originated? Wonder no more. Demons are the bodiless, restless spirits from the Nephilim. This is the reason they always seek a body to inhabit. Theirs were ripped away when their hosts entered the watery grave. Many people confuse the sons of God—the princes and high-ranking generals in the demonic realm—with demons. They're completely different. The *bene Elohim* are much higher ranking in the spiritual hierarchy, whereas demons are what we could label as "serfs" or "peons." The sons of God give the orders; demons, having much less power and authority, take the orders of their superiors and carry them out.

Rebellion #3: The Tower of Babel

The third major incident of rebellion involving the spiritual realm and humanity occurred sometime following God's rescue of Noah. In the Flood's aftermath, God commanded Noah to repopulate the earth and take dominion over it just as he had told Adam and Eve. After an appropriate period of time in which humanity replenished itself, in contradiction to God's command, men gathered on the plains of Shinar and built the Tower of Babel. History tells us this structure was a ziggurat, a pyramidal temple tower that functioned as a divine abode. As we learn in Genesis 11:4, the builders of this project had a specific purpose in mind:

Then they said, "Come, let us build ourselves a city and a tower with its top in the heavens, and let us make a name for ourselves, lest we be dispersed over the face of the whole earth."

They did this so that:

1. The tower would reach the heavens. Their intent was to approach the spiritual realm in order to bring God down to them. In their darkened state, they thought they could manipulate and control Yahweh.
2. They could exalt themselves. This was ego—self-realization—pride and arrogance on steroids. Their purpose was to show other humans how powerful they were by being able to reach the heavens and exercise such authority.
3. The way of life they wanted, rather than what God decreed, would continue. Apparently, they realized if they didn't take control of their situation through dominance over Yahweh, He would force them to scatter from this central location.

Another interesting aspect of this event was that God came down to investigate the goings-on. Genesis 11:7 provides us with Yahweh's intriguing statement:

Come, let us go down and there confuse their language, so that they may not understand one another's speech.

From this sentence we learn two things:

1. Yahweh personally visited earth. Once more we see this must be the Second Person of the Trinity who came in bodily form. God the Father is Spirit and is never seen.
2. This may not have been God in the Trinity talking to Himself. God's words, "let us," have been the subject of debate in biblical

circles for a long time. Is it God talking to Himself and inviting the other two Persons of the Trinity down with Him? Or, more reasonably, is it Yahweh engaging some members of the heavenly host to accompany Him? I favor this second interpretation because of what happened next.

God did what He said He would do; we learn exactly what occurred in Deuteronomy 32:8:

When the Most High gave to the nations their inheritance,
when he divided mankind,
he fixed the borders of the peoples
according to the number of the sons of God.

This verse is the specific reference to God scattering men into nations when He also confused their language. In dispersing mankind, He created nations into which He placed them. Note the last phrase of the verse: "according to the number of the sons of God." This is key. Note as well that if you read this in any Bible translation other than the English Standard Version (ESV), you will miss the entire context. The ESV translates this from the gold standard of scriptural antiquity, the Dead Sea Scrolls.

Other earlier translations don't reflect this more recent scholarship. In fact, they greatly confuse the narrative and cause people to miss how this big picture of rebellion in the Bible develops. Typically, you'll see this verse phrased as "sons of Israel" (NIV, NASB) or "children of Israel" (KJV). If you think about it, this makes no sense. God never placed Israel in a position of authority over nations. In addition, in this context, Israel wasn't even a nation at this time.

Yahweh placed His sons (*bene Elohim*) as conservators over the nations. By this time, God had effectively grown tired of man's choices to do anything other than what He said. This became the Father's time-out for mankind, where He sent them to their rooms (i.e., the nations) to think about their actions. He disassociated Himself from the general populace so that He could do something very special. He intended to raise up a nation wholly devoted to Him. Deuteronomy 32:9 shows us this:

> But the Lord's portion is his people,
> Jacob his allotted heritage.

Immediately following the Tower of Babel incident, God called Abram out of Ur to bring the nation of Israel into existence (Genesis 12).

The sons of God whom He placed over the nations were high-ranking spiritual entities. They were trusted and competent. Doesn't the king always place the princes—his sons—into positions of power and favor?

Unfortunately, something awful happened. We don't know how, but literally every one of God's sons over the nations rebelled. Psalm 82 shows us that God has judged this mass insurrection, but the condition of the world demonstrates He has not yet carried out His punishment.

Here's the entire text of this key psalm:

> God has taken his place in the divine council;
> in the midst of the gods he holds judgment:
> "How long will you judge unjustly
> and show partiality to the wicked? Selah
> Give justice to the weak and the fatherless;
> maintain the right of the afflicted and the destitute.
> Rescue the weak and the needy;
> deliver them from the hand of the wicked."
> They have neither knowledge nor understanding,
> they walk about in darkness;
> all the foundations of the earth are shaken."
> I said, "You are gods,
> sons of the Most High, all of you;
> nevertheless, like men you shall die,
> and fall like any prince."

Arise, O God, judge the earth;
for you shall inherit all the nations!

This is what's known as a Divine Council scene. There are numerous others in Scripture. Consider any time we're shown God's holy throne room with the heavenly host present (e.g., 1 Kings 22:19; Isaiah 6:1), and we encounter this holy assembly.

In this psalm, God condemns the gods (lowercase *elohim*). Why? The princes He placed over the nations to judge righteously did just the opposite. They lorded it over their human charges and caused them great distress. They took advantage of the trust God invested in them to point humanity toward Him; instead, they became the gods over the nations. This is where the gods we see throughout the Bible originated. Their ranks include Baal, Chemosh, Molech, Rimmon, and others.

The actions of His disobedient sons caused God to declare something grievous upon them. The batch of sons in Rebellion #2—because of the depraved severity of their actions—brought immediate judgment and banishment. Their fate was exactly like what will happen with these sons, only this is a delayed punishment. God decrees that for the sin of presuming to become gods in His stead and deceiving mankind, they will die like any mere human being. However, the timing is critical. Their deaths—i.e., their banishment for eternity in the Lake of Fire—have not yet occurred. They remain in their positions to this day and are integral to the Ephesians 6:12 hierarchy along with Satan:

For we wrestle not against flesh and blood, but against principalities, against powers, against the rulers of the darkness of this world, against spiritual wickedness in high places.

We have only to think about Daniel's interaction with the angel Gabriel in Daniel 10:13:

The prince of the kingdom of Persia withstood me twenty-one days, but Michael, one of the chief princes, came to help me, for I was left there with the kings of Persia.

The very powerful prince of Persia certainly wasn't human to thwart Gabriel's journey for so long. This demonstrates the power of these malevolent spiritual sons of God. They exercise immense authority and command significant resources in the spiritual realm to this day.

The impact of this rebellion on mankind is significant. Every person who is not a believer in Jesus Christ on the planet, in every nation, is subject to the voice and influence of the wickedness of this kingdom of darkness.

This brings us to today's world, and how these potent beings are working overtime to exercise total dominion over mankind to destroy God's plan of redemption through Jesus Christ.

For our purposes in this essay, Rebellion #3 is the most important.

Babylonian Global Storm

As mentioned earlier, a globalist cabal plans to rule the world, and its tentacles have a long reach. When we consider the scope of groupthink among so many people—be it corporate executives, national leaders, legislative bodies, court systems, embedded personnel within government bureaucracies, celebrities, sports figures, and literally any other group one can imagine, even the church—everyone seems to be singing from the same demonic hymnal. In any other context, these same people would be accusing others and shouting, "Conspiracy theory!" from the rooftops. For so many to parrot the same lines in widely diverse circumstances, is there a JournoList group they all check when they get up in the morning for their daily marching orders and canned speeches? (FYI, JournoList was a private forum from 2007–2010 whose members were some four hundred left-wing journalists. At this online site that banned conservatives, political issues were discussed among the members, often resulting in similar talking points.)

Of course, nothing like this is remotely possible—in the natural— among the vast expanse of people who espouse globalist thinking.

But, as we've seen thus far, we're addressing the intertwining of spiritual and human rebellion. Given how disobedience in the spiritual realm flows downhill to infect humanity, it shouldn't shock us to think that globalism's ideas and designs aren't necessarily from human origin. Neither should we be surprised that the extreme coordination among the elites of the world is directed from a demonic origin.

The question that should arise in this context is: How does this happen? We tend to think of our enemy as being Satan. Surely, he is. But we know he's not omniscient, omnipresent, or omnipotent. Yet, look at all that we attribute to him...all over the world. How does he cause the evil he does when he lacks the various characteristics that make God unique? If you're tracking with our argument so far, the answer is simple: Satan has help—lots of it.

Just think about that Ephesians 6:12 hierarchy again. Consider the mighty princes God placed over the nations after Babel. They wield great power and authority. One truth each of them knows is that the Bible foretells their doom at the end of the age. The rock in Nebuchadnezzar's dream (Daniel 2:31–35) that destroyed the image of these powerful earthly kingdoms, supported by mighty spiritual entities, is Jesus Christ. These sons of God, just like Satan, hate their Father—the One who created them. They all want to be god(s) in His place. Every single one of them is also looking out for number one. If God succeeds as He has said, these powerful beings will all die like mere men. Each will be relegated to the Lake of Fire for eternity. For their own preservation, they must not allow God to win.

Although each of these beings is an independent entity, they all have a common goal. Because Satan somehow rose to the top of the heap, they generally cooperate with him and take his directions. No doubt, just like God has Divine Council meetings, these beings have their own version of this assembly as well. From these summits they have surely developed the grand strategy for the globalist takeover we see moving forward today.

Because they have so many minions—underlings of lesser power and thus subject to their decrees—they surely dispatch this demonic horde with the same message to all those they influence in the flesh.

There is a grand conspiracy. It originates in the spiritual realm. It involves millions of fiendish creatures who do their masters' bidding. Every unbeliever is subject to their counsel. (Just imagine the old meme of an angel sitting on someone's right shoulder providing righteous guidance while the devil sits on his left giving ungodly advice.) More importantly, they target the elite of the world because they are the influencers and shapers of culture. Each of these Christ-haters is ripe for deception. It's not hard to believe they're all hearing, spouting, and implementing the same message.

What is that message? Steal, kill, and destroy. Anything from God must be countered and turned upside down.

Globalism was well on its way toward fulfillment with the probable election of Hillary Clinton in 2016; she was the elites' dream candidate at the time, and they anticipated she'd pave the way for their many and varied plans. *But God....*

The Lord had another plan. It seems like He wanted to give this sin-drenched nation one more opportunity to turn from its wicked ways. Many people prayed and believed 2 Chronicles 7:14 to that end. From my perspective, I think God didn't bring this deliverance to bear because we've gone too far; the evil that infests our nation has turned gangrenous and rotten. Where among America's leaders do we find any desire to please God rather than cast Him away? Depravity has contaminated us from the top down. There is no hint of repentance. Despite this, He placed Donald Trump in a position to slow down the landslide. But he couldn't. He was only one man. His support should have come from the church to pray against his enemies; instead, many churches embraced them. The evil of the Deep State was too deeply embedded. This was obvious from the extent of fraud in the 2020 election with literally no one, or no responsible body, acting to give truth a chance.

God has now given the US what it wanted, and we're seeing the fruit of that. A globalist storm has been brewing since the Biden regime came into power. What was held somewhat in check for four years under President Trump is now coming against everything godly. The spiritual powers in high places see little to thwart them. Their human minions are acting in concert and putting every one of their evil plans into place.

Yet, God has a Word about all that is happening. This is what He says in Isaiah 14:9–11 about those who believe they'll overcome Him:

Sheol beneath is stirred up
to meet you when you come;
it rouses the shades to greet you,
all who were leaders of the earth;
it raises from their thrones
all who were kings of the nations.
All of them will answer
and say to you:
"You too have become as weak as we!
You have become like us!"
Your pomp is brought down to Sheol,
the sound of your harps;
maggots are laid as a bed beneath you,
and worms are your covers."

Moreover, in Isaiah 14:22–23, the Lord makes clear that this evil world system begun on the plains of Shinar will not stand:

"I will rise up against them," declares the Lord of hosts, "and will cut off from Babylon name and remnant, descendants and posterity," declares the Lord. "And I will make it a possession of the hedgehog, and pools of water, and I will sweep it with the broom of destruction," declares the Lord of hosts.

Both the demonic host of Heaven and their lackeys on the earth think they will succeed. They believe they'll shape the world to the way they want it, and God will be tossed upon the trash heap. Instead, He will be the One to sweep the evil out of existence and clean up this world.

It is God's will—and His alone—that will prevail.

CHAPTER 8

DANIEL'S END-TIMES TORRENT: THE TERMINAL GENERATION

By Daymond Duck

DOES THE BIBLE REALLY TEACH that Jesus will come back and establish a kingdom on earth? The Old Testament prophets said He would:

> Behold, the days come, saith the LORD, that I will raise unto David a righteous Branch, and a KING SHALL REIGN and prosper, and shall execute judgment and justice IN THE EARTH. In his days Judah shall be saved, and Israel shall dwell safely: and this is his name whereby he shall be called, THE LORD OUR RIGHTEOUSNESS (Jeremiah 23:5–6).[70]

> And the LORD shall be KING over all the EARTH: in that day shall there be one LORD, and his name one (Zechariah 14:9).

> For unto us a child is born, unto us a son is given: and the government shall be upon his shoulder (Isaiah 9:6).

Israel's righteous King must reign over all the earth, not just over Israel. But if this righteous King is going to reign on earth, where will He live?

- The Lord's name is on Jerusalem (2 Kings 21:7).
- The Lord will dwell in Jerusalem (Psalm 132:13).
- The Lord will teach, and His Law will go forth out of Jerusalem (Isaiah 2:3).

These and similar verses are why the Jews expected the Messiah to be a great king (or a great political leader). They were not expecting the Messiah to be executed; they believed He would occupy a throne in Jerusalem.

The New Testament writers also said the Messiah will reign over a kingdom on earth. God sent the angel Gabriel to a virgin named Mary.

And in the sixth month the angel Gabriel was sent from God unto a city of Galilee, named Nazareth, To a virgin espoused to a man whose name was Joseph, of the house of David; and the virgin's name was Mary. And the angel came in unto her, and said, Hail, thou that art highly favoured, the Lord is with thee: blessed art thou among women. And when she saw him, she was troubled at his saying, and cast in her mind what manner of salutation this should be. And the angel said unto her, Fear not, Mary: for thou hast found favour with God. And, behold, thou shalt conceive in thy womb, and bring forth a son, and shalt call his name JESUS. He shall be great, and shall be called the Son of the Highest: and the Lord God shall give unto him the throne of his father David: And he shall reign over the house of Jacob for ever; and of his kingdom there shall be no end (Luke 1:26–33).

Gabriel told Mary God would give Jesus the throne of His ancestor David; that throne was on earth in Jerusalem.

At that time, they shall call Jerusalem the throne of the LORD; and all the nations shall be gathered unto it, to the name of the LORD, to Jerusalem. (Jeremiah 3:17)

Jesus taught us to pray, "Thy KINGDOM come. Thy will be done in earth, as it is in heaven." (Matthew 6:9–13)

Jesus will come back to this earth as King of Kings and Lord of Lords (Revelation 19:16) to establish a kingdom on earth in Jerusalem.

When Jesus was crucified, Roman soldiers dressed Him in a purple robe, put a crown of thorns on His head, and put a sign on the cross that said THIS IS JESUS THE KING OF THE JEWS IN THREE LANGUAGES. (Matthew 27:28–29)

After He was raised from the dead, Jesus met His disciples in Jerusalem one last time before He ascended into Heaven.

When they therefore were together, they asked of Him, saying, Lord, wilt thou at this time restore again the kingdom to Israel? And He said unto them, it is not for you to know the times or the seasons, which the Father hath put in His own power. (Acts 1:6–7)

Notice Jesus didn't say the kingdom would not be restored to Israel. He said it was not for His disciples to know the times or the seasons when the kingdom would be restored to Israel. The times and the seasons are in God's hands. We don't know the day or the hour that it will be restored to Israel, but we know a lot more than many realize.

Three Things to Know

Three things will help readers understand what is written in this chapter.

First, know that before Israel was captured by Babylon, the prophet Isaiah revealed that God would return Israel to the land twice (Isaiah 11:11–12). Two returns required Israel to be put off the land twice so it could return twice. This is a prophecy in the Word of God, so the removal of Israel twice and the return of Israel twice had to happen, and history and the Bible reveal that:

- Israel was first removed from the land by Babylon, but seventy years later, Israel returned to the land from Babylon and other nations in the area (first return).
- Israel was removed from the land the second time and was scattered all over the world by the Roman Empire, but in the 1800s, Israel started returning to the land from Europe and the remainder of the world (second return).

Second, know that the prophet Jeremiah said Israel would spend seventy years in captivity at Babylon, then Babylon would be destroyed and God would cause Israel to return to the Promised Land (Jeremiah 25:8–13; 29:10).

This whole land [Israel] shall be a desolation, and an astonishment; and these nations shall serve the king of Babylon seventy years. And it shall come to pass, when seventy years are accomplished, that I will punish the king of Babylon, and that nation, saith the LORD, for their iniquity, and the land of the Chaldeans, and will make it perpetual desolations. (Jeremiah 25:11–12)

For thus saith the LORD, That after seventy years be accomplished at Babylon I will visit you, and perform my good word toward you, in causing you to return to this place. (Jeremiah 29:10)

Third, know that Jesus gave the Olivet Discourse (Matthew 24) and the book of Revelation. Many verses in Revelation are a commentary on things in Matthew 24. For example:

- There are false Christs today (Matthew 24), but the ultimate false Christ will be the Antichrist (Revelation 6:1–2).

- There are wars today (Matthew 24), but the ultimate war will be the Battle of Armageddon (Revelation 19).
- There are famines today (Matthew 24), but the ultimate famine will be the third horseman of the Apocalypse (Revelation 6:5–6).
- There are pestilences today (Matthew 24), but the ultimate pestilence will be the fourth horseman of the Apocalypse (Revelation 6:7–8).
- There are earthquakes today (Matthew 24), but the greatest earthquake to ever happen on earth will take place during the Tribulation Period (Revelation 16:18).
- There are deceivers today (Matthew 24), but the greatest deceivers will be the Antichrist and False Prophet (Revelation 13).

This is not new; prophecy teachers have known these things for many years. But this just scratches the surface. Many verses in the book of Revelation add to what Jesus said in the Olivet Discourse. This will become obvious as we progress in this chapter.

The Fig Tree

There should be no speculation or disagreement about the identity of the Bible's fig tree.

God said, "I found Israel like grapes in the wilderness; I saw your fathers as the first-ripe in the fig tree at her first time." (Hosea 9:10)

Israel's fathers (Abraham, Isaac, and Jacob) were the first ripe in the fig tree, or the beginning of the nation of Israel (also see Jeremiah 24:1–10). Jacob's name was changed to "Israel" by God.

In the New Testament, the Apostle Paul asked, "Hath God cast away his people?" (Romans 11:1). Then, he answered his own question: "God hath not cast away his people which he foreknew" (Romans 11:2). God is not through with the nation of Israel (the fig tree).

But don't miss this point: In the Bible, trees are symbols of nations. The fig tree is a symbol of the nation of Israel, but other kinds of trees are symbols of other nations.

All the Trees

In Luke's account of the Olivet Discourse, concerning His Second Coming and the Kingdom of God, Jesus said:

> Behold the fig tree [the nation of Israel], and all the trees [all the nations]; When they now shoot forth, ye see and know of your own selves that summer is now nigh at hand. So likewise ye, when ye see these things come to pass, know ye that the kingdom of God is nigh at hand. (Luke 21:29–30)

Jesus was saying, "Watch the nation of Israel (the fig tree) and all the nations (all the trees). The Bible prophets said Israel will come back into being. A world government will come into being. The Roman Empire (EU) will be revived and oppose Israel. Russia, Iran, Turkey, and others will unite and oppose Israel. The kings of the East (perhaps China and others) will unite against Israel. Watch for the trees (the nations) to line up the way the prophets predicted.

"When you see Israel and all the nations (Israel and all the trees; the earthly kingdoms) lining up the way the prophets predicted, you are to know that the Second Coming and earthly kingdom of God is near."

Jesus did not say, "Know that the kingdom of God might be near," or "Know that it could be near." He emphatically said, "Know that the kingdom of God IS near."

When people talk about the Second Coming of Jesus, a common remark is, "Jesus said no one knows the day or the hour." That is true. But He also told us to watch Israel and all the nations because we can know when it is *near*. If we believe one of these statements, we should believe both.

The Parable of the Trees

In the Old Testament parable of the trees, the trees (nations) are looking for a king to rule over them (Judges 9:7–21). The nations even ask the fig tree (Israel) to rule over them.

The Parable of the Barren Fig Tree

In the New Testament, Jesus told the parable of the barren fig tree, which is usually interpreted as a warning to Israel to accept Jesus as the Messiah or be destroyed (Luke 13:6–9). The day after His triumphal entry into Jerusalem, Jesus and the twelve were going to the Temple when they came across a barren fig tree (Israel). Jesus cursed it (Mark 11:12–14). The next day, they passed it again and it had withered (Mark 11:20–21).

One or two days later, Jesus was on the Mount of Olives, and His response to a question about the signs of His coming was, "Watch the fig tree and all the trees." This is why some prophecy teachers talk about Israel, the European Union, world government, the battle of Gog and Magog, the kings of the East, etc.

How to Get the Point Across

Aristotle, an ancient Greek philosopher and scientist, said, 1) "Tell them what you are going to tell them, 2) tell them, 3) then tell them what you told them."

Here's what I'm *going* to tell you: It is my opinion that this present generation is the first and only generation that could have living people on earth at the Second Coming of Jesus. The Second Coming and kingdom on earth could not happen in any generation but the current one. It cannot happen now, but it appears to be very close, and it's likely to happen in this current generation.

Now, here's what I *am* telling you: Jesus was talking about His Second Coming and the Tribulation Period when He said the following:

Jerusalem shall be trodden down of the Gentiles, until the times of the Gentiles be fulfilled. (Luke 21:24)

Know that the Temple Mount is in East Jerusalem, and to this very day, the top of the Temple Mount is controlled by Gentiles (Muslims, not Jews).

This is important: Almost two thousand years ago, Jesus said the Gentile influence in Jerusalem will not end until the "times of the Gentiles be fulfilled." We will soon learn that Jesus told us this will happen when history reaches the tip of the toes on a certain statue. He even told John to write that the outer court area of the Temple will be controlled by Gentiles during the last half of the Tribulation period (Revelation 11:2).

And there was given me [John] a reed like unto a rod: and the angel stood, saying, Rise, and measure the temple of God, and the altar, and them that worship therein. But the court which is without the temple leave out, and measure it not; for it is given unto the Gentiles: and the holy city shall they tread under foot forty and two months. (Revelation 11:1–2)

Why does God allow Muslims on the Temple Mount today? Because Jesus said Gentiles will control part of the Temple Mount until His Second Coming and the establishment of His kingdom on earth.

Nebuchadnezzar's Dream

The second chapter of Daniel records Nebuchadnezzar's dream of the great statue, which is a timeline of the Gentiles. It doesn't reveal the day or the hour of the Second Coming. But it does disclose some important information about the Second Coming and Jesus' kingdom on earth.

When Daniel was called in to reveal Nebuchadnezzar's dream and its meaning, he told the king, "There is a God in heaven that revealeth secrets, and maketh known to the king Nebuchadnezzar what shall be in the latter days" (Daniel 2:28). God has let us know what shall be in the latter days, and His revelation has information about when Jesus will establish His kingdom on earth.

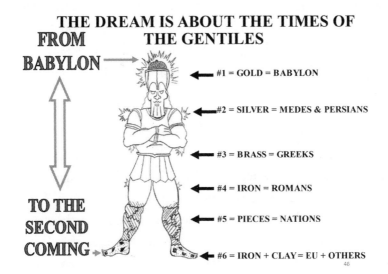

THE DREAM IS ABOUT THE TIMES OF
FROM THE GENTILES
BABYLON

#1 = GOLD = BABYLON

#2 = SILVER = MEDES & PERSIANS

#3 = BRASS = GREEKS

#4 = IRON = ROMANS

TO THE
SECOND #5 = PIECES = NATIONS
COMING

#6 = IRON + CLAY = EU + OTHERS
46

Daniel said a stone (Jesus) struck the statue on the toes of its feet; it became like chaff and the wind blew it away (Daniel 2:36–42). Then, "the stone (Jesus; see Deuteronomy 32:3–4, 15; Psalm 18:2, 31; Romans 9:33; 1 Corinthians 10:4) became a great mountain and filled the whole earth. (Jesus will establish His earthly kingdom when the stone strikes the tip of the toes.)

Jesus cannot establish His earthly kingdom until every detail—jot and tittle—of this prophecy is fulfilled. This prophecy is the Word of God. It must be fulfilled from the top of the statue's head to the tip of the statue's toes; otherwise, the Bible is wrong.

Notice it doesn't matter when the Scripture was given (two thousand or three thousand years ago) or who said it (Jesus, a prophet, etc.), what has been written or said has been right every time. Peter said, "We have also a more sure word of prophecy; whereunto ye do well that ye take heed" (2 Peter 1:19). The prophecy in Nebuchadnezzar's statue is sure (certain, accurate). We are wise to believe this.

Kingdom Established When Jesus Strikes the Tip of the Toes

The angel Gabriel told Daniel, "Seventy weeks are determined upon thy people and upon thy holy city, to finish the transgression, and to make an end of sins, and to make reconciliation for iniquity, and to bring in everlasting righteousness, and to seal up the vision and prophecy, and to anoint the most Holy." (Daniel 9:24)

The kingdom of righteousness will not be established on earth until Israel has gone through the Seventieth Week of Daniel and Jesus is anointed as the King. The return of Israel is setting the stage for the terminal generation, the Tribulation period, the coming King of Kings and Lord of Lords, and the thousand-year reign of Jesus on earth.

Some commentators suggest Israel went through the Tribulation period in AD 70, but there is no evidence in that year of a seven-year covenant, of anyone tracking all buying and selling, or of anyone who could come close to destroying all flesh, etc. The Tribulation has not happened, and it cannot happen until all the conditions are met.

Kingdom Not Established During Babylonian Empire

Israel and Jerusalem did not exist, so Jesus couldn't establish His throne in Jerusalem. The Temple did not exist. It was a long way to the tip of the toes. Jeremiah said Israel's captivity would last seventy years, Babylon would fall, and Israel would be released (Israel had to be in captivity for seventy years, Babylon had to be replaced by another kingdom, etc.; Daniel 2:39). Isaiah said Israel would be put off the land twice and return twice (this was Israel's first time off the land). They would have to return to the land and be put off again. Gabriel said Israel would have to go through the Tribulation Period (the toes). Gabriel said a command to rebuild Jerusalem would be given, then sixty-nine weeks of years (483 years) would pass, then Messiah would appear, but would be killed. It would still be hundreds of years before He would reign on earth.

Confirmation

About two or three years before the fall of Babylon, Daniel had a vision that started with the Medes and Persians and went all the way to the Antichrist and the Tribulation (Daniel 8:1–15).

> The angel Gabriel appeared unto Daniel and said, "I will make thee know what shall be in the last end of the indignation: for at the time appointed the end shall be." (Daniel 8:19)

Gabriel revealed the rise and fall of the Antichrist at the time of the end. He told Daniel to shut up the vision because it would be many days (a long time) before the appointed time arrived (Daniel 8:25–26).

After revealing many amazing prophecies in the book of Daniel, God said:

> Go thy way, Daniel: for the words are closed up and sealed til the time of the end. (Daniel 12:9)

The Lord's return was still in the future. We do not know the day or the hour it will occur, but since the days of Daniel, we have known that it will be:

- At the tip of the toes.
- At God's appointed time.
- After many days.

The disciples asked Jesus about the signs of His coming and He answered:

But of that day and hour knoweth no man, no, not the angels of heaven, but my Father only. (Matthew 24:36)

Kingdom Not Established During Medo-Persian Empire

The command to rebuild Jerusalem was given about 445 or 444 BC. After the command, 483 years still had to pass before Messiah appeared the first time (about AD 32–33). Messiah still had to die (the appointed time, tip of the toes, and earthly kingdom were still many years in the future).

Kingdom Not Established During the Greek Empire

The Greek Empire ended about ninety-five years before Messiah entered Jerusalem to be killed. Messiah still had to appear the first time and die before the appointed time to establish His kingdom.

Kingdom Not Established During the Roman Empire

The Messiah entered Jerusalem on the exact day the 483 years were fulfilled, but He said Jerusalem would be destroyed because the Jews did not know what day that was. A day or so later, Jesus said the Temple would be destroyed (not one stone would be left upon another). He said after two more days (Matthew 26:2), He would be killed (it was too early for the earthly kingdom).

When Jesus was asked about the signs of His coming and the end of the age, He replied that there will be false Christs (plural), wars and rumors of wars (plural), but the end was not yet. (This confirms the appointed time could not have occurred in past generations, because it was still in the future when Jesus walked the earth.)

Jesus said there will be famines, pestilences, and earthquakes (all plural) in diverse places before the end. History would go through many false Christs before the Antichrist arrives; many wars and rumors of wars before the Battle of Armageddon; many pestilences before the fourth horseman of the Apocalypse; many pestilences and famines before the third horseman of the Apocalypse comes forth; and many earthquakes before the greatest earthquake ever. History must go through many events before the appointed time at the tip of the toes.

Jesus said the end will come after the gospel goes all over the world (Matthew 24:14) and, in the book of Revelation, He said an angel will preach the gospel all over the world during the Tribulation period (Revelation 14:6).

Jesus said the Jews in Judea should flee into the wilderness when the Antichrist defiles the Temple (Matthew 24:15–16), and in the book of Revelation, He said they will be there three and a half years. He told them to flee because Satan will be cast to this earth and try to kill them (Revelation 12:12–17). This is fascinating. Before Michael and his angels go to war in Heaven with Satan and his angels, and before Satan is cast down to this earth, God will give the Jews in Judea a sign to flee into the wilderness, because Satan will try to persecute and kill them when he is cast down to this earth. Think about this. Jesus said there will be a generation that will not pass away until everything is fulfilled. Satan will try to kill these Jews, so God will have them flee into the wilderness and supernaturally protect them so Satan cannot kill them. Some in that generation will not pass away, and the Tribulation period will be cut short for them. At this point, Satan will know that his time is short (Revelation 12:12).

When asked about the signs of His Coming, Jesus said to watch the fig tree (Israel) and all the trees (nations). The lower part of the legs (Roman Empire) still had to break into pieces (nations). The nations still had to come back together. The lower legs, feet, and toes still had to be fulfilled before the appointed time at the tip of the toes.

About AD 32 or 33, Jesus said those who want to know when He will come back to establish His kingdom on earth should watch Israel and all the nations. Great! But what do Israel and all the nations have to do with the appointed time? We are coming to that.

Daniel told the king, "There is a God in heaven that revealeth secrets, and maketh known to the king Nebuchadnezzar what shall be in the latter days" (Daniel 2:28). In his sermon on Pentecost, Peter indicated that the last days had started with the beginning of the Church (Acts 2:16–17). Later, the apostle said, "Be not ignorant of this one thing, that one day is with the Lord as a thousand years, and a thousand years as one day" (2 Peter 3:8).

Some early Christians believed there were about two God-days of history (two thousand years) from the creation of Adam to Abraham; about two more God-days of history (two thousand years) from Abraham to the First Coming of Jesus; and about two more God-days of history (two thousand years) from the First Coming of Jesus to the Millennium (tip of the toes). We are approaching two thousand years (two God-days) of Church history.

After saying, "Behold the fig tree and all the trees," Jesus said, "Heaven and earth shall pass away: but my words shall not pass away" (Luke 21:33). The Word of God is more stable than Heaven and earth. The kingdom will be established on earth after Israel has gone through the Tribulation period and history reaches the appointed time at the tip of the toes.

Jesus was talking about His Second Coming in the Olivet Discourse when He said, "Wheresoever the body is, there will the eagles be gathered" (Matthew 24:28).

In the book of Revelation, He explained that birds will be gathered at the Battle of Armageddon to eat the bodies of kings, captains, mighty men, animals, etc. (Revelation 19:17–18). Jesus will establish His kingdom on earth after his Second Coming (after the Tribulation period).

Kingdom Not Established During the Lower Part of the Legs of Iron (Church Age)

The Roman Empire had broken into pieces (nations). The nations still had to form one last world government. Israel still had to come back into existence and return to the land the second time. Jerusalem and the Temple had to be rebuilt. History had not reached the appointed time at the tip of the toes, but it was getting close.

A Sprouting Fig Tree and All the Trees (Nations)

On October 24, 1945, the UN came into being with a charter calling for the establishment of a world government. (The UN began with a few trees [nations], but it now has more than 190 trees [nations]). On January 1, 1948, an agreement by three European nations to unite went into effect (it now has twenty-seven trees or nations). On May 14, 1948, Israel officially came back into being as a nation.

After saying, "Behold the fig tree and all the trees," Jesus said, "Heaven and earth shall pass away: but my words shall not pass away" (Luke 21:33). The Word of God is more stable than Heaven and earth. The kingdom will be established on earth after Israel has gone through the Tribulation period and history reaches the appointed time at the tip of the toes.

The importance of Israel (the fig tree) coming back into being in 1948 cannot be overemphasized. This is when history started moving into the feet of iron plus clay on the statue when Israel (the fig tree), the EU (the iron), and the UN (the clay) started forming in the late 1940s. The feet of iron plus clay have been forming for more than seventy years. History is now approaching the toes of the statue.

It can be said like this:

- Israel—the fig tree—exists.
- The EU, the iron—the revived Roman Empire, the group of trees that the Antichrist will come from—exists.
- The UN, the clay—a group representing all the trees—exists.

These things were written in the Scriptures about 2,600 years ago in the days of Daniel (Daniel 9:26).

How to Know When the Kingdom on Earth Is Getting Close

Now learn a parable of the fig tree; When his branch is yet tender, and putteth forth leaves, ye know that summer is nigh: So likewise ye, when ye shall see all these things, know that it is near, even at the doors. Verily I say unto you, This generation shall not pass, till all these things be fulfilled.

Instead of saying more prophecy must be fulfilled, Jesus said when the fig tree appears, everything will be fulfilled before that generation passes away. When the fig tree sprouts, there will be people on earth who will not die before everything is fulfilled; some flesh (people from the terminal generation) will survive.

The Point

Because every detail of Bible prophecy must be fulfilled, Jesus' earthly kingdom could not have been established in any other generation. But the fact that history has moved into the feet on the statue means that this generation may be the appointed one.

We should not be dogmatic, but some believe the terminal generation sprouted when the fig tree (Israel) declared independence and was recognized as a nation on May 14, 1948. Based on Psalm 90:10, some believe a generation is seventy to eighty years, but that is opinion, not a clear statement. Israel's seventy-third year of existence was May 14, 2021.

Messiah will destroy the statue and establish His kingdom when history reaches the tip of the toes.

One-World Government Forming

In September 2015, the UN (all the trees) met and adopted seventeen sustainable development goals that will establish a world government by 2030, but that is just part of the story. When history reaches the toes, there will be three global systems on earth at the same time: a global political system (under the Antichrist), a global religious system (under the False Prophet), and a global economic system (to track all buying and selling). These three great systems are coming on the scene now.

- Global political system: The UN, socialism, etc.
- Global religious system: Pope Francis is trying to merge Christianity, Judaism, and Islam.
- Global economic system: A global currency that can be tracked.

When Antichrist Will Appear

Antichrist will appear:

- After the Rapture
- After the ten toes appear
- On the same day he confirms a covenant with many for seven years of peace in the Middle East

When the Kingdom on Earth Will Begin

The kingdom on earth will begin seven years (2,520 days) after the Antichrist confirms the covenant with many for seven years of peace on earth. This will be three and a half years (1,260 days) after the Antichrist defiles the rebuilt Temple at the middle of the Tribulation period.

The triumphal entry happened on the exact day it was prophesied. The crucifixion and death of Jesus happened on the exact day and at the exact hour prophesied. Jesus was crucified, dead, and buried, and it looked like God's people could forget about a kingdom on earth.

Then Jesus was raised from the dead on the exact day it was prophesied. He came out of the tomb and appeared to Mary and others.

The trees are sprouting today, and there are now more than 190 trees (all the nations) in the UN. The EU trees are sprouting and there are now twenty-seven trees (nations) in the UN. The fig tree sprouted (May 14, 1948). This was Israel's second return, just like Isaiah said.

Other Must-Be-Fulfilled Prophecies on This Timeline

- Judah had to be conquered. (Judah was conquered.)
- Judah had to be conquered by Babylon. (Judah was conquered by Babylon.)
- Jerusalem and the Temple had to be destroyed twice. (Jerusalem and the Temple were destroyed by Babylon the first time.)
- The Jews had to be deported to Babylon. (The Jews were deported to Babylon the first time.)
- The Jews had to spend seventy years in Babylon. (The Jews spent exactly seventy years in Babylon.)
- The Jews had to return to Israel after seventy years in Babylon. (The Jews returned to Israel after seventy years in Babylon.)
- Babylon had to be conquered. (Babylon was conquered by the Medes and Persians when the hand wrote on the wall.)
- Babylon had to be conquered seventy years after Judah was conquered. (Babylon was conquered exactly seventy years after Judah was conquered.)
- Someone had to issue a command for Jerusalem to be rebuilt. (Artaxerxes issued a command for Jerusalem to be rebuilt; Nehemiah 2:1–8.)
- The Temple had to be rebuilt. (The rebuilt Temple was completed about 516 BC.)
- Jerusalem and the Temple had to be destroyed a second time. (Jerusalem and the Temple were destroyed a second time by the Roman Empire in AD 70.)
- Israel had to be put off the land a second time. (Israel was put off the land and scattered all over the world by the Roman Empire in AD 70.)
- Jerusalem had to be rebuilt a second time. (Jerusalem has been rebuilt a second time.)
- The Temple must be rebuilt a third time. (The architectural plans for a Third Temple are complete.)

- The animal sacrifices must resume. (Priests have been trained to resume the animal sacrifices as soon as they can get government permission.)
- There must be peace negotiations to produce a seven-year covenant. (Peace negotiations have been ongoing for many years.)

History has now moved into the feet, and all prophecy must be fulfilled by the time it reaches the tip of the toes. This explains why there are calls for a world government, a world religion, a world economy, and a world tracking system. History is approaching the appointed time, and the birth pains are becoming more obvious.

What I Said

I stated earlier that I would tell you what I was *going* to say. Then I *said* it. Now I'm telling you *what I said*: Our generation is the first and only generation that could have living people on earth at the Second Coming of Jesus and the beginning of His kingdom on earth. History is approaching the appointed time at the tip of the toes.

Remember the former things of old: for I am God, and there is none else; I am God, and there is none like me, Declaring the end from the beginning, and from ancient times the things that are not yet done, saying, My counsel shall stand, and I will do all my pleasure. (Isaiah 46:9–10)

Let us hold fast the profession of our faith without wavering; (for he is faithful that promised;) And let us consider one another to provoke unto love and to good works: Not forsaking the assembling of ourselves together, as the manner of some is; but exhorting one another: and so much the more, as ye see the day approaching. (Hebrews 10:23–25)

The Best Is Yet to Come

The kingdom on earth will last one thousand years (Revelation 20:1–6). Satan will be bound and chained. Resurrected and raptured Christians will come out of Heaven with Jesus for the marriage supper and to reign on earth with Him (Revelation 19:7–9). Resurrected Christians, Jews, and Tribulation saints will be in their new bodies.

The kingdom on earth will eventually transition into the eternal kingdom. Jesus will rule over the kingdom on earth and the eternal kingdom (2 Samuel 7:12–16; Daniel 7:27; Luke 1:26–35). The earthly kingdom will include every nation on earth (Isaiah 2:1–4). The earthly capitol will be in Jerusalem (later New Jerusalem).

The throne will be on the Temple Mount. Jews who survive the Tribulation will serve Jesus. Jerusalem, the Temple Mount, and the Jewish people will be holy (Isaiah 52:1; Zechariah 8:3). People from all over the world will worship Jesus at the Temple Mount (Isaiah 66:18–23; Zechariah 14:16)). Jesus will teach, and His Word will go all over the world.

The wicked will be removed from the earth (Matthew 13:36–43). There will be peace, justice, righteousness, and joy on earth (Isaiah 11:1–9). The curse will be removed from the earth. People will live longer. Humans and animals will coexist in peace.

Crops will flourish, and more.

How to Qualify to Enter the Kingdom

Humble yourself, repent of your sins, put your faith in Jesus, and honestly ask Jesus to save you. You have until death or the Rapture to do that. But you could be running out of time due to the closeness of the Rapture.

SECTION III

JOHN PREDICTS END-TIMES TURBULENCE

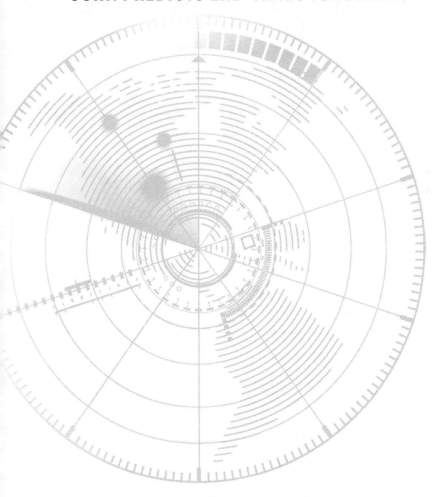

CHAPTER 9

REPORT ON THE ROARING SEAS

By Pete Garcia

SEVERAL YEARS AGO, I was driving down the road when I came across a radio program in progress. Intrigued, I listened as the narrator began intensely describing a woolly mammoth hunt with the sound of tribal drums beating in the background. He described how *early men* knew they couldn't kill the mammoth with spear and stone alone, so they had to improvise. As the group closed in on a herd, the tribesmen would begin to beat their drums, shouting and making a loud commotion to catch the animals off-guard. This in turn would cause the agitated mammoths to panic and start moving in the opposite direction. The direction in which they began moving was stationed with more hidden hunters with drums along the way. As the mammoths approached, these hunters would also begin making noises, beating drums, and shouting as loud as they could. This effectively began to channel the unsuspecting mammoths toward a ravine or cliff, sending them to a frenzied death.

Pretext

While I do not subscribe to caveman theories, I do, however, recognize this is as a valid hunting technique used by many indigenous tribes, and the example has been stuck in my mind ever since. Although I am no fan of Mr. Alex Jones' sensationalist programs or his post-Trib eschatology, I do agree that we're now witnessing the same technique being used against the general population by those with globalist agendas. Those who want a New World Order must perpetually beat the drum of crisis to get the masses (the herds, in their opinions) to move in the direction they want them to go. They do this by creating unnecessary panic regarding:

- A planet with several years of below-normal temperatures? *Global cooling*!
- A planet with several years of above-normal temperatures? *Global warming*!
- A planet with no predictable "doom and gloom" weather phenomena? *Climate change*!
- A pandemic with a 99.7 percent survival rate? *Existential crisis*!
- Capitalism and a free-market economy? *Inequality*!
- White people, conservatives, Christians, and Jews? *Catastrophe*!
- A nation bound by a Declaration of Independence and a Bill of Rights? *The horror*!

Now, all this begs questions as to who these globalists are and what they're trying to achieve. First, the globalists are those who are in power now and want to keep that power forever. They might be out in the open or operating behind the throne, but they hold the reins. They are the *establishment* Republicans and Democrats, the Bilderbergers (big business and media), the Trilateral Commission (powers behind the thrones), the George Soros family, the Rockefellers, European bureaucrats, climate-alarmist prophets, United Nations advocates, the international banking cartel, and so on.

They are throwing crisis after crisis at us in an attempt to get us agitated and panicked, to channel us onto a predetermined path. Ultimately, their goals are to get us to suicide our national sovereignty by trading our liberties for security. We all witnessed this in 2020 with the global COVID lockdowns. Countless cities, states, and nations essentially surrendered their political capital and their economic livelihoods to the most survivable pandemic in human history. It was a surreal process to witness, and the tragedy in it was not just the dismantling of our constitutional republic, but of Western civilization at large. Nevertheless, the COVID-19(84) pandemic may have just been the final test run of a hundred-year process globalists have been perfecting to ensure the United States abdicates its throne as leader of the free world. Once that happens, the rest of the world will fall in line rather quickly and embrace the new normal of the Great Reset. This means accepting a new global government controlling every facet of life on the planet.

This is where they (the enlightened and elite globalists) want to take us. Yet, their plan isn't really their own. This is where the Bible said they would take us nearly two thousand years ago.

> Then I stood on the sand of the sea. And I saw a beast rising up out of the sea, having seven heads and ten horns, and on his horns ten crowns, and on his heads a blasphemous name. (Revelation 13:1)[71]

Background

In the book of Revelation and its Old Testament predecessor, Daniel, the sea represents humanity, and the multi-headed beast represents the final world government (see Daniel 2, 7–8; Revelation 17). The image John is shown is this government rising out of the sea of humanity and becoming an all-consuming, all-powerful, totalitarian government. It manages to harness complete control over the three pillars of civilization: government, religion, and economics. In all of human history, no kingdom or empire has ever been able to control all three for the entire planet. In fact, those who came closest to achieving this were the Romans. Interestingly, the final world empire will be a revival of the old Roman one, with some major overhauls.

First, it will have the technology to do so. With the legacy twentieth-century fiat currencies on the way out, digital currencies promise to deliver an Orwellian level of control of what people can buy and sell—everywhere. Second, the world has been rushing toward a one-world government since before World War II ended. Last, the push for total religious ecumenism has plateaued, seemingly waiting for some final and mysterious dam to break.

However, let's get back to the drumbeats. Now, these represent different things at different times and are often interchangeable, depending on what exactly the globalists need them for. At times, the drums have been used to ratchet up tension through *crisis*; other times, the drums have beat rhythmically to just keep the world moving in a particular direction via *incrementalism*. Either way, the drums were always beating, and the world has always marched to the beat. For the remainder of this chapter, we'll call the soothing drumbeat *incrementalism*, and the later, louder, annoying drumbeat *crisis*. The two work in tandem and complement each other's end-state, which is global government.

Incrementalism, thus far, has been the most effective and corrosive method by which these globalists have crept into our universities; local, state, and federal governments; the media; and big business. Slowly and steadily they seeded these positions of power with like-minded people in the hopes of the big payoff one day. That day was September 11, 2001, and in the months and years that followed, massive transitions began to reshape our nation. Incrementalism is the slowly but steadily increased application of heat to the water in the proverbial pot of frogs. Little by little, the temperature heats up, and by the time we begin to notice that the water has become too uncomfortable, it is too late.

Most Americans are unaware of a decline in our individual liberty, and the reason is obvious: the decline rarely takes the form of sudden deprivations, but instead takes the form of unnoticed erosion; thus we come to regard whatever state we are in as a normal condition.[72] —Leonard E. Reed

If you've read many articles like this one and have kept up with current events over the last ten years, most of what I'm saying isn't any real surprise. You know that government control has only ever been expanding. This is why the Constitution was designed to limit governmental power because the founders understood how power corrupts institutions. This is why those who are true believers in a global agenda have used incrementalism to creep into all the necessary organizations and institutions under the radar. They knew if they told people their real intentions, they would have been run out of town on a rail long ago. But incrementalism is painstakingly slow. They needed to marry those long stretches of slow growth with short bursts of major growth. As the old saying goes, nothing creates opportunity faster than a crisis, which is why everything becomes a crisis.

The real question is: Why?

Why would the people in power try to destroy the very system that put them in power? Because the powers that be (pick an administration) seem to know something the rest of us don't, namely, that if they don't act quickly, they may not get a seat at the global table. Granted, none of these globalists would point to Revelation 13 as to why they are doing what they are doing. They are simply being driven by much older and darker unseen forces: Satan and his army of principalities, powers, and spiritual wickedness in high places (Ephesians 6:12).

Now, I say all of this regarding America's predetermined fall not because I want it to happen or believe America is the center of Bible prophecy or last-days events. I do, however, believe the collapse of the United States is key to allowing for the revival of the Roman Empire 2.0, which cannot begin with the US in its present position as the global leader.

Thus, understanding how much time we have left as a nation will in large measure determine how much time the world has left in its present state. According to Acts 17:26, God has "determined the nations' pre-appointed times and the boundaries of their dwellings," and for nearly one hundred years, He has used the United States to halt the spread of tyrannical governments and has used us to slow-roll this rush towards global government. He has done this to allow for the rebirth of the nation of Israel and reestablish its role in last-days events.

While the United States is not a covenant nation (this honor belongs only to Israel), God has blessed the US as long as we have continued to honor Him. But from the ashes of the victory of World War II and our subsequent explosion of wealth and leisure in the 1950s, that honor we paid Him became increasingly superficial…and we began to pay the price. From the late 1960s onward, this honor seemed to be more and more replaced with hostility towards God. Correspondingly, He began to remove His hand of protection from us while we began to nationally suffer *death by a thousand cuts*. In fact, our nation has so many existential issues at the present that it would be impossible for us to recover without God's divine interference.

As the principle in Luke 12:48 states, those to whom much is given, much is required. America has been blessed like no other nation in history, so our end will come swiftly and severely. In our absence, the floodgates for globalism will open to fill the void left in our wake. The globalists, driven by their satanic overlords, can sense this collapse as imminent and are salivating at the prospect. On the other hand, those who are not yet ready to yield their position sense it as well, and are readying themselves.

For this reason, we are every bit in the throes of a *cold civil war*, with both sides digging in for the long fight. This cold civil war, given the right trigger, will turn hot before the end comes as people wake up to the reality that the American dream is being intentionally destroyed. But even if the pro-change side loses (as expected), the globalists will win anyway, because our nation will, at that point, be too fractured and weakened to ever recover. Such will be the swiftness of our demise that our national collapse will go from impossible to inevitable, without ever passing through improbable. However, there is one possible solution, or way through this, without having to go through another bloody civil war.

If one thinks about how America's cold civil war could be resolved, there seem to be only five possibilities. One would be to change the political subject. Ronald Reagan used to say that when the little green men arrive from outer space, all of our political differences will be transcended and humanity will unite for the first time in human history. Similarly, if some jarring event intervenes—a major war or a huge natural calamity, for example—it might reset our politics.[73] —Charles R. Kesler

Context

We know, according to Revelation 13, that the world will eventually end up under a singular global system run by a man identified as the "little horn" (also known as the "rider on the white horse," the "man of sin," the "man of lawlessness," the "son of perdition," the "Beast," etc.) This man will control the entire earth and will use religion, politics, and economics to do so. I estimate he will be able to recover or assume control over America's vast wealth and military arsenals to then force three other regions/areas to concede. He will have access to or control over a powerful, 5G or 6G, quantum-based, artificially intelligent, information network. Lastly, he will have the entirety of the fallen angelic hosts (including Satan) aiding him in his rise to power.

So, how do we get from where we are today—a world divided and tossing like a roaring sea—to where the Scripture says we will be tomorrow (whenever that tomorrow might be)? This coming of the Beast rests on two foundations: *infrastructure* and *opportunity*.

1. Infrastructure

And in the latter time of their kingdom,
When the transgressors have reached their fullness,
A king shall arise,
Having fierce features,
Who understands sinister schemes. (Daniel 8:23)

In 1980, a mysterious man under the pseudonym R. C. Christian appeared in Elbert County, Georgia, with cash in hand, requesting that a local granite company create a unique monument. To this day, the man (and the organization he represents) remains anonymous, and the monument remains a tribute to what the United Nations would later adopt as almost identical to its Sustainable Development Agenda. It is comprised of *ten commandments*, written in eight languages, with each language carved into the face of each of the four giant granite slabs. The languages, perhaps in tribute to the Tower of Babel, are English, Spanish, Swahili, Arabic, traditional Chinese, Russian, and Hebrew. Here is the list of the commandments:

1. Maintain humanity under 500,000,000 in perpetual balance with nature.
2. Guide reproduction wisely—improving fitness and diversity.
3. Unite humanity with a living new language.
4. Rule passion—faith—tradition—and all things with tempered reason.
5. Protect people and nations with fair laws and just courts.
6. Let all nations rule internally resolving external disputes in a world court.
7. Avoid petty laws and useless officials.
8. Balance personal rights with social duties.
9. Prize truth—beauty—love—seeking harmony with the infinite.
10. Be not a cancer on the earth—Leave room for nature—Leave room for nature.[74]

Aside from the disturbing and anonymous nature of its existence, the first commandment should send shivers down the spine of everyone who reads it. How does a world with a population of around eight billion drop down to a population of a half billion? I believe this is where the four horsemen of the Apocalypse enter the equation. Once they begin their apocalyptic rides (inside the confines of the beginning of the Seventieth Week of Daniel), nearly 2.5 billion people (or one-quarter of the world's population) will lose their lives. Their ride may even be pointed to by those alive then as a fulfillment of these *Georgia Guidestones* as part of the end-times delusion.

However, for a singular world government to rule and reign for seven years very soon, global infrastructure for global governance must first exist. It will have to control the Internet and global commerce, and must have established regionalized political and military arrangements already in place. Were it not for five major world powers, the world would vote tomorrow on some new form of global government. The five holdouts are the United States, China, Russia, Turkey, and Iran. We know, according to Scripture, that at least three of the five powers will be utterly decimated in the Gog-Magog conflict (Ezekiel 38–39) before the Beast's ascendancy to total global control.

Presumably, the US will have abdicated its throne long before that, since, as a longtime ally of Israel, we must be in such a weakened position to not even rise above a diplomatic protest as this massive coalition marches against Israel. This leaves only China, who has an eventual role to play later in the book of Revelation as it continues to ready its two hundred million-man army (Revelation 9:15–16; 16:12).

2. Opportunity

The other thing that must follow the framework is **opportunity**. If we here in the twenty-first century have learned anything, it is that power corrupts, and absolute power corrupts absolutely. In terms of how the Beast comes to power, there must be opportunity, and that opportunity must come in the form of crisis. Whoever this Antichrist ends up being, he will stand far apart from the rest of the political herd and will appear to be (at least initially) completely trustworthy, ethical, transparent, intelligent, and competent. His oratory skills will make Barack Obama's appear infantile, and he will step up and solve the seemingly insolvable issues surrounding said crisis.

We've seen how the global system has tried time and again to present something, anything, as the crisis of record they can somehow use to their advantage: war, global cooling, global warming, climate change, Ebola, COVID-19, and other pandemic diseases, banks too big to fail, oil, water, food, immigration, AIDS, Islamic terrorism, information wars, etc. That's not to say these aren't issues, but none of these were ever big enough for the Great Reset the globalists and the UN have hoped for. They need a crisis of true global calamity, yet one crisis is coming that I believe will be used as THE crisis to force the nations to realign. I am so sure it is THE crisis because it's the one thing none of them (the godless, Christ-rejecting leadership) are even talking about. If it is mentioned at all, it's only used as a punchline to be laughed at and mocked.

The crisis?

The Rapture of the Church.

While Mr. Kesler, in his aforementioned quote, does present five *potential* scenarios in his brief (should you choose to read it), only two are feasible. Either we (the US) go through another civil war or some outside event interrupts our present political polarity. Although "little green men" are not going to be the cause preventing the next American civil war, President Reagan's logic wasn't far off. Should the Rapture of the Church occur in the next decade, this will in fact present the perfect global calamity the globalists didn't know they needed.

Not only will it collapse the United States, but it will also rid the world of all of those troublesome Christians (a good deal of whom make up conservative movements). This extraordinary, supernatural event will, seemingly, hand the globalists the world on a silver platter as they greedily dive in to redistribute the wealth left behind by hundreds of millions of Christians. In the case of the United States, they would redistribute (or confiscate) the wealth of some thirty million Americans from all walks of life (e.g., assuming a 10 percent Rapture percentage).

Subtext

All of this *roaring of the seas* thus far (the incrementalism, political polarity, globalist infrastructure, and crisis-opportunism) has been fear-based stage-setting for what is to come. Namely, Satan will use the incessant roaring of the seas to channel man's unending desire for peace, security, and utopia into this final world government. This artificially induced anxiety is critical to get populations to hand over their liberty before the beginning of the Seventieth Week. This form of social conditioning, like movies, is desensitizing the masses to embrace totalitarian governance. While this is the norm in most of the world, Western civilization has been (historically speaking) more reluctant to give up hard-fought freedoms—that is, until our postmodern era.

Postmodernism and the destruction of objective truth have been the greatest success for globalists in the past two millennia. They have followed a carefully scripted strategy of introducing ambiguity into the public arena of ideas to intentionally cause confusion. This confusion was intended initially to divide a population (making it easier to conquer) and then target groups according to their social and ethnic assemblages. These are the three areas Satan is using to drive humanity off the cliff and into his final world government.

1. Global Godlessness

Almost by definition, secularism cannot be a future: it's a present-tense culture that over time disconnects a society from cross-generational purpose. Which is why there are no examples of sustained atheist civilizations. "Atheistic humanism" became inhumanism in the hands of the Fascists and Communists and, in its less malign form in today's European Union, a kind of dehumanism in which a present-tense culture amuses itself to extinction. Post-Christian European culture is already post-cultural and, with

its surging Muslim populations, will soon be post-European.[75]
—Mark Steyn

The Apostle Peter remarked that, in the last days, scoffers would come
mocking that Christ had not yet returned (2 Peter 3:3–4). Paul wrote that,
in the last days, perilous times would come (2 Timothy 3:1). Paul's definition of "perilous," interestingly enough, does *not* include war or natural disasters, but how treacherous and wicked men would become. Jesus
stated that, in the last days, because lawlessness will abound, the love of
many will grow cold (Matthew 24:12). Furthermore, Jesus said the days
surrounding His return will be similar to the days of Noah and Lot—both
of whom were noted for being exceptionally violent and wicked—yet
things will appear as normal (Luke 17:26–30).

Satan realizes government without a spiritual component is an empty
suit. This means all the world's present varied religions and philosophical ideologies are not going to exist during the Tribulation. Rather, Satan
will use these until they no longer serves his purposes. Satan knows we
humans are designed to worship, so he will give the world's itching ears
what it wants to hear: a dead religion that offends no one and saves no
one. The two (politics and religion) must go hand in hand in order to
be effective. With the Restrainer no longer restraining (the Holy Spirit-
infused Church), the False Prophet (religion) will be imbued with supernatural powers to deceive the masses; he will lead them into this final
world religion to promote global peace and harmony.

Juxtaposed to this foregone end state is how, at present, *human secularism* rules the day. It rules governments, the media, the entertainment
industry, and academia. However, the final years will not be filled with
atheists, agnostics, or pagans. It will be filled with those who will embrace
the ecumenical system set up by *Mystery Babylon* (the religious harlot
of Revelation 17) who arrives in force after the Rapture of the Church.
Granted, this will change at the midpoint when the Antichrist declares
himself to be God and will demand everyone, everywhere, to worship

him on threat of death. However, those who are too proud to kneel to Jesus Christ today will one day willingly kneel to the Antichrist.

2. Global Instability

> And you will hear of wars and rumors of wars. See that you are not troubled; for all these things must come to pass, but the end is not yet. For nation will rise against nation, and kingdom against kingdom. (Matthew 24:6–7)

The terms "nations" and "kingdoms" used above might seem a bit redundant, but they mean two different things in their original Greek form. "Nation" is *ethnos*, by which we get the word "ethnicity." "Kingdom" is *basileia*, which conveys a political or governmental element. In true Hegelian dialectic fashion (thesis→antithesis→synthesis), Satan uses these violent, useful idiots to drive people into the arms of a totalitarian government. Islamic terrorism, communism, fascism, and violent political activism have become the antithesis by which globalists increasingly introduce invasive and constrictive legislation on the world who is ready to trade freedom for security.

Similarly, the twentieth and twenty-first centuries have been rife with economic turmoil. Satan has used this to hopelessly entangle the global economies so that a global currency is the only solution. This is what makes the prospect of an American collapse so appealing (to Satan). So much of the world today depends on a strong American dollar. However, our dollar has been on the decline due to massive government debt and the outsourcing of our economy to hostile nations. Thus, to sum up the past two centuries in a brief summary, it would be this:

The nationalism, socialism, capitalism, Marxism, and other isms of the nineteenth and twentieth centuries resulted in two world wars, two major revolutions (Bolshevik and Maoist), the embracing of postmodernism, and numerous economic depressions, all resulting in the deaths of over five hundred million people and the total restructuring of the global order. The ideological and economic chaos is forcing the world to abandon nationalism in favor of regionalization and, ultimately, globalization as a means to avoid the mistakes of past generations. Aided by the meteoric advancements in technology, this is the framework (infrastructure) on which the Beast will cement his authority over the entire face of the earth. All he needs now is the perfect crisis...the Rapture.

3. Global Peace and Security

> For you yourselves know perfectly that the day of the Lord so comes as a thief in the night. For when they say, "Peace and safety!" then sudden destruction comes upon them, as labor pains upon a pregnant woman. And they shall not escape. (1 Thessalonians 5:2–3)

The drumbeat of the past two centuries has hinged largely on peace and security. Since 9/11, we have increasingly come to bear witness to the fact that one cannot have peace and security (Greek: *asphaleia*, "safety") without giving up rights and liberty. Granted, these freedoms had been steadily eroding with the onset of the Industrial Age, the rise in Marxist and socialist governance, and the decline in true faith in God. Nevertheless, the most successful experiment in human freedom and liberty, the United States, has become unsustainable, both for practical and existential reasons.

> And there will be signs in the sun, in the moon, and in the stars; and on the earth distress of nations, with perplexity, the sea and the waves roaring; men's hearts failing them from fear and the expectation of those things which are coming on the earth, for the powers of the heavens will be shaken. (Luke 21:25–26)

The globalists elite (think Prince Charles, Al Gore, Bill Gates, etc.) have been attempting to gin up an existential threat since at least the

1970s, and unfortunately for them, "mother nature" has not cooperated with their global ~~cooling~~ warming climate-change schemes. This is not to say the world doesn't face numerous seemingly unsolvable problems, because it does. However, these elite are ignoring the real problems and replacing them with the fake problems—such as climate change, racism, objective truth, fake pandemics, and nationalism—to drive their agendas.

The world has real issues, such as growing economic instability, exploding population growth, mass immigration and displacement, the decline of fiscal currencies and other twentieth-century legacy institutions, increasingly hybrid forms of terrorism and crime, artificial intelligence, cosmic threats (asteroids, solar storms, etc.), real pandemics, and real natural disasters (super-volcanoes, tsunamis, mega-earthquakes, etc.).

The fact that governments are placing fake threats above real threats shows how out of touch these leaders really are and how this will exacerbate their unpreparedness when a real crisis comes. The average man on the street sees this, and it is causing great anxiety and increased distrust with elected officials. The rise in anxiety is also cause for the dramatic increase in the destruction of the family unit, which is the pillar of any nation. This means an increase in substance abuse, divorce, fatherlessness, violence, crime, and many other existential dilemmas for the human race.

Closing Thoughts

> But you, Daniel, shut up the words, and seal the book **until the time of the end**; many shall run to and fro, and knowledge shall increase. (Daniel 12:4, emphasis added)

The book of Daniel, written over 2,600 years ago, was designed specifically so that it would not make sense until the earth enters the time in which it will make sense—i.e., *the time of the end*. It is one of the most underrated signs that we would even have the capacity to understand Bible prophecy as we do today; that should be a bright, glowing, neon sign that the end is near. It wasn't until the dispensationalist movement in the early nineteenth century that men like John Darby, Cyrus Schofield, Sir Robert Anderson, and Clarence Larkin **rediscovered** the three fundamental truths of biblical hermeneutics. The late Charles Ryrie coined these, the *sine qua non* ("without which there is not"), who codified the three fundamental truths below:

a. The bible requires a consistently literal interpretation (using a normal or plain sense of the language)
b. The church is not Israel, nor did it replace her
c. God does everything for His glory[76]

Once these dispensational pioneers did this, the prophetic Scriptures began to make sense. Furthermore, our place on the timeline began to make sense. And with so many prophetic trajectories converging over the twentieth and twenty-first centuries, we soon transcended from one underappreciated era into another as we moved from the *signs of the time* to the *time of the signs*.

Paradoxically, this unprecedented transition began occurring while a growing majority of professing Christendom was asleep at the wheel. Their prophetic drowsiness, as it were, was due to their preponderance of denominational leaders refusing to either teach the prophetic text or even acknowledge its reality. This profound ignorance by so many has been exacerbated by pulpits' unwillingness to sound the alarm as to the lateness of the hour. The same preachers and pastors who confidently teach that Jesus calmed the sea while aboard a boat with disciples even now refuse to teach the even greater miracle of Jesus one day calming the sea of nations at His Coming.

However, not all is lost. At no other point in history have so many believing and watching remnant believers been so convinced that we are living in the last moments of the last days. I believe this is one of the most underrated signs of our times, and it speaks volumes to the Holy Spirit's witness to all of us who are prophetically awake. The fact that the Holy Spirit is confirming the nearness of His coming in so many should be a wake-up call for all believers. Although we will not be here on the earth to hear it then, we hear it even now—the angelic proclamation reverberating through our souls that "the kingdoms of this world have become *the kingdoms* of our Lord and of His Christ, and He shall reign forever and ever!" Therefore, although we see the world falling apart, let us not despair. These things were predicted to come to pass in order for the end to come.

And let us consider one another in order to stir up love and good works, not forsaking the assembling of ourselves together, as is the manner of some, but exhorting one another, and so much the more as you see the Day approaching. (Hebrews 9:24–25)

CHAPTER 10

BEASTLY PROPHETIC WEATHER AHEAD

By Jeff Kinley

SATAN'S GOAL IS TO DOMINATE the world and be worshiped by it. This has been his unholy ambition since the moment sin entered his heart and he attempted to overthrow God's throne (Isaiah 14:12–14; Ezekiel 28:1–19).[77] Throughout history, he has sought to achieve this objective through men. The most near successful example of this was demonstrated during World War II in Nazi Germany. There, out of obscurity, arose a dictatorial tyrant named Adolf Hitler. Even today, more than eighty years later, the very mention of his name evokes repulsion in the hearts and minds of sane and decent people. However, Hitler was not able to push forward his vision of world dominance on his own. He had help. His minister of propaganda, Joseph Goebbels, was a strategic player whose bold tactics effectively brainwashed the German populace via the Nazi marketing campaign. Movies, posters, flyers, radio, and bullhorns mounted on trucks combined to blast the masses with the maniacal leader's message. This public-relations blitzkrieg eventually produced a mind-numbing effect, so much so that an overwhelming majority bought into the insanity of the racial superiority of the Aryan race, the supremacy of Germany itself, and the justification for invading Europe.

But it also could be argued that the dominant right hand of Germany's iron fist was actually another man named Heinrich Himmler. The bespectacled Himmler, whose official title was *Reichsführer* of the SS (Hitler's bodyguard), commanded his dreaded storm troopers (also known as the "brownshirts") into an elite police unit. He also ruled over the Gestapo (Secret State Police), and the Waffen SS (the military branch of the SS).

However, Himmler's ultimate evil legacy was achieved through founding the *Einsatzgruppen*, or paramilitary death squads, whose sole duty was to begin the systematic extermination of all Jews in Germany and the rest of Europe. This diabolical doctrine eventually led to death camps like Dachau, Sobibor, Birkenau, and Auschwitz, where some six million innocent Jews were rounded up, deceived, and sent to their deaths.

In order to do what he did, Hitler needed a Himmler.

Virtually no Bible teacher today would contest the idea that this duo served as a precursor to what Bible prophecy claims will occur in the last days. The devil's weakness, however, is his limitation of knowledge. He cannot know *when* God will permit him to fully pursue and achieve his long-held ambition to rule the world, be worshiped, and destroy many of the Jewish people.

For that reason, it is fair to speculate that Satan has groomed an Antichrist candidate in every generation, and would especially be doing so in these last days. Whenever the Rapture occurs (and we believe it is imminent), Satan must be prepared to catapult the man of his own choosing onto the global political stage. And, unlike Hitler before him, he will not achieve his agenda alone. By his side will be another man, another "Beast" (Revelation 13:11), also called the "False Prophet" (Revelation 16:13). Together, they will do what no tandem has ever done—bring the planet to its knees before the Prince of Darkness.

But precisely what will their nefarious agenda look like? And can we see any of it in formation right now?

The "Beauty" of the Beast

I believe the next prophesied event on God's calendar is the Rapture of the Church. As I search the Scriptures, I can find nothing specifically forecasted to occur between the rebirth and return of Israel to the Holy Land and the beginning of the Tribulation period. Therefore, because of this and because we understand Jesus' return for His Bride to occur prior to that Tribulation (pre-Trib Rapture), it stands to reason that it will be the next prophetic fulfillment. This too, plays a role in the rise of Antichrist. The impact of the Rapture will devastate the world like no other single happening in human history. Here's how:

1. **It will be *unexpected* (John 14:3).** Tragically, much of the church either has no knowledge of the Rapture doctrine, or willfully chooses to reject or ignore it. But even more ignorant is a world unaware of its coming reality. Many of those in culture who have heard of it (perhaps through preachers, books, or movies) gleefully mock and scoff at it, as they do Christ's Second Coming (2 Peter 3:3–4). But there will be no immediate warnings. No signs. No advance notice. It will simply happen, catching an entire planet off-guard.

2. **It will be *sudden* (1 Corinthians 15:51–52).** Scripture tells us that the Rapture will happen "in a moment, in the twinkling of an eye." It will happen so fast, in fact that before we realize it's happening, it will be over. In a millisecond, Jesus will descend, shout, and snatch away His beloved Bride. The word "moment" (Greek: *atomo*) refers to "that which cannot be divided," or an "infinitesimal measure of time." Like a flash of light, it's here and then is gone.

3. **It will be *global* (1 Thessalonians 4:13–18).** Every believer in Jesus Christ, from the largest nations to the most obscure neighborhood, will feel its impact as hundreds of millions instantly

vanish from earth's terrain and gravitational hold. Wherever there are Christians, there will suddenly be none. John records that a post-Rapture Heaven is populated by saints "from every tribe and tongue and nation" (Revelation 5:9; 7:9).

4. It will be *devastating* (1 Thessalonians 1:10). Because its reach is global, its impact will be global as well. Christians will disappear from every economic class, every walk of life, and every strata of society—from the working class, industry, sports, medicine, education, transportation, military, entertainment, and government. Virtually no segment of society will be left without a massive void from this "vanishing." This one truth alone will ignite a panic heretofore unknown and unexperienced in world history. Commerce will abruptly grind to a halt. Industries will be paralyzed. Travel will be halted. Governments will scramble to readjust and address the crisis. Militaries will be thrown into turmoil. Economies will take a sharp nosedive. Evil men will attempt coups. Evil nations will attempt invasions. Terrorists cells will launch attacks in a bid for power and dominance. The general public will panic. And dwarfing the COVID aftershocks we have seen in the supply chain flow, the transport of goods will be halted, with food and other commodities becoming scarce. And considering the collective week mental and emotional state of humanity, suicide and violent crime will surely spike.

Consider this: If current cultural appropriations, racist or gender "triggers," and offensive tweets can turn whole people groups into emotional cripples and angry mobs that incite violent protests, anarchy and "canceling" of anyone who merely disagrees with their ideology or agenda, how do you suppose they will react when life as they know it is snatched out of their hands? For at least a time following the Rapture, our entire planet will lose its collective mind, becoming unhinged.

And the devil will wring his hands in glee. For, you see, this is precisely the level of crisis he has tried to incite in recent history. Only now, he will spend this global turmoil into a welcome mat for the man who will incarnate his evil end times agenda.

Profile of a Spiritual Predator

Appearing on the horizon of this hopeless moment in history will be a single individual. He may or may not have previously been established politically. Scripture indicates he will likely be a Gentile, having come up out of the "sea" (literally, "nations," i.e., non-Jewish; see Revelation 13:1; 17:15). The Bible calls him a "beast," a word in the original Greek referring to a "wild, ravenous animal." Yet, he does not at first glance match such a description, for his platform and agenda are one of "peace and safety" (1 Thessalonians 5:3). He arrives to conquer, albeit peacefully (Revelation 6:1), bringing calm to earth's post-Rapture chaos. He understands the bigger the crisis, the more susceptible the masses will be to a leader who promises them relief from their anxious suffering. Like other rulers before him, he will no doubt pledge financial relief to those buried under the rubble of a collapsing economy. He will promise peace to a world teetering on the brink of nuclear annihilation—and he will deliver on these pledges. We are not told precisely how he will posture himself as the viable candidate to fill the global leadership void. But Scripture does give us clues that allow us to connect some of the dots.

How will he succeed in his nefarious scheme? And how will his persona feed into his success?

First, he will be a man of supreme arrogance and self-confidence. The prophet Daniel reveals he is a man who speaks boastfully and does whatever he wants (Daniel 7:8; 11:36). But Scripture's names for him actually uncover more of this man's unprecedented arrogance. He is called:

- The little horn (Daniel 7:8)
- The insolent king (Daniel 8:23)
- The prince who is to come (Daniel 9:26)
- The one who makes desolate (Daniel 9:27)

- The king who does as he pleases (Daniel 11:36)
- The foolish, worthless shepherd (Zechariah 11:15–17)
- The man of lawlessness (2 Thessalonians 2:3)
- The son of destruction (2 Thessalonians 2:3)
- The lawless one (2 Thessalonians 2:8)
- The antichrist (1 John 2:18, 22; 4:3; 2 John 1:7)
- The deceiver (2 John 1:7)

Second, he will be a man of persuasive speech. In his early days, I believe the full expression of his arrogance will be throttled back in order to win favor with people and governments. He will inspire, cajole, and convince others of his ability to lead a chaotic world to a better place. Like the evil one who empowers him, he has the ability to convince others of his vision with alluring eloquence and inspiring speech. This oratory skill will be essential not only in winning the populace, but also in convincing other world leaders to join him in his plan for planet earth.

Third, by all indications, what initially puts this man on the map is a particular peace treaty he forges with the nation Israel. Daniel 9:27 states, "and he will make a firm covenant with the many." In Daniel's immediate literary context, the "many" can only refer to the Jewish people (9:7, 11, 15, 19, 24, 25, 26).

What is unknown is the actual immediate situation Israel finds itself in during the interim following the Rapture and leading up to the signing of this unprecedented document. Some have speculated that it is during this time when the Gog-Magog war of Ezekiel 38–39 occurs. We do know that such an invasion of Israel did not happen in the Old Testament, and could *not* have happened since the first century, because there was no "Israel" to invade!

But it seems most plausible that the signing of Antichrist's covenant with Israel would *precede* the Gog-Magog war, as Ezekiel makes it clear that this invasion occurs when Israel is "living securely in the land" (38:8, 11, 14). This security would presumably be brokered by Antichrist's peace treaty. As for the invasion, it could be viewed as an attack on Antichrist himself because of the alliance he has with the Jewish people. The resulting supernatural deliverance of Israel from its enemies by God could be used as a marketing tool by the Beast to further his own image and agenda. In other words, he may even somehow spin the narrative to take credit for Israel's victory in the war!

Fourth, he will lead the nations together in unity. On the heels of the 2020 COVID crisis, calls for global unity came forth from a host of current and former world figures. Though not fully successful, they did manage to greatly raise global awareness among the nations, namely, that in order to defeat a worldwide threat (in this case a viral pandemic), there must be international cooperation and unity. I believe the Rapture and the ensuing chaos will raise the global level of emergency to the degree that one man will be able to seal the deal and finally bring them together. This multinational coalition will, in many ways, fulfill the vision of the current European Union, the World Economic Forum, and other international entities. Specifically, Antichrist's government will consist of ten primary nations that mirror the former geographical and political dominance of the former Roman Empire (Daniel 2:36–45; 7:1–28). Further, Revelation 13:1–2 describes this future kingdom as having "10 horns and seven heads" (cf. Revelation 17:3, 7). The seven heads are explained in Revelation 17:9 as "seven mountains" and "seven kings." Who might these mountains and kings refer to? The angel explains to John that, of the seven, "five have fallen, one is, and the other has not yet come." From John's historical perspective, these would correlate to Egypt, Assyria, Babylon, Medo Persia, and Greece—five former world empires that were no more by the first century—"five have fallen."

The Roman Empire—"one is"—doesn't lay in John's day. The future revived Roman Empire of Antichrist—"the other has not yet come."

As for the ten horns of Antichrist's kingdom, Revelation 17 reveals them to be "ten kings who have not yet received a kingdom, but they receive authority as kings with the beast for one hour. These have one purpose, and they give their power and authority to the beast" (17:12).

This end-times, united world government will be responsible for global policy in the last days, wielding unprecedented political and military authority across the planet.

So to summarize, the Antichrist will be:

1. A man of supreme self-confidence.
2. A man of powerful persuasion.
3. A man who is a friend of Israel initially.
4. A man who is the architect for global unity.

We also know that Antichrist will derive his power from Satan himself (Revelation 13:2) and miraculously return from the dead following a fatal head wound (Revelation 13:3). This supernatural occurrence supplies him with the credentials necessary to proclaim himself as God (2 Thessalonians 2:4), prompting "all who dwell on the earth to worship him and the Dragon" (Revelation 13:3–4). This declaration of deity lasts forty-two months, or three and a half years (13:5). And because of the authority of his platform, all those who refuse to worship him instantly become enemies of the state, and war is declared on them. This will primarily involve Christians and Jews during the second half of the Tribulation (12:13–17; 13:7).

The Second Beast

As previously mentioned, the Antichrist will be accompanied by a second man, also known as the False Prophet (Revelation 16:13; 19:20; 20:10). Jesus had earlier warned in Matthew 24:11, 24 and Mark 13:22 that, in the last days, "many false prophets will arise and show signs and wonders, in order, if possible, to lead the elect astray." This sidekick is called "*another* beast," meaning another (Greek: *allos*) of the same kind. In other words, he will be like the first beast in at least two ways: 1) he will also derive his authority from Satan (13:12, 15), and 2) his true character eventually reveals that he is a wild, ferocious monster (Greek: *therion*, or "beast"; Revelation 13:11).

The difference between the two men is while the first beast (Antichrist) will primarily be a political and military leader, the second (False Prophet) will exercise authority in the world of religion. His number-one objective is to cause the world not merely to honor, venerate, or applaud Antichrist, but to actually worship him as God in human flesh.

> He makes the earth and those who dwell in it to worship the first beast. (Revelation 13:12)

But how? How does he accomplish this? First, because his chief role is to promote worship, he no doubt will spearhead a movement highlighting the global leader's return from the dead following his fatal head wound. This most likely will have been an assassination attempt (Revelation 13:3). In doing this, the people of the earth will actually be worshiping Satan himself (13:4). The False Prophet will promote Antichrist as God, for who but God can overcome the grave and conquer death? Granted, it was previously believed by millions that Jesus Christ had already done this. But that was two thousand years ago. Who can know if it really happened? There are no documented videos to support such a claim. But this resurrection will be in the now; it will likely be witnessed by the entire world. He will be the Messiah every unredeemed soul can believe in.

Second, to substantiate his claims, the False Prophet will provide supernatural, miraculous as proof of the divine power residing in this "devilish duo" (2 Thessalonians 2:9).

> He performs great signs, so that he even makes fire to come out of heaven to the earth in the presence of men. (Revelation 13:13)

These miracles will be observable, supernatural, verifiable, and believable.

Third, he manufactures an "image" of the first beast. Actually, he so convinces the world of Antichrist's deity that he persuades "those who dwell on the earth" to make this image for him in order to honor and exalt the first beast (Revelation 13:14). The specific nature of this image is unknown, whether it be some sort of giant statue (like that of Nebuchadnezzar in Daniel 3) or some other, more technologically advanced, hologramic expression. Perhaps it will be something akin to the recent revelation of the "Giant," a ten-story, programmable, and movable statue proposed by an Irish company, and one outfitted with millions of LED pixels, allowing it to take the form of any person. This traveling wonder is set to appear in twenty-one major cities across the globe. It speaks, sings, and is billed as "the world's most captivating billboard."[78]

But whatever the beast-image's eventual form and composition, it will be epic, massively oppressive, and appealing.

Fourth, along with this, the False Prophet will use his powers to "give breath to the image of the base, so that the image of the beast would even speak" (Revelation 13:15). No doubt this will also be perceived as a supernatural, divine act (whether it actually is or not is not known). Regardless, its presence and function will be to inspire worship of Antichrist. Anyone who refuses to do so will be summarily put to death (Revelation 13:15).

Fifth, *666*. The False Prophet's crowning achievement will be to enact what is popularly known as the "mark of the beast" (Revelation 13:16; 14:9, 11; 15:2; 16:2; 19:20; 20:4). This "mark" (Greek: *charagma*) originally referred to a tattoo or some type of identifier that committed the wearer to a commanding officer or slave owner. Despite recent speculation that implanted chips or the so-called COVID vaccine could be the mark, this is not supported by Scripture for several reasons:

1. Antichrist's mark is implemented only *after* his identity is known to the world.
2. It occurs at the midpoint of the seven-year Tribulation, meaning, for the COVID jab to be the mark, we would have already endured the first three and a half years of the Tribulation, and at least the seal judgments of Revelation 6.

3. The Bible makes it clear the mark will specifically be "*on* the right-hand or the forehead" (Revelation 13:16). The mark, therefore, cannot be a hypodermal (under the skin) application.

This makes sense, as Antichrist would presumably want his brand on humanity to be visible and obvious to everyone. Further, the mark will directly represent "the name of the beast or the number of his name" (Revelation 13:17–18). The False Prophet's job will be to ensure all of mankind receives this mark, which signifies the wearer as a worshiper of the Beast and part of the privileged class permitted to participate in commerce ("buying and selling"; see Revelation 13:17). It is in this way that Satan can seal the deal and realize his centuries-long ambition of being worshiped by those who were created to worship God alone. Through controlling people's financial freedom and spiritual allegiance, he finally, at long last (at least in his mind), will have "raised his throne above the stars of God...ascended above the heights of the clouds, and made himself like the Most High" (Isaiah 14:13–14). But for those who do submit and receive his mark, they will effectively seal their doom, as not one person who accepts it will enter Heaven (Revelation 14:9–10; 20:4). They will all have heard the "last gospel" through the judgments, the two witnesses (11:3–13), the 144,000 Jewish evangelists (14:1–5), and an angel who encircles the earth proclaiming the way of salvation one last time (14:6–7). Therefore, they will have no excuse on the day of judgment (Revelation 20:11–15). Indeed, as Revelation 16:6 states concerning God's awful wrath, "they deserve it."

What is particularly tragic is, in that day, they will actually *know* they deserve it. But there's nothing they can do about it. It will be too late.

Thus, the legacy of the two beasts is that they will have deceived billions into rejecting the Creator and Savior, and dragged those same billions with them into the eternal fire.

CHAPTER 11

RELIGIOUS END-TIMES TSUNAMI

By Mike Gendron

OUR GREAT GOD AND SAVIOR gave us His prophetic Word to magnify His divine attributes and bring greater glory to His name. Only God, who is sovereign over everything in His created universe, can know the end from the beginning. He alone knows and controls the trajectory of human history. That is why no other religious book contains prophecy that foretells the future. The gods of other religions do not govern anything and therefore they don't know the future. For this reason, the God of the Bible revealed the future and put His perfect and holy character on the line "so that you may know and believe Me and understand that I am He. Before Me there was no God formed, and there will be none after Me" (Isaiah 43:10).[79] Only our True God deserves all blessing and glory and wisdom and honor! God's prophetic Word was given to encourage us with hope:

> Everything that was written in former times was written for our instruction, so that through endurance and through encouragement of the Scriptures we may have hope. (Romans 15:4)

Our hope is in the true God whose Word can be trusted and whose promises will bless those who obey His Word. That's why John wrote:

> Blessed is the one who reads the words of this prophecy aloud, and blessed are those who hear and obey the things written in it, because the time is near. (Revelation 1:3)

Two Men Will Initiate Satan's Global Agenda

God's prophetic Word reveals human history will continue to move in a trajectory towards a global kingdom that will be under the power of Satan. As the god and ruler of this world, his agenda includes the formation of a one-world religious system empowered by a one-world government that will arise from the revived Roman Empire. These two global systems will be headed by the final False Prophet and the final Antichrist. The religious system will worship a man claiming to be the long-awaited Christ, who will rule the world as he is empowered by Satan. He will perform miracles, signs, and wonders that will persuade many to worship him as God. The Bible describes him as the "son of perdition" and the "man of sin."

> All who dwell on the earth will worship him, everyone whose name has not been written from the foundation of the world in the book of life of the Lamb who has been slain. (Revelation 13:8)

The Coming Religious Tsunami

The precursor to these events is now taking place throughout the world. Satan's plan will include what will look like a global religious tsunami that will bring about the convergence of apostate Christianity with all the world's non-Christian religions. The demonic deception will be so powerfully effective that it will deceive even the elect, if possible. The Lord Jesus warned us deception would be one of the visible signs that will precede His Second Coming (Matthew 24:4, 11, 24). Many false teachers will help create a global religious system that will give its allegiance and worship to the Antichrist. This satanic kingdom will encompass all the nations of the world. It will be Satan's final attempt to be worshiped as the Most High God and to receive the glory he has desired from the beginning. Satan's political leader will join hands with his spiritual leader, who will seduce the world with the promise of peace and prosperity. The False Prophet "causes the earth and those who dwell in it to worship" the False Christ (Revelation 13:12).

Man's First Organized Rebellion against God

As we study the formation of the global religion and man's rebellion against the True God and Creator, we need to consider the first worldwide rebellion (recorded in Genesis 9–11). After the Flood, God commanded Noah's descendants to "be fruitful, and multiply, and replenish the earth" (Genesis 9:1). Instead of obeying God, they took up permanent residence in Shinar with no intention to fill the earth. The settlers put down roots in one place to make a name for themselves. They would do this by building "a city and a tower whose top will reach into heaven" (Genesis 11:4). Clearly, it was the height of absurdity for man to think he could bridge the gap between the physical world and the spiritual world by his own efforts. Yet, it was the Tower of Babel where mankind first joined hands in an organized way to turn its worship away from God. They attempted to dethrone the eternal God and Creator and usurp His sovereign authority for the purpose of self-worship. The leader of this foolish rebellion against God was a willing pawn of Satan named Nimrod. However, Satan and his willing partners could not thwart God's will to fill the earth. The Sovereign Lord accomplished His purpose by confusing the language of the rebellious people and scattering them over the face of the earth. As they were dispersed, Nimrod's idolatry gave birth to many other pagan religions. Now, four thousand years later, there is a demonic movement to unite them all again.

Today, another great city with a pagan tower is motivated by the same desire of the people of Babel. Vatican City, also a sovereign nation, has a four thousand-year-old pagan obelisk, or tower, in St. Peter's Square. This obelisk came from Heliopolis, Egypt, where it was built by a Pharaoh in 1835 BC in honor of the sun god. It was brought to Rome in 37 BC by Emperor Caligula and erected in the circus he built. Pagans saw the obelisk as a symbol that represented a way of communicating with the divine. The re-erection of the 135-foot-tall structure required a workforce of some nine hundred men and almost one hundred horses, and it took over a year to complete.

Who Is the Woman on the Beast?

Satan's ambition to unite the people of the world in a global religion is describes by the Apostle John in Revelation 17:3–6:

> I saw a woman sitting on a scarlet beast, full of blasphemous names, having seven heads and ten horns. The woman was clothed in purple and scarlet, and adorned with gold and precious stones and pearls, having in her hand a gold cup full of abominations and of the unclean things of her immorality, and on her forehead a name was written, a mystery, "BABYLON THE GREAT, THE MOTHER OF HARLOTS AND OF THE ABOMINATIONS OF THE EARTH." And I saw the woman drunk with the blood of the saints, and with the blood of the witnesses of Jesus. When I saw her, I wondered greatly.

The Apostle John was stunned at such an incredible vision of a mystery woman with roots in Babylon.

Throughout Scripture, we see women often used as symbols of religion. Some examples include the Mother of Harlots as a symbol for Satan's false religion. In another passage, a woman is a symbol of Israel giving birth to the Messiah (Revelation 12:1–6). The Apostle John describes another woman as the Bride of Christ, a symbol for His Church.

Let us rejoice and be glad and give the glory to Him, for the marriage of the Lamb has come and His bride has made herself ready. It was given to her to clothe herself in fine linen, bright and clean; for the fine linen is the righteous acts of the saints. (Revelation 19:7–8)

If we are in the season of our Lord's return, there is overwhelming evidence that Roman Catholicism has been, and will be, a powerful player in the formation of the one-world religion described in Revelation. The woman sitting on a scarlet beast is full of blasphemous names. We can only speculate what those names might be that insult Almighty God and rob Him of His glory. Surely there is no greater insult to the Triune God than to steal His divine titles. Yet, the papacy has done this by brazenly stealing the titles "Holy Father," "Head of the Church," and "Vicar of Christ." There is only one Holy Father, and He is the Father of our Lord Jesus Christ and all who have been adopted into His family (John 1:12; 17:11). There is only one Head of the Church, and He is the Lord Jesus Christ who purchased the Church with His own blood (Acts 20:28). And there is only one Vicar of Christ; He is the Holy Spirit, whom Jesus promised to send after He ascended into Heaven (John 15:26).

Other characteristics of the harlot religion are shared by the Roman Catholic religion. The woman's adornment with gold, jewels, and pearls is a picture of her great wealth. Many have said the Roman Catholic religion is one of wealthiest institutions on the face of the earth. Much of her incalculable wealth has come from the sale of indulgences for releasing souls from a fictitious place called purgatory. The blasphemous selling of God's grace through indulgences was the spark that ignited the Reformation in 1517. Today, the Vatican Museum is filled with treasures of diamond-studded, gold crowns and jewels of past popes. Its investments and accumulated wealth are upwards of $15 billion. Many of its assets, such as priceless works of art by Michelangelo and Raphael, are nearly impossible to value because they will never be sold. In addition to its vast wealth, we also see the harlot of Satan adorned with the colors worn by the Roman Catholic clergy: Bishops wear purple robes and cardinals wear robes of scarlet.

The harlot has in "her hand a gold cup full of abominations." Of all the abominations that could fill the cup, none are greater than a deceptive sham of the precious blood of Jesus Christ shed two thousand years ago for the remission of sins. Catholic priests have been deluding people with the power to change wine in a golden chalice into the blood of Jesus. The gold cup or chalice may be seen at every Roman Catholic communion service. This vile and detestable cup of abominations is worshiped by deluded Catholics and consumed by fraudulent priests. Catholic popes have embraced the harlot with the chalice as a good thing. Pope Leo XII had a coin minted in the eighteenth century that shows a woman with a chalice in her hand declaring her authority over the entire world. Six other popes minted coins depicting the woman with the chalice. Other papal medals were minted with the same woman and chalice by Pope Innocent XI, Leo XII, Pius VIII and XII, John XXIII, and Paul XI. It is indeed fascinating that Roman Catholic popes have embraced the woman of Revelation 17 as their very own.

The "woman drunk with the blood of the saints, and with the blood of the witnesses of Jesus" is another characteristic shared by the apostate Church of Rome. While the Roman Catholic religion isn't the only religion that has murdered saints of the Most High God, its history reveals the persecution of over fifty million Christians—far more than any other religion. Pope Innocent III murdered more Christians in one afternoon than any Roman emperor did in his entire reign. Eighty consecutive popes, beginning in the thirteenth century, created the cruelest means of torturing "heretics" who were witness of Jesus. On August 24, 1572, during the St. Bartholomew's Day Massacre in France, approximately one hundred thousand Protestants were murdered by orders of the pope. Blood flowed like a river throughout the streets of Paris. Pope Gregory XIII had a medal struck to celebrate the slaughter of Protestants. One side of the medal shows an angel with a cross and sword murdering the Huguenots. By the

end of the seventeenth century, roughly three hundred thousand Huguenots had to flee France because of persecution by Catholics.

Dr. Martyn Lloyd-Jones wrote:

Roman Catholicism is the devil's greatest masterpiece. It is such
a departure from the Christian faith and the New Testament
teaching that her dogma is a counterfeit, she is the whore. Let me
warn you very solemnly that if you rejoice in these ecumenical
approaches to Rome, you're denying the blood of the martyrs.
There are innocent people who are being deluded by this kind of
falsity and it is your business and mine to open their eyes.[80]

The Roman Catholic religion seduces people with its dazzling show-
case of pomp and pageantry; the splendor of its clergy dressed in expensive
costumes; its deceptive liturgies; idolatrous shrines and relics; repetitious
chanting of beaded rosaries; counterfeit representations of Christ's crucifixion; adoration of a mythical "sinless" Mary; and prayers for the dead.
None of these have anything to do with the simplicity of true worship
taught by Christ and His apostles.

We see the global scope of this satanic religion in Revelation 17:15:

The waters that you saw, where the prostitute is seated, are peoples and multitudes and nations and languages.

This world religion will sit in the commanding position over all the
peoples of the world. Babylon the great, the mother of harlots, has influenced every religion in the world. She is the mother of harlots because
she gave birth to all false religions. All her religions are bonded by the
same spirit and share a common DNA—a works-righteousness salvation. All these religions will be reunited with the mother of harlots: Islam,
Roman Catholicism, apostate Christianity, apostate Judaism, Hinduism,
Buddhism, the cults (including Mormonism and Jehovah's Witnesses),
Taoism, Confucianism, Shinto, Sikhism, Bahá'í Faith, Jainism, Unitarian

Universalism, Scientology, Zoroastrianism, and others. Satan is using his harlot to gather all unbelievers to worship the Antichrist.

The Vatican and the Kings of the Earth

Another characteristic the harlot shares with Roman Catholicism is her relationship with the kings of the earth. John writes:

> The woman whom you saw is the great city, which reigns over the kings of the earth. (Revelation 17:18)

This harlot religion has seduced government leaders with her religious power. Only one global religious institution has a history of riding the backs of kings. Beginning in the fourth century, Constantine made Christianity the official religion of the Roman Empire. Many pagans and their traditions entered the Church with no call to repentance or faith. Many would say this was the genesis of the Roman Catholic Church and its deliberate apostasy from the faith of the apostles. Since then, the Catholic religion has continued its alliances with kings, presidents, emperors, dictators, and prime ministers. Popes used their armies and navies to defeat other kingdoms and build their own. Throughout the Middle Ages, emperors and kings would beg the pope for forgiveness and absolution, and they often had to pay for it.

The Vatican, the headquarters for the Catholic Church, is also a sovereign nation that sits on seven hills. Thus, it is not only a religious capitol but a political one as well. It is an apostate theocracy with a pope who rules over all who belong to his church. Ambassadors from nations all over the world come to the Vatican to meet with the pope who has become one of the most powerful and influential rulers on earth. Since 1959, all the US presidents have traveled to the Vatican to consult with the pope.

In the twentieth century, the Vatican signed concordats with two of history's most wicked leaders—Benito Mussolini in 1929 and Adolf Hitler in 1933. Hitler and Mussolini were both Catholics, and were praised by the pope as men chosen by God. The Church virtually put both wicked dictators in office. Catholics were forbidden to oppose Mussolini and were urged to support him. Adolf Hitler said, "The world has never known anything quite so splendid as the hierarchical structure of the Catholic Church. There were quite a few things I appropriated from the Jesuits for the use of the party."[81]

Is the Papacy the False Prophet?

Many have said the papacy is the seat of Antichrist because he usurps God's infallibility, condemns all who believe God's gospel, and receives worship due only to God. The Reformers knew the harlot better than anyone, since they all came out of the apostate religion. They knew Catholicism was the ungodly harlot and a bitter enemy of the Bride of Christ. Luther exposed the papacy by saying:

> The Pope is the very Antichrist, who has exalted himself above, and opposed himself against Christ because he will not permit Christians to be saved without his power. To lie, to kill, and to destroy body and soul eternally, that is where his papal government really consists.[82] (Article IV, *The Smalcald Articles*)

The 1560 Geneva Study Bible described the harlot this way:

> She is full of idolatries, superstitions and contempt for the true God. This woman is the antiChrist, that is, the pope with the whole body of his filthy creatures.[83]

Charles Spurgeon said:

> It is the duty of every Christian to pray against Antichrist, and... if it is not the popery in the Church of Rome, there is nothing in the world it can be.[84]

John MacArthur wrote:

Pope after Pope engaged habitually in wholesale mayhem and
murder, pillage, rape, incest, sodomy and corruption of the worst
sort. So the mother of all harlots found her way to Rome…and the
final form of world religion may well be centered there. Roman
Catholicism today is the old paganism of Rome surviving under a
thin veneer of Christian terminology.[85]

Of all the popes throughout history, Pope Francis has had the most
aggressive agenda to unite professing Christianity and all the religions of
the world. He has been building bridges and suppressing Catholic doctrine in his global pursuit of unity. Francis asked that we open ourselves
to each other and unite as human beings and as brothers and sisters with
those who pray according to other cultures, other traditions, and other
beliefs. He is seeking full fellowship with brothers and sisters of other
religions. Many of his bizarre theological statements and pronouncements
have been an attempt to suppress doctrines that would prevent unity.
Clearly, he has proven to be one of the most egregious false prophets of all
the popes throughout history.

Pope Francis Is a Universalist

In spite of the clear teaching of Christ and His Word, Pope Francis believes
it is God's will for all people to be saved. He declared:

The Lord has redeemed all of us, all of us, with the Blood of
Christ: all of us, not just Catholics. Everyone…even the atheists.
Everyone! The Blood of Christ has redeemed us all.[86]

The pope's belief that everyone will eventually be saved opposes not
only the teachings of his Church, but also the very words of Christ as

well. The Lord Jesus made it clear that few will enter Heaven; the greater majority will end up in a place of destruction. He said we must:

> Enter through the narrow gate; for the gate is wide and the way is broad that leads to destruction, and there are many who enter through it. For the gate is small and the way is narrow that leads to life, and there are few who find it. (Matthew. 7:13–14)

Pope Francis Denies the Existence of Hell

Not only has Pope Francis said everyone will eventually be in Heaven, but he also has stated there is no Hell: "There is no hell where sinners suffer in eternity." He added to this heresy by saying: "After death, those who do not repent cannot be pardoned, and they disappear." Then he declared, "Hell does not exist but what does exist is the disappearance of sinful souls."[87] By denying the existence of Hell, Pope Francis is calling Jesus a liar, because the Lord Jesus spoke of Hell more than thirty times in the New Testament. God's Word describes it as a place of torment where unbelievers suffer pain and unquenchable thirst from a burning fire. The horror and hopelessness is so great they want to warn their loved ones who are still alive. The punishment for their sins is irreversible; there is no second chance and no escape (Luke 16:19–31). The pope's denial of the existence of Hell also opposes Roman Catholic teaching that affirms the existence of Hell and its eternal fire where Catholics who die in mortal sin suffer.

Gathering All People in Unity

Several organizations have been working diligently to unite the people of the world, but none as aggressively as the Roman Catholic Church. The Second Vatican Council stated:

[The Catholic Church endeavors] to gather all people and all things into Christ, so as to be for all an inseparable sacrament of unity…expressed in the common celebration of the Eucharist.

Since then, the Vatican has been building strategic bridges to all Christian denominations and non-Christian religions to bring all people under the power and influence of the papacy. In 1986, many of the most influential religious leaders of the world responded to the pope's invitation to gather in Assisi, Italy, to discuss unity and peace. The pope, whom Catholics believe is the supreme head of the entire Christian Church, made all the leaders of non-Christian religions feel comfortable by removing all the images, crucifixes, and icons of Jesus Christ. Later, in a 1998 speech to the leaders of Islam, Pope John Paul II declared:

Dialogue between our two religions (Islam and Catholicism) is more necessary than ever. There remains a spiritual bond which unites us and which we must strive to recognize and develop.[88]

On the twenty-fifth anniversary of Pope John Paul II's initial gathering at Assisi, Pope Benedict assembled the world's religious leaders in the same "holy place" of Assisi for a "Day of Reflection and Prayer."

The papacy's push for a global religion will meet very little resistance after the Rapture of the Church when the Lord Jesus returns to take all born-again Christians to Heaven (1 Thessalonians 4:16–17).

Then that lawless one will be revealed…that is, the one whose coming is in accord with the activity of Satan, with all power and signs and false wonders and with all the deception of wickedness for those who perish, because they did not receive the love of the truth so as to be saved. For this reason God will send upon them a deluding influence so that they will believe what is false. (2 Thessalonians 2:9–11)

Who are the ones who "did not receive the love of the truth"? They are those who rejected God's gracious offer of salvation through faith alone in the finished work of Christ alone. All religions, with the exception of true biblical Christianity, are united in their outright denial of salvation by grace alone. This is one of the common bonds that will unite all the religions of the world when God sends them "a deluding influence so that they will believe what is false." Their rejection of the true Lord and Savior who came to testify to the truth will be the catalyst that will unite them in worship of the Antichrist, who will be very persuasive posing as Jesus. God's Word tells us he will perform miracles that will convince the majority of the world's population to worship him as God. They will pay for that fatal mistake when they are cast into the eternal Lake of Fire prepared for the devil and his angels (Matthew 25:41).

Common Bonds of Religious Unity

The New Testament has much to say about all the unbelievers who will be a part of the one-world religion. It will be made up of those who are blinded by Satan so they might not see the light of the gospel of the glory of Christ (2 Corinthians 4:4). They are ensnared by the devil and held captive by him to do his will (2 Timothy 2:24–26). Some may have been professing Christians who departed from the faith to follow deceitful spirits and doctrines of demons (1 Timothy 4:1). All are children of their father, the devil (John 8:44). They profess to know God, but by their deeds they deny Him, being detestable, disobedient, and worthless for any good deed (Titus 1:16). They will all worship and serve a False Christ when he appears in deceit (Revelation 13.12). The harlot religion of Antichrist will be united in a common hatred for the saints (Revelation 17:6). In the end:

> The devil who deceived them will be thrown into the lake of fire and brimstone, where the beast and the false prophet are also; and they will be tormented day and night forever and ever. (Revelation 20:10)

There is currently a dialogue among world religious leaders who are seeking common bonds as a basis for unity. One common bond of all religions is the teaching that salvation is attained by what men must *do* to appease their god instead of what the True God has *done* for man through His Son. A historic interfaith covenant was signed in the Middle East on February 4, 2019, between Pope Francis and Sheikh Ahmed al-Tayeb, considered the most important imam in Sunni Islam. They arrived at the signing ceremony in Abu Dhabi "hand in hand in a symbol of interfaith brotherhood." But this wasn't just a ceremony for Catholics and Muslims. The covenant, entitled "A Document on Human Fraternity for World Peace and Living Together," was signed in front of a global audience of religious leaders from Christianity, Islam, Judaism, and other faiths. There was a concerted effort to make sure all religions of the world were represented.

The covenant initiated construction on the Abraham House in Abu Dhabi, a structure that will become a worship center for Catholics, Muslims, and Jews. The complex will be a physical manifestation of the "Document on Human Fraternity." According to Sheikh al-Tayeb:

> This is a really special project that hits on the trinity of the Abrahamic faith that is influencing over half of the world's population.[89]

A statement by the organizing committee said the complex "recounts the history and builds bridges between human civilizations and heavenly messages." The complex was scheduled to open in 2022. We can only wonder what will happen as the world's two largest religions converge with Judaism. It may be a catalyst for all the other religions to unite with them.

Common Bonds between Islam and Catholicism

At first glance, Islam and Roman Catholicism appear to be vastly different, but under close inspection, they have ten common bonds that help facilitate their convergence.

1. **Both esteem and honor Mary.** Muslims and Catholics both call Mary "Our Lady" and venerate her as a pure and holy saint. Most people know the importance of Mary to Catholics, how she is the cause of their salvation, and how she delivers souls from death. But not many know of her prominence among Muslims. The most revered woman of the Muslim faith, her name is mentioned more often in the Quran (thirty-four times) than in the Bible, and an entire chapter in the Quran is named after her.

2. **Both seek messages from apparitions of Mary.** Muslims and Catholics flock to apparition sites to receive messages from Mary. Could these be some of the lying signs and wonders Satan will use to unite Catholicism with Islam? Many of the messages make it clear that Mary is coming for all her children—including Muslims, Catholics, and Protestants—and that people of all religions can be saved apart from Jesus Christ as long as they are "good." On average, five million people flock to apparition sites each year. Years ago, I was interviewed for a History Channel documentary on the apparitions of Mary. In the interview, I made a statement used in the opening segment:

> People travel thousands of miles and spend thousands of dollars to seek messages from apparitions when they can open their Bible right where they are and get a message from God.

3. **Both are anti-Semitic.** The Vatican has issued more than one hundred anti-Semitic documents and has taught that Jews should be cursed because they killed Christ. Mohammed's words recorded in a hadith say, "The last day will not come until the Muslims destroy the Jews." This is why Islam is determined to eliminate the Jews from Israel. As long as the Jews remain, it says to the world that Mohammed was a false prophet, Allah is a false God, and the Koran is a false revelation.

4. **Both embrace another Jesus.** Catholicism has a counterfeit Jesus, who returns to the earth every day at the beckoned call of Catholic priest to be transubstantiated into a lifeless piece of bread. His death on the cross

was not sufficient to save Catholics, so he has to be represented on an altar as a sin offering. The true Jesus cried out, "It is finished," and there are no more offerings for sin (John 10:30; Hebrews 10:14). Islam also has a counterfeit Jesus (Isa) who is not God; he is only a prophet who did not die on a cross.

5. **Both seek world dominion.** Both religions rule with an autocratic government and have a history of forced conversions and killing those who oppose them. Could these religions that control people with indoctrination, intimidation, and fear be a precursor to the rule of Antichrist? Why would the RCC single out the one religion of Islam and not another of the world's religions? Could it be that it is not only a religion, but a political ideology similar to the RCC? Islam is a controlling system that lays down detailed rules for society and the life of every person. Islam means "submission" and is not compatible with freedom and democracy. Could this be a precursor to a world that must submit to the strict control of an Antichrist?

6. **Both deny the authority of Scripture.** The pagan beliefs of both religions stand opposed to the Bible. Muslims reject the Bible as the final revelation from God, declaring God has revealed a final testament: the Quran, their supreme authority. Catholics use their "infallible" teachings to twist and distort Scripture to support their ungodly traditions. Whenever religions, cults, or denominations do not submit to the authority of Scripture, they are easily influenced by the lies of the devil. He is the master deceiver, schemer, and ruler of this age, so it is no wonder both religions are enemies of God's Word.

7. **Both use prayer beads to avoid punishment.** Catholics pray the rosary to remit punishment for sin. Muslims use ninety-nine beads that correspond to the names of God. Praying to Allah five times a day is an act of obedience to escape the punishment imposed on those who do not pray.

8. **Both take pilgrimages to obtain favor from God.** Catholics take pilgrimages for religious purification and the promise of indulgences. Muslims take pilgrimages to Mecca, a mandatory religious duty that must be carried out at least once in their lifetime.

9. **Both have human mediators.** Catholics rely on the priesthood to dispense salvation through sacraments and seek Mary to intercede with God on their behalf. Muslims rely on the intercession of Muhammad on judgment day. He will prostrate himself before Allah, who will say, "O Muhammad! speak, it will be heard; and be given; intercede, and it will be approved."

10. **Both have a works-righteousness salvation.** Allah will place one's good and evil works on the divine scale: "Those whose scales are light are those who lose their souls in hell" (Sura 23:102, 103). Good works by Muslims are determined by their performance of the Five Pillars of Islam. In Catholicism, sacraments, good works, and obeying the law are necessary for salvation. Catholics obtain the joy of Heaven after they "merit for themselves and for others all the graces needed to attain eternal life" (Catechism of the Catholic Church, para. 2027).

A works-righteousness salvation will be the common bond that unites all the religions of the world. By embracing this lie of the devil, they reject God's only way to be saved—by grace alone, through faith alone, in Christ alone, according to Scripture alone, for the glory of God alone.

What Are Christians to Do?

As the Vatican continues to seduce Christians with its ecumenical movement, we must contend earnestly for the faith of the apostles. There is no stopping the winds of apostasy that will continue to draw people into a false Christianity. We need to stand firmly on the truth and warn those who are being deceived. We cannot be silent! Our voices must be heard for the glory of our Savior, the purity of His gospel, and the sanctity of His Church.

Christians who have read this chapter need to be aware that time is running out to rescue those who are perishing. We must confront them in their deception and tell them about God's one and only provision for their sins. They must repent and trust the Lord Jesus Christ alone. He is God's eternal Son, who left the glory of Heaven to be conceived by the Holy

Spirit in the womb of a virgin to take on human flesh. He lived in perfect obedience to the God's Law, then was crucified as the perfect sacrifice to satisfy divine justice for sinners. He bore man's sins, suffered God's wrath, died in man's place, and was raised on the third day to show that divine justice was satisfied. There is no other Savior and no other way to be saved (John 14:6).

CHAPTER 12

TRIBULATION TEMPEST: END-TIME MONEY ENTRAPMENT

By Wilfred J. Hahn

WE MUST ALERT THE READER.

We are dealing with the topic of the end-times role of Money…a deliberate strategy hatched a long time ago to carry out the dark intentions of the Conspirator. It is a topic that is neither well understood nor acknowledged.

Therefore, before we delve into this urgent treatise, we need to establish some key scriptural perspectives on Money.

Did you know God Himself has designed His Creation in such a way that it allows the universe to choose to rebel? Mankind (and also the angels) are free to make choices and are enabled to use various means to organize a controlling, universe-wide insurrection against God.

So, Money plays a key and necessary role in the cosmological agenda aimed at the entrapment of mankind. The reader must understand that, were there no such thing as Money—in all of its guises, its financial systems, and roles—the Conspirator would have little means (possibly none at all, in my view) of implementing a scheme that successfully entraps and enlists mankind into his final and great (premillennial) conspiracy.

Furthermore, mankind's proclivities to worship Mammon instead of God greatly aids the agenda.

Money is a many-faceted entity. Important to grasp is that Money, from a biblical perspective, is also a metaphysical force.

We here are not just dealing with the simple math of currencies and transactions or a medium of exchange or a store of value, etc., but rather with something inhabited by many spirits, chief amongst them the Destroyer. Again, Mammon has a metaphysical and spiritual dimension. (That is why I always capitalize its name.) As the case may be, a number of Bible translations use the terms "Money" and "Mammon" interchangeably.

Very few recognize there are malign spirits behind Money. As such, the biblical concept of Money is grossly misunderstood in our societies today. This may be even more so in the case of societies that have had Christian influence.

Why? Many (if not all, to some degree) have been lured by prosperity theology (PT)—a malignant corruption. People living in wealthy countries such as the US and Canada have their minds thoroughly riddled with this nonbiblical bias. It is a key reason most Christians are blind to the end-time strategies of the Conspirator. It creates a false, one-sided perspective of Money, as we will show.

People in poor countries, on the other hand, do not readily fall into the deceptions of this teaching for obvious reasons. For one, this so-called doctrine that promises everybody can be rich is just too fantastical and preposterous to them.

Indeed, everyone may want to be rich, for example, but we all know not everyone can be rich. It is a relative measure. So, it is only logical that never will everybody be rich in this current dispensation. Jesus even prophesied that the poor will always be with us—see John 12:8.[90] This amorphous dynamic of Money—something that disappears once one reaches to grasp it—is just one such dimension of its metaphysical characteristics.

Prosperity Theology

Briefly described, prosperity theology (PT) says material prosperity is the right of all Christians, and moreover, serves as proof-positive of being blessed by God. We are to believe that all so-called Christians will be materially rewarded for their faith and obedience. This reward is to accrue in the physical dimension of the here and now upon earth.

The mortal flaw of this view is that Satan also powerfully uses Mammon (Money and wealth) as a key catalyst and incentive to bring about his aims.

Other formulaic notions of PT abound. For example, one is the belief that we will receive a return in the multiples of what we may have tithed or given to the church.

We do witness a strange specter: Prosperity theology flourishes in the richest nations of the world (the United States uppermost) while not in the lesser-developed countries. We wonder why this is not the opposite. This would seem to be one other indication the prosperity theology is a false doctrine.

As always, Scripture has the final word. We need only view the lives of the twelve apostles to ascertain that prosperity theology is mostly bogus. None of the apostles would have endorsed this view.

In fact, not one of the apostles was materially rich. None sought to become wealthy. There was no easy street promised to them, though they played key roles in spreading the gospel; their names are to be put on the twelve foundations of the New Jerusalem (Revelation 21:14).

Reality could not have been more opposite for the apostles compared to what the false PT purveyors teach. All of them experienced difficult trials and persecutions. Eleven died from unnatural clauses. Prosperity theology did not save them from trials. To the contrary, the Apostle Paul said about his ordeals:

Five times I received from the Jews the forty lashes minus one. Three times I was beaten with rods, once I was pelted with stones, three times I was shipwrecked, I spent a night and a day in the open sea, I have been constantly on the move. I have been in danger from rivers, in danger from bandits, in danger from my fellow Jews, in danger from Gentiles; in danger in the city, in danger in the country, in danger at sea; and in danger from false believers. I have labored and toiled and have often gone without sleep; I have known hunger and thirst and have often gone without food; I have been cold? (2 Corinthians 12:24–26).

What then motivated the apostles? Their eyes were fixed upon the prize—their heavenly reward that was not expected in the here and now. (Philippians 3:14).

Actually, one of the very proofs one is a Christian is persecution, not personal riches or material blessings here on earth: "Indeed, all who desire to live a godly life in Christ Jesus will be persecuted" (2 Timothy 3:12; also see Matthew 24:9).

Mortal Deceit of Prosperity Theology

Why have we mentioned PT in this discussion? Readers will be surprised to learn the answer: It plays a key role in assisting the Conspirator to bring about the end-time Money trap. All of its false teachings produce a deep blindness in both Christians and non-Christians. Here we connect the dots between corrupt teachings (doctrines of demons) such as PT and the prophesied end-time Money schema presented in the Bible.

Tragically, hardly any pulpits have not been influenced by the infectious disease of PT in one way or another, blatantly or subtly.

We observe that the end-time roles of Money are complex and potentially spiritually dangerous. Like a chameleon, it can change its visage. Money lures and entices.

Satan and his cohorts use the promise of wealth and power as strong motivational incentive to participate in the end-time Money trap, as we will further see. The Conspirator very well understands human weaknesses. Mankind is a rather simple creature that can be easily buffeted and coerced.

Therefore, we will want to continue to unveil the tactics and deceits of the realm of Mammon and Money—key actors in this cosmic battle.

Current Financial Affairs

Policymakers and economists around the world are gnashing their teeth. Indeed, unprecedented times are upon the world's financial markets and economies. Many professionals are bewildered as to what has happened… and what will yet happen.

Very definitely, what is being experienced today is a unique expression of the signs of the times. Indeed, developments are of biblical scale. Why are two-thirds of the world's bond market suddenly paying negative interest rates? It is a cause of massively rising financial asset values. In the worst of times, therefore, participants are lulled by the apparent but false view of prosperity

Much of the financial perversion and warping we witness today is really of no surprise. It is, for the most part, a direct cause of the choices mankind has made.

To no one's surprise, there exists today a large contingent of "doomsters" (also called "anxiety merchants") who are inciting financial and economic fears. A huge cottage industry exists to peddle these views into book sales, newsletters, and the sales of survival supplies, etc. These so-called analysts can make a tidy living by fomenting and inciting fears and panic about economies and financial developments.

Many of these purveyors are likely well-meaning. To be sure, doom merchants have always existed. However, it must be noted that these sirens have been largely wrong, going back ten years, fifty years, a hundred years and more. Predictions of investment analysts and economists are haphazard at best.

What is grievous most of all is that Christians almost everywhere also feel pressured and fearful. This is a serious malady, especially as Christians are specifically instructed not to fear:

For God hath not given us the spirit of fear; but of power, and of love, and of a sound mind. (2 Timothy 1:7, KJV)

Why then are Christians robbed of their God-given promises? The reader will be surprised to discover the answer.

But why should Christians be caught up by worries…being cast "to and fro"? After all, we are charged to "be no more children, tossed to and fro, and carried about with every wind of doctrine, by the sleight of men, and cunning craftiness, whereby they lie in wait to deceive" (Ephesians 4:14).

Then why has much of Christianity lost its peace, "the peace of God, which passeth all understanding [which] shall keep [our] hearts and minds through Christ Jesus"? (Philippians 4:7). Why are Christians caught unawares by the Destroyer's tactics?

There are several reasons. For one, I suggest Christians are being unnecessarily distracted by human conspiracy theories. In general, these are highly speculative and undocumented. Those who spread these notions are, in effect, "warring against flesh and blood" rather than demonic "rulers in high places" (Ephesians 6). They have lost the primacy of Scripture in their lives.

A topic that has already been broached: Christians have been swept up by prosperity theology in one form or other. And, because of these errors, they are vulnerable to listening to false prophets and falling to Satan's wiles. In our view, these false doctrines create much harm, as many of their views are unbiblical. This is unfolding today as perhaps never before.

Who is to blame? There indeed is a great primordial conspiracy playing out in the cosmos. It is not a theory. Rather, it is the one conspiracy fomented by Satan as alluded to earlier. As such, I have generally avoided discussing "conspiracy theories" apart from the primordial one of the universe. We view all other conspiracy theories as unnecessary distraction and misdirection. We should keep in focus the dark, primordial "master" conspiracy.

Scriptures make clear that Satan ensnares the world through deception, taking advantage of traps, lies, and conspiracy. He understands the behavioral biases and vulnerabilities of mankind like no other strategist.

Crucially, therefore, the Destroyer takes advantage of human weaknesses, gullibility, and penchants. Expressly, Satan concentrates on manipulating human emotions of fear and greed.

To be sure, financial and economic crises and destructive developments are unfolding, through many of these are masked. But why? It is first necessary to understand that human economies and financial systems have always faced periods of flux and volatility. It must be recognized that financial and economic trends are "human phenomena."

These do not happen by accident or randomly. No, they are a direct function of human wants and decisions. Consider that there has been a massive humanist shift in values and wants for the human race (i.e., godlessness, lusts, humanism, independence from God, etc.) in recent decades.

These value shifts have consequences. Why? Because God proclaims there will be consequences. They cannot be escaped: "Do not be deceived: God cannot be mocked. A man reaps what he sows" (Galatians 6:7). Clearly, these consequences can already be identified today.

Indeed, end-time financial and economic market conditions are unfolding. Some of these developments being witnessed today are foreshadowed in the Bible. The ultimate outcomes—much of which is prophesied in Scriptures—will be grave.

But when does this all happen? A wrong answer to this question, sadly, will open the door to misdirection—in some cases, to Christians even being preyed upon. As already mentioned, the many "doomster" forecasts and prophecies have been wrong, spectacularly so. In our understanding of Scripture, a major world financial collapse will not happen until sometime during the Tribulation. Why?

The answer is very simple: Satan needs to disguise his agenda with the appearance of broad prosperity—for example, by rising financial markets—and smug humanism. This is the key deceiving tactic that hoodwinks most of the world. False prosperity is the bait in the end-time Money trap.

To remind, Satan is the primary spirit behind Mammon and Money. He has been given control over Mammon as well as all the kingdoms of the world. When he sought to tempt Christ, the Bible records the following:

> The devil led him up to a high place and showed him in an instant all the kingdoms of the world. And he said to him, "I will give you all their authority and splendor; it has been given to me, and I can give it to anyone I want to." (Luke 4:5–6)

Clearly, Satan has authority over all the worldly kingdoms on earth, these being enmeshed with Mammon. As such, the long-term courses of financial markets and economies are commandeered by the devil, though not directly. He has many human minions that aid him in this endeavor. The Bible suggests many of them, if not all, will be either wealthy or globally influential.

I see these elites mentioned in the Bible. Consider Daniel's account of those who will be honored by the Antichrist:

> He...will greatly honor those who acknowledge him. He will make them rulers over many people and will distribute the land at a price. (Daniel 11:30)

These are definitely motivated by price (Money).

An insightful perspective on the dynamics of these elites was mentioned to me by the late Dave Hunt (a well-known Bible teacher and Christian apologist). Just as Jesus Christ will discipline those He loves (Hebrews 12:6), Satan must also discipline his greedy minions. However, these latter actions must be done for different reasons. If Satan did not do so, global financial markets would likely have witnessed even greater manias…destruction…running far ahead of Satan's end-time agenda. There is no chastening like suffering steep financial losses.

Elites under the influence of Mammon/Satan are not the only players aiding in the end-time agenda. You'll likely be surprised to learn the identity of another major agent: doomsters both within and outside of the pulpit.

The Mission of Predicting Crisis

It is no surprise the "doomster business" appears to be prospering in this time of perplexity. We identify many "anxiety merchants." They see it as their mission to warn Christians (and others) about financial and economic crises. Some will even sell "emergency supplies."

In this consumer-weary world, every promoter knows one needs an emotionally charged sales pitch to "move the merchandise." Among the most effective strategies is to appeal to vanity, greed, or fear. Without a doubt, fear and greed drive the most urgent human responses and behaviors. However, fear generates the biggest reactions.

Fear sells. I (being in my fifth decade of managing money globally) will attest to that statement. Unfortunately, we also witness these types of sales tactics being endorsed in so-called Christian forums.

I have sat through more than a few presentations of "financial prophets" at Bible or prophecy conferences. All of them engaged in some measure of fearmongering. Some made outrageous claims—for instance, stating they were in touch with "inside high contacts" who confirm that a financial collapse is planned to occur "within a month." None of their predictions were accurate. From it.

Others who were financial advisers took advantage of their perceived legitimacy. After all, they were speaking at a conference, weren't they? They had staff ready on site with account-opening forms. Assuredly, gold bullion has always been a good seller on this circuit. Sadly, not many buyers will have made enduring gains as sales volumes are always best when prices (i.e., gold bullion) have already risen.

But what does the Bible say about the "doomster business"—the "anxiety merchants"?

The Bible on the Christian Doomster Business

The current state of affairs begs an all-important question: Just where can we find the biblical mandate for Christian leaders and preachers to be on the "watch" for financial crisis and to provide "doom and gloom" economic survival advice that wreaks emotional havoc?

Answer? Nowhere.

No Scripture implores us to provide a mission of forecasting economies and financial markets. Readers may do so, if they wish. However, said flatly, the New Testament does not urge Christians to "watch" for crises. Far from it. Not one command of this type can be found in the New Testament.

We must therefore ask: Just what were the great concerns Jesus and the apostles had during their day on earth? They watched out for false teachers and sought to correct them. The false teachers were promoting false teachings…countered and denied the gospel…and spread the "doctrines of demons."

ALL the commands to "watch" found in the New Testament concern spiritual issues and not once material matters. The focus of the apostles could not be clearer.

As it was, the Roman world of the Mediterranean during the time of Christ was experiencing enormous financial shakings. The massive credit collapse of AD 33 during the reign of Emperor Tiberius (according to the accounts of the historian Tacitus) couldn't have been more similar to the global financial crisis (GFC) that seized virtually the entire world in the late 2000s.

Consider the significance of the fact that the entire New Testament dedicates not one single word to a major financial crisis occurring in the

Roman world at that time. Jesus Christ and His disciples were responding to a completely different urgency—to "proclaim the good news of the kingdom of God" (Luke 4:43).

An Additional Doomster Flaw

There is yet one other unscriptural aspect of the "doomster business." It primarily only caters its wares to those who can afford it. Only people with financial means are eligible to be offered solutions and survival services. To the extent such services are offered as an accredited Christian activity, this is not biblical.

The exact opposite holds true: Says Isaiah: "Come, all you who are thirsty, come to the waters; and you who have no money, come, buy and eat! Come, buy wine and milk without money and without cost" (Isaiah 55:1). The spirit of prophecy gives testimony to the thirsty that they will be given "water without cost from the spring of the water of life" (Revelation 21:6).

God's salvation is free. He would not allow only the wealthy to be given access to His deliverance. The building up of supplies to survive the Tribulation period is not needed. (Nor will this be possible in any case? The Bible makes clear that all tribulational Christians will not survive).

God Has a Better Plan

Salvation is for ALL without cost. So is the Rapture. All premillennial Christians have equal access to the rescue of the Rapture. As such, Christians may relax. No purchase of a bomb bunker is necessary.

Should Christians worry about the world's fixation on money and wealth? Jesus had a practical answer. He said to leave earthly matters (of the spiritually dead) to the dead. He told them: "Follow me, and let the dead bury their own dead" (Matthew 8:22). We could draw a parallel here. Let the world worry about financial crises. These are dead matters, not leading to life. Therefore, churches and preachers should only focus on the important spiritual concerns.

As it is, one cannot love Mammon and God at the same time (Luke 16:3). Therefore, we must not mix up or merge these realms! It cannot be done without great harm. Trying to sit on the fence between these two opposing forces can only lead to a compromised testimony for Christians. We cannot be concerned about spiritual matters and worry about financial matters at the same time.

Anxiety Merchants Playing into Hand of Policymakers

Doomsters and crises forecasters (whether in the pulpit or not) will be surprised to learn they fulfill an important function for the Destroyer. After all, policymakers are not blind and do realize the grimmer the outlook for global economies and financial markets, the more interventions and ruses will be required.

When policymakers around the globe are trapped and desperate, we must not forget they can and will respond with virtually infinite monetary deceptions. Policymakers are also vulnerable to fear. They choose to err on the side of caution, pouring whatever amount of monetary liquidity (and government budget stimulus) into financial systems is needed.

This contributes to a perverse condition. The more negative the outlook, the more prosperous stock and bond markets will appear eventually. This indeed is a perversity that serves to deceive the masses. As mentioned, people assume all is well, so long as financial markets and economies reach new heights. In reality, however, the exact opposite is likely true. In the meantime, global fragility is being fostered, indebtedness continues to rise to ever-new heights, and global wealth distribution is becoming ever-more extreme. As such, the wealthy of the world are becoming even richer, thus concentrating global wealth and. influence.

Doomsters tend to forget that the Destroyer first must lure as many of humanity as possible into the trap before it suddenly snaps shut (Luke 21:34). That is best achieved through deceptively sweet (but deadly) entreaties and the warm glow of rising wealth.

As the case may be, most people actually will gladly be deceived so long as it offers the hope of more prosperity and slakes their lusts. That may sound perverse; it is.

Nevertheless, it is considered to be a bargain exchange. Why? Because a materialistic humanity wants to hear that prosperity (as they may perceive it) will continue for as far as the eye can see. They will not care that it is false wealth. This is the same type of mistake people will make in the Tribulation period. They will take the mark in order to gain the promise of "buying and selling."

As mentioned, mankind has made choices that have had and will have great consequences. This is already unfolding today in the most treacherous of ways. Conditions are already far advanced.

Choosing to Abandon Values

The reader may be asking: "Just what is really going on? Why are there are so many financial precedents unfolding now? Where do we find the connections in the Bible?"

Popular values and beliefs, and their "ripening." have enormous consequences. In my opinion, these are likely to play a role in creating the conditions likely to reach full catharsis later in the Tribulation period.

This being the case, what then are the most critical "human factors" or proclivities contributing to the ongoing development of an end-time money snare? We will examine just two: human demographics and ingrained human behavioral biases. The latter refers to the responses and reactions seemingly hardwired into our fleshly brains. Experts have come to call this field of study "neural finance."

However, we will first tackle the former of the two human factors that we chose. We then ask: Just what is demographics? We referred to a condensed definition from www.investopedia.com: Demographic analysis is the study of a population based on factors such as age, race, and sex.

What is unfolding today that demographics reveals? There are two main contributing trends—one good, the other bad. First, human longevity (length of life) has continued to increase for much of the world...

to the continued surprise of actuaries. This trend is largely the outcome of advancing medical technology and prosperity. Its main impact is to increase the average age of the population.

Lengthening longevity, traditionally, has been considered to be a positive development. This past century, people are living longer than ever before. A "good old age" was once considered a blessing according to the Bible. But sadly, today, a long life has begun to be regarded as a curse. How so?

Before answering this question, we must first connect the first of the two demographic developments we cited—plunging fertility. It is a highly malignant factor that will continue to accelerate worldwide.

Increasingly, households are deciding not to have children (or cannot have more children). This is partly attributable to post-familialism. More and more, people choose not to have children or to marry. Families are under attack.

Shockingly, not only are female fertility rates at new lows, male fertility is also decaying rapidly. In this case of the male decline in fertility, it is not a result of human choice. For some (still unexplained) reason, sperm counts have declined at a steep pace over recent decades.

Lengthening longevity and post-familialism are the major causes to the aging of the world's population. Critically, this trend is remarkably fast. However, this related development really shouldn't be news. After all, as the saying goes, "demographics is destiny."

How do these demographics trends connect to the worldwide money trap?

Today the future has arrived, the chickens having come home to roost. So, the time has arrived for the crisis to be more widely evident to most. This has unleashed desperate responses.

People are clamoring to save for their retirement years and find sufficient future financial income. With interest rates so low and investment prices so high, this is virtually impossible. A very large cohort of older people will experience difficult retirement years. They will not be able to afford a comfortable retirement as they had anticipated.

At the same time, workforces and pension systems must rely on the support of a young group of people. However, that will not be workable. Quoting a report by Fabius Maximus (a respected political research organization), the future impact will be shattering:

The 2nd generation after the present one will be only 40% as large as today's. The 4th generation will be only 15% as large. These are astonishing numbers. The worst large-scale pandemics killed 1/4 to 1/3 of the affected population. Only the most severe inflicted such damage.

There can be no doubt: The scale of these demographic trends is unprecedented. The resultant financial and social pressures upon the world are truly profound.

Eventually, as simple math confirms, financial markets will become greatly distressed. Seen overall, pension funds cannot adequately deliver income if succeeding generations are less populous than the previous. This is already in evidence. We dubbed this trend the "global income crisis" some three decades ago.

Again, how does this all connect? In response to the world's demographic disaster, what are we likely to see? Again, rising markets and yet lower interest rate levels. Why? Policymakers have no choice. They must pump up the value of shares and assets by pushing interest rates even lower. Here again, we witness the deception of the global income crises. Negative trends are masked so to appear as a wealth-enhancing development.

Thoughts to Ponder

Financial markets and economies are "human constructs," after all. They do not exist in isolation of humanity. Global financial markets start and end with humans.

Financial problems and cracks in the economic superstructure will be masked by the corrupted and enticing monetary and fiscal interventions.

Therefore, what seems to be bad is spun into an apparition of growing wealth and financial security.

Also, what most observers do not realize is that "doomsterism" (the constant shrill predictions of economic doom whether by so-called experts or even from the pulpit) actually contributes to the opposite outcome— an alluring financial market trend. This is end-time deception at work.

None of our perspectives here denies the veracity of Bible prophecy. All Bible prophecy has been and will be fulfilled. But even with the inviolable foreknowledge of prophecy, we are admonished, "Do not go beyond what is written" (1 Corinthians 4:6). While prophecy provides a light in a dark place (2 Peter 1:19), it offers no guidance as to short-term events.

Sadly, though teachers and preachers may be well-meaning in their warnings and prophecies about predicted financial, geopolitical, or economic trends, they are on thin ice.

A perfectly prescient forecaster does not exist in this field of endeavor. Therefore, the doomsters and other forecasters must all be categorized as false prophets. In our view, they create much harm as many of their views are unbiblical and plain wrong. Moreover, they play an unwitting role in the facilitation of a worldwide end-time trap.

Not only do they discredit the pulpit, they are inadvertently aiding the agenda of the Destroyer who uses fear and greed as agents to bring about advances in his agenda.

This writer has witnessed many ill-advised financial and economic predictions from the pulpits of North America. These may have induced their congregations to buy gold, buy the Iraqi dinar, sell the US dollar, and participate in a host of other possible investment schemes. The damage has been great, in monetary as well as reputational terms.

Then, what advantage do pastors or ministry leaders bring with their predictions? The answer? None. In fact, the risks of harm are great, though their motivations to do so may have been benevolent.

As it is, secular professionals who may specialize in geopolitics or currency markets, for example, are also often (if not almost always) wrong in their predictions.

We must conclude such types of "crisis" prophecies are likely to be unreliable. They may also betray a lack of Bible-rooted perspectives. It is no surprise that some securities-market regulators these days require wealth-advisory professionals to declare whether they have influence over their congregations.

To repeat, what we observe today is a worldwide shifting in human values…a shift like no other in history in terms of scale and rapidity. It surely is symptomatic of a godless end that is coming "like a flood" (Daniel 9:26).

Gone are the days when "children's children are a crown to the aged, and parents are the pride of their children" (Proverbs 17:6). Global demographics today are bringing about this view. It plays a major role in bringing about deceptive trends of last-days financial market. Beware.

Oswald Spengler, German historian and philosopher, once observed, "When the ordinary thought of a highly cultivated people begins to regard 'having children' as a question of pros and cons, the great turning point has come." That point has most certainly arrived for most developed nations. The trend will not reverse as the point of return has passed.

Today's financial perversions are attributable to worldwide godlessness, denial of truth, and transgressions against God. A final and inevitable financial collapse should be seen as part of God's wrath and judgment upon mankind unfolding in the Tribulation period.

The final collapse is therefore not yet. The great Conspirator's agenda is not finished. He requires conditions that appear deceptively prosperous. Beware. What many forecasters forget is mankind's capacity and penchant for delusion, perversion, and sin.

The Bible says: "As fish are caught in a cruel net, or birds are taken in a snare, so people are trapped by evil times that fall unexpectedly upon them" (Ecclesiastes 9:12). Trials and adversities fall upon all, just as the Lord allows it to rain on both the righteous and unrighteous. "In this world you will have trouble" (John 16:33).

EZEKIEL FOREWARNS NORTHERN STORM FRONT

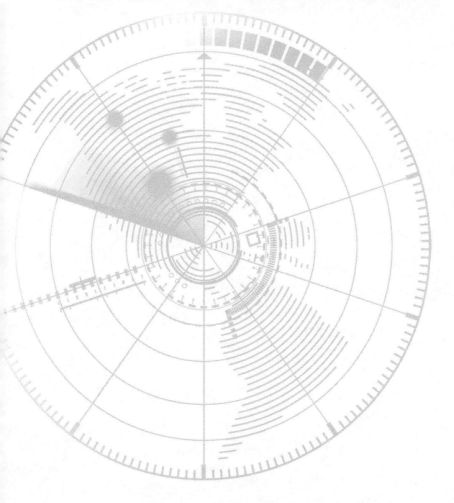

CHAPTER 13

COALESCING SUPER CELLS APPROACH

By Nathan Jones

"IF BIBLICAL PROPHECY TEACHES us anything, it is that God is in complete control of human history and its culmination."[91] If this quote by Dr. Ron Rhodes highlights one of the greatest benefits of studying God's prophetic Word, fulfilled Bible prophecy provides an indisputable apologetic for the existence of God. "For prophecy never came by the will of man, but holy men of God spoke as they were moved by the Holy Spirit" (2 Peter 1:21).[92] Intertwined with that apologetic is an evangelistic message that effectively proclaims the triune God of the Bible alone stands apart as the one true God, and only as revealed in Scripture.

While prophecy constitutes a whopping 27 percent of the Bible, God's overall plan for the ages appears to be rather like a one hundred-piece puzzle, and so far, He has only provided seventy-five pieces. One can definitely make out the outline of a picture, but until certain events unfold that add other new pieces to the puzzle, the picture remains incomplete.

These absent proverbial puzzle pieces have thrown a stumbling block before students of Bible prophecy in their attempt to properly see the big picture of God's redemptive plan for mankind. To overcome this obstacle and better understand God's forewarnings, students of the Bible must dive into the complete Word and utilize the one dirty word missing in much of today's "newspaper exegesis" so unfortunately equated with the field of eschatology: "study." Followers of God's Word must be able to study a particular biblical prophecy and, much like they would inspect a diamond, then carefully examine the many glistening facets in order to discern exactly what revelations the Bible imparts.

One such "incomplete" prophecy can be found in Ezekiel 38–39, which concerns what is called the Gog-Magog battle or the war of Gog and Magog. At first read, as one theologian so colorfully commented, the book of Ezekiel can appear as if a "perplexing maze of incoherent visions—a kaleidoscope of whirling wheels and dry bones that defy interpretation," causing readers to "shy away from studying the book and to miss one of the great literary and spiritual portions of the Old Testament."[93] And, he would be right.

That is why this chapter will 1) take a deep dive into identifying just who the Gog-Magog players are, and 2) examine the clues as to when this prophesied war will likely occur. But, before we get started, it'd be best if you first read Ezekiel 38–39. As we mine the book for its "rich spiritual truths that strike with peculiar force upon the hearts of men," my hope is that you will be "brought face to face with a transcendent God, a self-existent being who has absolute power and is constantly revealed in glory."[94]

The Battle

The Prophecies

A long 2,600 years ago, the great Hebrew *nabi*, Ezekiel ben Buzi of the priestly family of Zadok, was exiled to Babylon in 597 BC.[95] There he unveiled a prophecy the Lord God had divulged to him concerning the future of the nation of Israel. Recorded in the book of Ezekiel ,chapters 36 and 37, the prophet revealed that God would fulfill His promise to regather the Jewish people "out of all [the] countries" of the world where they had been dispersed "and bring you into your own land" that had been promised to their forefathers Abraham, Isaac, and Jacob (36:24).

Like dry bones reanimated into a living person, Israel did indeed become a nation once again on May 14, 1948, after nearly 1,900 years since the Romans in AD 70 destroyed Jerusalem and exiled the Jewish people across the globe. But, this reanimation would still lack a soul—the national belief in Yahweh and His Son. As one commentator noted:

> The bones came together. The flesh crept up over them. They were ready for life, but as yet there was no life in them. It was still a congregation of corpses.[96]

After all these centuries, this prophecy found its fulfillment in our modern generation! But, God wasn't finished unveiling the future of Israel to Ezekiel and the world, for the following two chapters portray a great trial for the newly established nation of Israel—the Gog-Magog battle—a trial that would lead towards granting that reanimated body a soul.

The Details

The Gog-Magog battle is set between a massive coalition of nations descended from Noah's sons Japheth and Ham against Israel (Genesis 10:2–7). The nations are from the territories of ancient Rosh, Magog, Meshech, Tubal, Persia, Cush, Gomer, and Beth-Togarmah (38:2–6). Their leader is called "Gog, the prince of Rosh, Meshech, and Tubal" (38:2–3). The battlefield is on "the mountains of Israel, which had long been desolate" (38:8). The purpose of the invasion is to "plunder and to take booty" and attack the people of Israel (38:12–16).

The result of such a massive invasion by a seemingly invincible army on an unprotected Israel ends up surprising the invaders and shocking the world. The invading nations are, in truth, being manipulated by God, pulled out of their lands as with "hooks in your jaws," so that those nations feel the sovereign Lord's fury (38:4, 18). God drags these specific nations to the "mountains of Israel" to "bring him to judgment with pestilence and bloodshed…flooding rain, great hailstones, fire, and brimstone" (38:21–22). God's ultimate purpose for supernaturally obliterating the invading coalition is so:

> Thus, I [God], will magnify Myself and sanctify Myself, and I will be known in the eyes of many nations. Then they shall know that I am the LORD. (38:23)

God's supernatural victory over the Gog-Magog invaders allows Him to reintroduce Himself to the world and declare in no uncertain terms that Yahweh is personally defending Israel. Should the people of the world doubt, they only have to look on Israel who "will go out and set on fire and burn the weapons…and they will make fires with them for seven years" (39:9). As for the invaders' corpses, "for seven months the house of Israel will be burying them, in order to cleanse the land" in the newly named "Valley of Hamon Gog" by a newly built "town called Hamonah" (39:11–12, 16).

The Leader

Ezekiel provides the prophetic name of the leader of this coalition of nations—"Gog, of the land of Magog, the prince of Rosh, Meshech, and Tubal" (38:2–3). Whether Gog is a real name, as was used of a descendent of Reuben (1 Chronicles 5:4), or a title for a supreme position such as king or president remains to be seen. Some historians even point to King Gyges of Lydia, who asked King Ashurbanipal of Assyria for help in 676 BC, but then joined an Egyptian-led rebellion against Assyria, as a historic type.[97] Gyges' name in that era became synonymous with terror, bloodshed, and homelessness.[98] Others point to Genghis Khan—who, during the 1200s, ruled the Mongolian empire, which covered a fourth of Asia—as another historic type.[99] Whether Gog is historical or the prophesied Antichrist yet to come depends on the timing of this epic battle. Either way, the identity of Gog truly lives up to the meaning of his name: "hidden or covered."[100]

The Nations

Ezekiel provides the ancient names of the territories that comprise the invading nations: Rosh, Magog, Meshech, Tubal, Persia, Cush, Put, Gomer, and Beth-Togarmah (38:1–6). If only the prophet had gone the extra mile and given their contemporary names, a lot of debate over their modern identities would have been saved. Nevertheless, God prefers students of the Bible to do their historical research, and the following list of equivalent names is the fruit of that research.

Magog: Some historians point to the former Soviet nations of Kazakhstan, Kyrgyzstan, Uzbekistan, Turkmenistan, Tajikistan, as well as Afghanistan, as encompassing the land of Magog. Historian Edwin Yamauchi explains that Magog was the "ancient Scythian northern nomadic tribes who inhabited territory from Central Asia across the southern steppes of modern Russia."[101] These nations, today consisting of a population of sixty million, are united by one commonality—Islam.[102]

Meshech: The ancient Moschoi or Muschki or Musku tribe settled in Cilicia and Cappadocia, now part of modern-day Turkey.[103] Ezekiel earlier noted that these people traded in slaves to Tyre and refers to them as an ancient bandit nation (27:13; 32:26).

Tubal: The people of Tubal would have hailed from the ancient Tibarenoi tribe.[104] For those who have equated Tubal as the Serbian city of Tobolsk, along with Meshech as the Russian city of Moscow, Hebrew Scripture experts claim there is "no etymological, grammatical, historical, or literary data in support of such a position."[105] This land also resides in modern-day Turkey.

Gomer: Jewish historian Josephus identified Gomer, who "founded those whom the Greeks now call Galatians [Galls], but were then called Gomerites."[106] Some theologians point to Germany as the land of Gomer, leading one theologian to ask, "What if a united and anti-Semitic Germany were to seek its future fortunes while allied to an anti-Semitic Russia?"[107] The Jewish *Midrash Rabbah* and Talmud also call Gomer "Germania" indicating today's Germany.[108] Not a commonly held view, but one Oxford historian even suggested Gomer's son who became the ancestor of the Celtic people necessitates including the Cymry of Wales and Brittany, meaning Great Britain.[109] Gomer most popularly looks to reference the Gimirrai of the Assyrians, or Cimmerians, who lived in the Black Sea area adjacent to Turkey.[110]

Beth-Togarmah: Togarmah, or Beth-Togarmah, which means the "house of Togarmah," contains an etymological connection between the name "Togarmah" and the names "Turkey" and "Turkestan."[111] The Tilgaimmu resided between ancient Carchemish and Haran, which is modern-day Turkey and possibly the lands of Azerbaijan and Armenia.[112]

Persia: The land of Persia is ancient and long-running and the easiest to identify, only having changed its name to Iran during the last century in 1935.

Cush: Cush is another area easy to identify, having split into Ethiopia and the Sudan in more recent history.

Put: While the *Midrash Rabbah* claims Put is not Libya or Lub, but rather Somaliland or Somalia bordering on Ethiopia, the scholars reviewed all claim that Put is indeed Libya, with the possibility that the land also includes Algeria and Tunisia.[113]

Many Nations: Ezekiel describes "Sheba and Dedan, the merchants of Tarshish, and all their young lions" as just observing the battle (38:13). Sheba and Dedan were Shem's descendants who settled in modern-day Saudi Arabia.[114] Tarshish could refer to Tarsus, located just northwest of Israel, or the island of Sardinia, located just north of Carthage in the Mediterranean Sea.[115] But, more than likely, the inhabitants of Tartessus, located on the southwest coast of Spain, denotes the Phoenician merchants who sailed as far as Britain.[116] The "young lions" could then be referring to Spain and Great Britain's colonies in the New World.

Noticeably absent from this list of Middle Eastern nations are those surrounding modern-day Israel, such as Syria, Lebanon, Jordan, Egypt, Gaza, Iraq, and the Arabian peninsula nations. Why these "many nations" are not also actively involved in the Gog-Magog Battle is open to speculation, but a Psalm 83 scenario where the seer Asaph foresaw Israel subjugating their surrounding neighbors could be the one that grants Israel the peaceful condition Ezekiel describes that precedes the Gog-Magog invasion (38:11).

Rosh: The final nation to be explored in Ezekiel's list is Rosh. Could it be modern-day Russia? As one author queried, "Will the old Russian Bear come out of its quarter-century hibernation and again sound a roar that shakes the world?"[117]

The Translations

The word "Rosh" or "Ros" appears noticeably absent from the list of nations provided by Ezekiel in the King James Version, the New International Version, the English Standard Version, and others (38:3). But, it can be found in Ezekiel's list of nations in the New King James Version, the New American Standard Version, the Amplified Version, the Darby Translation, and others. Why the difference in translations?

The difference derives from the challenge for translators to either interpret the Hebrew word "Rosh" as a noun indicating an actual land mass or as an adjective indicating "an exalted one" such as a king, sheik, captain, chief, or prince.[118] The NAS translators chose the noun form of "Rosh," while the NIV translators chose the adjective form. Translations based on the Greek Septuagint (LXX) follow the noun form, while those based on the Latin Vulgate follow the adjective form.

Support for Rosh Equaling Russia

Support for the use of the noun interpretation of "Rosh" as a distinct land mass identifiable as modern-day Russia points to the validity of this interpretation for several reasons.

For one, various Hebrew scholars such as G. A. Cook believe the noun form of "Rosh" is true to the original Hebrew.[119] Another scholar, John Walvoord, explains:

In the study of how ancient words came into modern language, it is quite common for the consonants to remain the same and the vowels to be changed. In the word "Rosh," if the vowel "o" is changed to "u" it becomes the root of the modern word Russia.[120]

The Septuagint (LXX) translation predates the Latin Vulgate by seven hundred years and is only three centuries removed from the time of Ezekiel, making it a translation more contemporary to the prophet.

Tenth-century Byzantine writers such as Ibn-Fosslan identified a group of Scythians dwelling in the northern parts of Taurus upon the river Volga as the Ros.[121] Ninth-century BC Assyrian texts predating Ezekiel's time also refer to the Rosh or Rashu.[122] Even farther back, as early as 2600 BC, ancient Egyptian and other Middle-Eastern inscriptions and texts—such as in Sargon's inscriptions, on a cylinder by Assurbanipal, in an annul by Sennacherib, and five times in Ugaritic tablets—all record the existence of the Rosh/Rash/Reshu people.[123]

The early Byzantine church claimed the Ros were the people who lived far north of Greece in the area today known as Russia.[124] Rosh is supposed to originate "from the remotest parts of the north" (39:1–2). No other nation exists more directly north of Israel and is more remote than modern-day Russia.

Today's news reports repeatedly show that Russia has very quickly solidified economic and military ties with the nations involved in the Gog-Magog coalition. Russia is building a nuclear reactor in Iran and is arming Islamic nations, and has gained a foothold in Syria due to the Syrian civil war for the purpose of controlling the Middle East's vast oil reserves. Israel's Mediterranean gas deposits are seen as a direct threat to Russia's monopoly of the natural gas supply to Europe.

And, finally, Russia nationally has held a long and historic anti-Semitic violent streak that God would not leave without a response. When all arguments for Rosh being Russia are put on the table, it is clear that Russia descended from the Rosh people.

General Timing

While many books have been written to debate the specific timing of the Gog-Magog battle, students of the Bible can be positive about its general timing, which is clearly spelled out in Ezekiel's account as events that must happen to set the stage for the battle.

The first general-timing clue concerns Ezekiel's use of the terms "latter years" and "last days" (38:8, 16). The Gog-Magog battle must happen in the prophetic scheme of the end times as it relates to the nation of Israel. The key verse that unlocks the understanding as to what these terms mean can be found in the Pentateuch: "When you are in distress, and all these things come upon you in the latter days, when you turn to the Lord your God and obey His voice" (Deuteronomy 4:30). "Distress" is also translated as "tribulation." It is the Tribulation, also called Daniel's Seventieth Week (Daniel 9:20–27), that brings the Jewish people as a nation back to a belief in Yahweh and later to acceptance of Yeshua as their Messiah. The Tribulation leading up to the millennial reign of Christ is what the Old Testament prophets consistently and repeatedly taught. So, these key phrases point to the Gog-Magog battle happening in relation to the Tribulation and the Millennial Kingdom.

The second general-timing clue rejects the claim that the battle has already happened. Never in the history of the Middle East have the nations described in the coalition united in a concerted attack against Israel. In no time has such a specific group of nations been destroyed by inclement weather. And, in no time has Israel named a valley Hamon Gog, nor has the adjoining town called Hamonah ever existed where the Jews buried their invaders' dead bodies (39:11–12, 16). Lack of historical support leaves only a future timing for the battle to occur.

The third general-timing clue is given in Ezekiel 36 and 37 and involves the regathering of the Jewish people back into their homeland "from out of all countries" of the world (36:24). Like the valley of dry bones reanimated into a living person the prophet envisioned, Israel did indeed become a nation once again. Out of the 14.5 million Jewish people in the world today, 47 percent reside in Israel, making up 6,841,000 (74 percent) of the population dwelling in the Holy Land.[125] And, the Jews must have control of "the mountains of Israel," which they gained when they took control of the mountains from the Jordanians during the Six Day War (38:8).[126]

The fourth general-timing clue involves the developments nationally that have to occur to make the nations of the coalition unite in an invasion of Israel. Two factors have made this coalition possible today. The first is the religion of Islam uniting these nations in satanic hatred of the Jewish people. The second is the economic bounty Israel now has with its revitalized land and newly discovered gas deposits.[127] The coalition nations now see a viable motivation to unite for the singular purpose of plundering Israel's wealth.

The fifth general-timing clue reads:

You will say, "I will go up against a land of unwalled villages; I will go to a peaceful people, who dwell safely, all of them dwelling without walls, and having neither bars nor gates." (38:11)

Israel must be living without walls, peacefully, and unsuspecting of an attack. Israel today lives in constant fear of attack and is always prepared for an invasion by the sixty-plus million hostile Muslims surrounding their borders. Because of this turbulent climate, this part of the prophecy can be argued to have yet to be fulfilled.

Discarded Timings

As for the question of when the Gog-Magog battle will occur, two obvious answers can be eliminated from the onset. The first presupposes the battle has already occurred, but that would be historically incorrect. That the Gog-Magog battle was fulfilled in Ezekiel's day by an invasion of the Scythians, Babylonians, or Greeks fails to fulfill the roster of nations that comprise the Gog-Magog invasion force. Also, it fails to address Ezekiel chapters 36–38, which prophesy a regathering of Jews to Israel from all over the world using the end-timing clues given as the "latter years," or "last days." A past invasion just does not fit the Ezekiel 38–39 description.

The second concludes the Gog-Magog battle will never occur and also can be discarded. A literal interpretation being replaced with a metaphorical interpretation that postulates Ezekiel 38–39's description is somehow "apocalyptic symbolism" representing a struggle between good and evil is replacement-theology spiritualizing.[128] As Semitic languages expert Charles Feinberg once said, "It is either the grammatical, literal, historical interpretation or we are adrift on an uncharted sea with every man the norm for himself."[129] Prophecy fulfilled is always prophecy fulfilled literally, and the words concerning the Gog-Magog Battle should be interpreted no differently.

Before the Tribulation

The following timing views are founded on the premillennial interpretation of Scriptures as they relate to the order of future events. Premillennialism was the dominant view during the first three centuries of church history and was later reinstated by German Calvinist theologian Johann Heinrich Alsted in his book *The Beloved City* (1627).[130]

Before Both the Rapture and the Tribulation

Some theologians believe the Gog-Magog Battle will occur before both the Rapture of the Church and the seven-year Tribulation. A few of the supporters of this view are Tim LaHaye and Jerry Jenkins of the popular *Left Behind* series and Joel Rosenberg, who wrote *Epicenter*. Another supporter, David Cooper, noted with confidence back in 1940, years before Israel had even become a nation again, that "there will be a time between now and the beginning of the Tribulation when the Jews will be dwelling in the Land in unwalled cities and will be at rest."[131]

While many positive supports are inherent in this timing view, the most poignant concerns leaving Israel to burn the invaders' weapons for seven years, which equals the length of the Tribulation. Negatives involve placing this event outside of the Tribulation, postulating how Israel could be living unsuspecting and in peace, and the argument for the imminency of the Rapture.

After the Rapture but Before the Tribulation

Popular supporters of this view are Ed Hindson and Tommy Ice,[132] as well as Arnold Fruchtenbaum of Ariel Ministries, who reasons the Russian invasion will take place "some time before the Tribulation," because "God will punish Russia for her… long history of anti-Semitism."[133]

A well-supported view, the most telling positive, postulates that the world will be thrown into chaos due to a pre-Tribulation Rapture, so Russia and its Islamic coalition could seize the opportunity to attack a friendless Israel. The largest negative would be placing this battle outside of the Tribulation if a strict "latter-years" interpretation is taken.

During the Tribulation

The following timings place the Gog-Magog battle during the Tribulation.

First Half or Middle of the Tribulation: Supporters of this view include John Walvoord, J. Dwight Pentecost, Charles Ryrie, Herman Hoyt, Charles Dyer, and Mark Hitchcock. As Pentecost explains, "To place the events in the middle of the week is the only position consistent with the chronology of these extended passages (Isaiah 30–35; Joel 2–3)."[134]

This view's most promising point is how the Antichrist's peace treaty with Israel could easily provide Israel her peaceful precondition.[135] The negative wonders why Israel would be burning the fuel well into the Millennial Kingdom. It also questions why God would rescue Israel so dramatically from the Gog-Magog nations only to hand Israel immediately back over to the intense persecution by the Antichrist.

End of the Tribulation (Armageddon): Supporters of this view, including Louis Bauman and Charles Feinberg, believe the Gog-Magog battle and the final battle of Armageddon are one and the same.[136]

Proponents of this timing view point to how the Gog-Magog battle (38–39) and the Battle of Armageddon (Revelation 19:19) are described as taking place during the "latter years." Ezekiel and Revelation both describe dead invaders being eaten by birds and wild animals. And, Ezekiel and Zechariah both declare that, due to the defeat of the invasion, Israel will again acknowledge God. This view stumbles over the peaceful precondition, as the Jews are being hunted by the Antichrist and many flee into the wilderness before Armageddon begins. And, the national makeup of Gog-Magog is more limited than all the countries of the world that comprise the Antichrist's invading forces. The nations in the two battles, the locations, the leaders, the opponents, and the overall account just do not match.

In Relation to the Millennial Kingdom

Three views place the Gog-Magog battle in relation to Jesus Christ's thousand-year reign on earth, often called the Millennial Kingdom. The first places the battle in a gap between the Tribulation and the Millennium, and the second at the very beginning. Too many problems exist with these timing views, so we will just skip over them and go right to the third, which is the end of the Millennium.

The majority of supporters of this view tend to come from a non-evangelical background.[137] Henry Halley is a proponent of this view;[138] so are George Knight and Rayburn Ray.[139] Frank Gaebelein also places the Gog-Magog battle at the end of the Millennial Kingdom.[140]

Supporters of this timing view stab their finger at this passage:

Now when the thousand years have expired, Satan will be released from his prison and will go out to deceive the nations which are in the four corners of the earth, Gog and Magog, to gather them together to battle, whose number is as the sand of the sea. (Revelation 20:7–8)

Clearly, similar terminology exists between Ezekiel 38–39 and Revelation 20 concerning the great number of invaders involved. The prosperity Israel possesses as Ezekiel described would be fulfilled by God's blessings on Israel during the Millennial Kingdom. And, God uses supernatural weather in both accounts to destroy the invaders.

But, that's where the comparisons end. The negative points far outweigh the supporting points. Ezekiel's chapters would be chronologically out of order with this view, as Ezekiel 33–39 covers the national restoration of Israel and is followed by chapters 40–48, which describe Israel's spiritual restoration entering and enduring throughout the Millennial Kingdom.[141] Revelation 20's chronology, along with many other aspects, does not harmonize with Ezekiel's account. Israel would have no need to burn weapons into the eternal state. So, John's use of "Gog and Magog" in Revelation 20:8 is more likely used to draw a comparison between Ezekiel's Gog-Magog battle and the one John is describing at the end of the Millennial Kingdom. In other words, the labeling acts as a kind of shorthand, saying, "It's going to be Gog and Magog all over again."[142]

Final Analysis

I will conclude by analyzing what I believe are the best views as to when the Gog-Magog battle will take place. Note that each of the timing views revolves around two yet-to-be-fulfilled key prerequisites:

1. Israel exists in a state of unsuspecting peace before the invasion (38:11).
2. Israel takes seven months to bury the dead invaders' bodies and seven whole years to expend the leftover fuel and weaponry (39:9, 12–16).

Placing the timing at the beginning, though not in the middle, of the Tribulation gives Israel the seven months to bury the dead invaders and the full seven years to burn the fuel. This view would then need to settle the peaceful precondition of Israel, possibly due to the peace covenant made with the Antichrist.

The two outlooks that place the timing of the Gog-Magog Battle squarely before the Tribulation perfectly grants the full seven years needed to burn the weapons. Israel's current military superiority or a Psalm 83 subjugation of Israel's hostile bordering neighbors could provide her a false sense of security.

My View

Obviously, all of the timing issues struggle over several particular points. Which perspective a person holds rests more on what he or she sees as the one that provides the most logical harmonization of the prerequisites. I have to agree with those who conclude that the timing of the Gog-Magog battle happens after the Rapture of the Church but just before or at the very onset of the Tribulation. This timing best fulfills these prerequisites and makes the most logical sense in the prophetic chronology, and I would see it playing out as:

1. The Rapture of the Church removes the Restrainer.
2. Israel subjugates its surrounding neighbors in fulfillment of Psalm 83.
3. The Gog-Magog battle destroys the Russian and Muslim influence in the Middle East, makes the world aware of God's presence, and restores Israel's belief in Yahweh.
4. The Antichrist makes a peace covenant with Israel, which starts the seven-year Tribulation, then conquers what is left of the Middle East, and births his revived Roman Empire.
5. Israel spends the seven years of the Tribulation burning the weapons.

6. Jesus returns at the end of the seven years to defeat His enemies at Armageddon, resulting in Israel acknowledging the newly returned Yeshua as God's Son.

7. Jesus gathers the people from all over the world for the Sheep-Goat Judgment, which results in only believers entering the Millennial Kingdom.

8. At the very end of the Millennial Kingdom, a final battle takes place that is reminiscent of the first Gog-Magog battle.

Time will tell when the Gog-Magog battle will truly take place. But, Israel exists as a nation as prophesied, and the coalition of invading nations is already working together for the first time in history. The scene is pretty much all set for this epic battle to be waged—and in the very near future.

CHAPTER 14

HOLY LAND PREPARES FOR UNHOLY LIGHTNING

By Jim Fletcher

Bible prophecy is a reason for faith.
—Joseph Farah

THE GOG-MAGOG INVASION of Israel in the last days is a popular subject for prophecy enthusiasts.

It's the timing we sometimes "argue" about.

On the very day Israel declared its independence in 1948, Egyptian planes bombed Tel Aviv (the city had also been bombed by Italy in 1940, under the orders of Mussolini). The few planes Israel had were destroyed, but incredibly, were rebuilt. The new state had no other choice.

From 4,500 troops on the day of partition in 1947 until the war began, Israel gained more than 30,000 for battle.

Iraqi troops also crossed the river Jordan on May 15, the first full day of Israeli independence. Crossing at Gesher—whose settlers had driven off an Arab Legion attack two weeks earlier—on the following morning, they attacked the British police fort and the village. The villagers held their fire until the attacking troops were almost upon them, then drove them back. But the settlement was besieged for seven days. On one occasion, an Iraqi armored vehicle reached the gate of the police fort and blew it up, but was itself hit by an Israeli Molotov cocktail and went up in flames.[143]

Today, if one looks at the terrain of Israel on the eastern side, facing Jordan, you will see a rocky, high ascent. But if an invading army can pierce this territory and reach the high point of the mountains of Israel, it has an easy two-thousand-foot descent to conquer the breadbasket of Israel.

Many armies have come from the east into Israel in ancient times, including Alexander's, but none have fulfilled the unique elements of Ezekiel 38—39.

The Case for Prophecy

Biblical accounts of certain events, such as Gog-Magog, are dismissed by critics for all sorts of reasons. They say it's symbolic of something else, usually a modern thing. Or the prophecy was already fulfilled in ancient times; critics don't mind those that are far back in the rear-view mirror. They detest it when we insist many are still future. This has to do with the sovereignty of God. Critics, even those in the church, do not like the idea of a God in complete control. They want to limit Him and claim that Bible prophecy is sometimes too fantastic to believe.

So they want to reinvent a God who knows all and sees all (Isaiah 46).

You see, we have had enemies from within the fort for many years… decades…a century, at least. Seminary professors have been filling young students' heads with the idea that the Exodus never happened. The Flood was either an invention of ancient editors or it was a small, regional event. Or the return of the Jews in the last days was in fact somehow a representation of the modern church!

All these examples involve prophecies. God told the Israelites He would lead them to the Promised Land. He told Noah the earth's population would be reduced to eight people. He told the Jews that, in the latter days, they would return from exile to reclaim their ancient homeland.

The enemies of the cross of Christ despise God. They despise His

Word. So they try to make it something it is not. They try to make it a human invention.

This is one of the reasons I've always been so interested in Bible prophecy. It is proof that God is sovereign and that He is the God of the Bible.

Before we can believe Gog will lead a massive coalition army against Israel in the last days, we must first believe the rest of the Bible. For this, we have several prophecies that are easily confirmed. Some are more obscure than others, and in fact make for some of the more interesting "future tellings" in Scripture.

You should also know I've had public and private dialogue with some of the more virulent critics of Bible prophecy, and I've never yet heard an effective response to the validity of predictive prophecy in the Bible.

I've talked to people who simply don't like Jews, so they don't like the specialness of the Jews as outlined in Scripture, including the promises of future restoration (such as we read with stunning clarity in Deuteronomy). I've talked to others who simply enjoy currying favor with the "intellectual" crowd, scholars and media figures who dismiss the Bible.

But in all these conversations, I've never heard anyone really refute prophecy. A story I've told before illustrates this perfectly.

In 2002, I attended a lecture in Fayetteville, Arkansas. Episcopal Bishop John Shelby Spong (now gone to his reward) made a career out of spewing blasphemy. He reveled in his supposed skill in relegating much of the Bible to myth.

The church that hosted this apostate loved him. The packed room laughed and clapped when he attacked Scripture. But in the Q&A, we had opportunities to ask the "good" bishop anything we liked.

I stood and mentioned his dismissal of Bible prophecy; he had even laughed at the "physics involved" in Jesus returning to earth.

I said, "Bishop Spong, in Exodus [Exodus 12:14], the Lord tells the Jewish people in Egypt that they will remember their final night as slaves, and they will do it forever. Today, all over the world, more than 90 percent of Jews stop what they're doing to celebrate Passover. This is a clear fulfillment of that 3,700 year-old prophecy. How do you answer that?"

Spong was caught off-guard, as were his hosts. This was supposed to be only a friendly crowd that would affirm his apostate remarks.

He turned his back and put his fingers to his lips as if deep in thought. He was stalling for time, to think of something to say. He knew what I had just said was true. By the way, this is an example of a learned man clearly rejecting truth by his own decision. He wasn't deceived; he was doing the deceiving.

Finally, he turned around, smiled, and said, "I just don't interpret it that way. I don't believe that."

His answer wasn't good enough; it wasn't sufficient. I hope some people saw that on that night. In fact, his response was so poor, I almost felt sorry for him.

Almost.

The point of that little story is to demonstrate that even the supposed lions of scholarship—those who stab at the faith and sow doubt among believers—have no place to hide when exposed to truth. This should be a signal that we can fight these apostates simply by reminding them of Scripture, which interprets itself constantly.

Now let's look at a few specific prophecies before we tackle the topic of Ezekiel 38–39.

Not One Stone Upon Another

The famous encounter the apostles had with Jesus on the Mount of Olives, when they asked Him several probing questions about the future, is one that thrills me.

Let's look at it here:

And Jesus went out, and departed from the temple: and his disciples came to him for to shew him the buildings of the temple. And Jesus said unto them, See ye not all these things? verily I say unto you, There shall not be left here one stone upon another, that shall not be thrown down. (Matthew 24:1–2)[144]

No one but the most stubborn critics would deny that Jesus said these things. He was telling His followers that in the future, this wonder of the ancient world would be thrown down, destroyed. They could not have yet known that, forty years into the future, Rome's Tenth Legion would do this very thing, finally destroying the city of Jerusalem and rabidly tearing down the walls of the magnificent Temple.

Ancient manuscript experts attest to the genuineness of copies of the New Testament dated to hear the first century. Now consider this:

If you visit Jerusalem today, you will see the evidence of the destruction of the Temple right in front of your face. Not so long ago, I sat a few yards away as families walked among the huge stones that litter the base of the Western Wall. This is part of the archaeological park located in the Old City. It was unearthed by archaeologists after the Six Day War of 1967, and offered crystal-clear proof of the presence of Jews there in ancient times.

Those stones are literally among the stones pushed over the edge of the Temple Mount by unhinged (because of hatred) Roman soldiers in AD 70. Ancient accounts of the event (such as those of Josephus) describe wildfires and destruction in the Temple complex. When it was over… nothing remained.

The so-called Arch of Titus, a bas-relief depicting Roman soldiers carrying treasures away from the Temple, including the golden menorah, is an accurate portrayal of this event.

Now, if you've had the privilege of visiting the Temple Mount, you've seen, about sixty feet above those littered stones, several famous structures, including the golden Dome of the Rock, the Muslim shrine to Mohammed. The Al-Aksa Mosque is also up there, along with various outbuildings.

But…if you know some history and allow your mind's eye to go back to AD 70, you will realize that at the end of that terrible day, absolutely nothing remained of the Temple on that site. It was scraped as clean as a tabletop.

Now, think about Jesus' words in Matthew. How do the critics refute this? This is a very plain description of an event that found fulfillment several years later. I've stood on this spot many times and had these thoughts. It thrills my soul.

(I have to say, at this point, that I believe a majority of people haven't yet actually rejected these Scriptures. They simply don't know about them. That's why teaching Bible prophecy responsibly [not wild speculation] is actually an evangelism tool. That's why it's so feared and loathed by the enemies of God, many of whom are found in the Church.)

A City Without Walls

One of the most remarkable prophecies I've ever come across involves a 2,700-year-old prediction from the book of Zechariah...and a nineteenth-century Jewish benefactor in Britain.

On my first trip to Israel in 1998, I was walking through a museum in the Old City of Jerusalem. Of course, there were many famous exhibits and a lot of great teaching. But it was what I'd call a benign scene that really knocked me out emotionally and mentally.

The stone ramparts of the city have many narrow windows, such as you'd see in a castle. I stopped at one particular narrow opening and noticed a plaque on the wall just to the right bearing the following:

> Then I looked up, and there before me was a man with a measuring line in his hand. I asked, "Where are you going?" He answered me, "To measure Jerusalem, to find out how wide and how long it is." While the angel who was speaking to me was leaving, another angel came to meet him and said to him: "Run, tell that young man, 'Jerusalem will be a city without walls because of the great number of people and animals in it. And I myself will be a wall of fire around it,' declares the Lord, 'and I will be its glory within.'" (Zechariah 2)

This passage called to the future, to a time when Jerusalem would see expanded dwellings outside the thick, protective city walls. At the time, hundreds of years before Christ's first appearing, such a thing was unthinkable. No one would live outside the walls, because outlaws, wild animals, and invading armies would be roaming around.

And yet.

By AD 1860, living conditions inside Jerusalem had become so cramped, so unhealthy, that something had to be done for the inhabitants. Disease was rampant, with sewage running down the streets.

A British businessman, Moses Montefiore, decided to use part of his wealth to help. He proposed building apartment-style structures just outside the walls of Jerusalem's Old City. This was to be a planned community steps from Jaffa Gate, on the city's west side.

So that's what was done.

Notice the opening lines of the prophecy in Zechariah 2: A man stands with a measuring line, literally surveying the city to see how wide and long it is. Surely, this is an odd passage from the Old Testament.

Flash forward more than two thousand years.

In the era of Montefiore's plan came the decision from the British government to see what could be done to somewhat modernize Jerusalem. Both Israelite and Roman structures and ingenuity brought clean water into the city, but over time, the extremely compact dwellings inside had created serious problems.

Around the time the American Civil War was concluding, a British army officer, Charles William Wilson, undertook a survey of Jerusalem. The result was a "perfectly accurate map" of the city.

The record of the survey itself is quite fascinating. (One particular note of fascination is that it was discovered that, underneath the Temple Mount, the area was "honeycombed with cisterns," perhaps lending credence to the theories of the current resting place of the Ark of the Covenant.)

So here we have the nineteenth-century account of the first major effort to "measure Jerusalem," the very thing being spoken of in Zechariah. The next step is to build those dwellings outside the city walls.

On another visit to Jerusalem, I thought about all this and decided to ask around. Sure enough, I was told that, if one looks across the road from Jaffa Gate, one can see an old stone windmill and an outcropping of buildings. This is the famed *Mishkenot Sha'ananim* ("Beautiful Dwelling"), the very small community built with the funds from Montefiore.

A row of apartments, with a porch, looks out over the Old City. This I believe is the direct fulfillment of Zechariah 2; we can see clearly both elements of that prophecy—the survey and the construction of dwellings (complete with vegetable gardens in the back).

This prophecy was fulfilled in the 1860s, and cannot be disputed, in my view. It is a remarkable fulfillment of prophecy, not one well-known.

I spent a few nights in one of those apartments, and could barely sleep because of my awe over the site!

Today, just down the slope, is a magnificent community, Yemen Moshe, filled with stunning stone houses decorated with lush foliage and flowers. It is some of the priciest real estate in the world.

The fulfillment of Zechariah 2 is a stunning display of the sovereignty of God, and helps prove His existence, if I may say it that way.

The Scoffers

Brian McLaren is a clever fellow—*too* clever, by half, as they say.

A pastor who began his professional life as an English teacher, he has become so successful as an author/speaker that he gave up the pastorate and moved to Florida.

I hardly blame him for that.

Where I take issue is with the liberties he takes with the Bible.

McLaren is one of the most famous "progressive Christians" in the world today, very popular with college-age Millennials. He is the spiritual successor to John Shelby Spong, Marcus Borg, and other heretics/apostates.

In particular, he loves to display his animus for Bible prophecy. He also of course believes in Darwinian philosophy, or evolution.

Of prophecy, McLaren has stated:

These doctrinal formulations often use a bogus end-of-the-world scenario to create a kind of death-wish for World War III, which—unless it is confronted more robustly by the rest of us—could too easily create a self-fulfilling prophecy.

McLaren does not believe in the Second Coming of Christ, as traditional, evangelical Christians have understood it for hundreds of years. He is a mocker.

So it is then that I find 2 Peter 3:3–7 so compelling:

Knowing this first, that there shall come in the last days scoffers, walking after their own lusts, And saying, Where is the promise of his coming? for since the fathers fell asleep, all things continue as they were from the beginning of the creation. For this they willingly are ignorant of, that by the word of God the heavens were of old, and the earth standing out of the water and in the water: Whereby the world that then was, being overflowed with water, perished: But the heavens and the earth, which are now, by the same word are kept in store, reserved unto fire against the day of judgment and perdition of ungodly men.

Wow! The apostle was describing the last days of the Church, when evil men would appear to attack the Scripture and the faith. Notice the two characteristics: these would be people who deny first the Creation and Flood accounts in Genesis, they then would move to a logical conclusion by denying the glorious coming of Christ.

Brian McLaren is just such a teacher. Like Spong, he particularly has disdain for the Rapture and Christ's Second Coming. These men seem to have no fear of the Living God. Yet they serve as the fulfillment of Peter's prophecy!

Gog and Magog

Now we turn our attention to one of the most famous prophecies in the Bible, the one found in Ezekiel 38 and 39.

The fearsome description here is of an evil leader from the far north who will cobble together a coalition army of various nations to attack a sovereign Israel.

I took time with the opening part of this chapter—the three separate, compelling fulfilled prophecies—to set the groundwork for a reason to believe Gog and Magog are yet future and deal with real nations.

I like to look through various Bible translations to see the editors' views of Bible prophecy. Unfortunately, since the 1970s, many have sought to throw cold water on prophecy. This is a reflection of the teaching from seminaries and the worldview of prominent celebrity pastors and ministries that focus on man's ability to help himself and the world.

The Quest Study Bible, published by Zondervan, is one such translation from the NIV. Here we see time after time an agenda to encourage readers to move away from traditional views of Bible prophecy. Cunningly, the editors of such books mix some truth with error. For example, the Quest Study Bible does allow that Ezekiel 38–39 speaks to a future time, but the message is garbled from that point, even noting that some do not believe it is literal, as in the future restoration discussed in Ezekiel 36:35–38. They state that while some believe it is a real future fulfillment, others believe it to be a "spiritual" fulfillment, and yet others believe it refers to the return from the Babylonian captivity and exile.

As to Gog-Magog specifically, the Quest Study Bible editors do state these passages seem to refer to the end times, yet they deal with the seven-year period of burning weapons (Ezekiel 39:9–10) by saying it refers to weapons made of wood and leather.

A study Bible much worse in its dealing with Ezekiel 38–39 is the Interpreter's Bible, a pastor's study series first developed by mainline sources in the 1920s. The editors of this version spiritualize virtually every example of Bible prophecy. They then wax poetic, going far afield by quoting Lincoln, Aristotle, etc.—anything to shift focus away from the subject of literal fulfillment of Bible prophecy.

The actual Scriptures dealing with Gog and Magog, however, are well known to prophecy students. The real question is: Can we believe this is a future fulfillment?

The scenario, of course, is that Gog (thought by many scholars to be a modern Russian leader) is suddenly taken with the idea of invading Israel. In fact, we are told that God puts a hook in his jaws and turns him around. This is an interesting detail, because it indicates Gog has not been planning this invasion for a long time; the idea comes to him suddenly.

He then assembles a coalition of willing allies: Persia (Iran), Cush (Ethiopia), Put and Libya (northern Africa), Gomer (Germany), Beth Togarmah (Turkey).[145]

It is interesting to note that, in Jewish tradition, Gog and Magog are enemies to be defeated by the Messiah to usher in the messianic age.

In essence, Gog doesn't seem to have a *specific* reason for invading Israel, though one can strongly argue that access to warm-weather seaports has long interested the Soviet Union/Russia. That the Russians have planted themselves in Syria seems ominous on this count.

The Israel Bible notes that Gog seems driven simply by hatred for the Jews/Israel, which I think is a plausible analysis. However, the reason he invades isn't the most important, at least for Gog's own motives. What is important is *God's reason* for letting it happen.

As Ezekiel 38 opens, God explains that this event will happen many years into the future, when Israel is restored and now lives "in safety" (verse 8). This is a clue about timing.

The answer as to why this happens is found in verse 16:

You will advance against my people Israel like a cloud that covers the land. In days to come, Gog, I will bring you against my land, so that the nations may know me when I am proved holy through you before their eyes.

That's it. Several times in Scripture, God says He will show His great power through the Jews to allow the heathen to see Him. He does this to display His own sovereignty and power in rescuing His people. This is finally so that no one on earth will have an excuse for not recognizing the True and Living God.

Now, about that timing. If Israel is living in safety, what does that mean? We don't have to overthink it, but there are a couple of possible interpretations.

Israel lives in safety today in that the country is a haven for Jews around the world. It is the first and only place in modern history where they can defend themselves. However, living in "complete safety" is not the case for Israel today. Iran and others threaten the nation on a weekly basis. So, certainly, we are not currently in a moment in which Israel lives in complete safety.

So, then, is this event occurring when Israel lives "safely" or "completely safe"? I don't think we know the answer to that. Many have debated it. I believe, in these situations, we must be flexible enough to allow for the possibility that we don't know all the details of the timeline. So, the Gog-Magog war can erupt in our time, fairly soon, or some distant point in the future.

For example, Putin's Russia would seem today to be a prime candidate to invade Israel one day. On the other hand, perhaps it will be several decades from now when geopolitical conditions exist that Israel feels completely safe and will "take chances" for peace.

What I want you to take away from this chapter is something else, apart from timing: The fact of Gog-Magog cannot be disputed. Read the two chapters for yourself. My personal view is that it clearly takes place in the future, and it will be fulfilled to the letter.

For example, the cleanup after the battle is a description of nuclear-type weapons. We know from recent history (the Yom Kippur War) that Israel was almost at the point of using so-called battlefield nukes in order to survive. Would they launch such weapons if an invading army arrived in-country?

Surely they would.

We also read of God's miraculous rescue of Israel: He specifically says that as soon as Gog's forces reach the peak of the mountains of Israel—as they straddle the peaks and look westward to Israel's weak point, the fertile valley, He will destroy them suddenly. He leaves a small portion of the forces alive, seemingly as witnesses to His power.

So, as we wrap up this brief survey of Ezekiel 38–39, I want to leave you with two thoughts:

First, it is easy, rather than hard, to believe Bible prophecy is true. We have too many examples of specifically fulfilled prophecies. Unlike other religions, which do have some prophecies but spotty records in fulfillment, God's predictions always come true exactly as He said they would. So, study Bible prophecy today and believe!

Second, the conditions for Gog-Magog are largely in place; the biggest piece of this puzzle was the return of the Jews to their ancestral land as a sovereign nation. They had to be there for this prophecy to be fulfilled.

That happened beginning in 1882 with the first large-scale immigration of Jews to modern Palestine. It was cemented with the establishment of the state in 1948.

Gog and Magog will arrive one day in the very heartland of Israel. There, they will raise their collective sword and prepare to strike.

Then God will kill them in an instant.

Book it.

CHAPTER 15

FAR-EAST EVIL

By Todd Strandberg

THE MOST DISASTROUS FOREIGN-POLICY move in American history was President Richard Nixon's decision to open relations with China. Since the signing of the 1972 Sino-American bilateral relations, the American economy has steadily become addicted to cheap Chinese imports. Whole American industries have been phased out as China became the source of common household items like phones, radios, and TVs.

The greatest damage occurred in 2020 with the COVID-19 pandemic. America is now $6 trillion deeper in debt because a virus was deliberately or accidentally released into the global population. Millions of retail businesses were wiped out because of COVID-19.

Another negative aspect of our relationship with China is the content theft of our intellectual property. We spend billions on research to develop a product, and the Chinese get it for free. China's typical modus operandi is to steal American intellectual property, replicate it, replace the US company originating that intellectual property in the Chinese domestic market, then displace the United States in the global market.

Prior to the Trump administration, it was the American State Department and previous administrations—both Democrat and Republican—

that made agreements that enriched the communist state. Our own negotiation blunders, in effect, have helped build the Chinese communist regime into what is becoming a massive force that has prophetic overtones—portending the destruction of much of the world's population.

China is not our friend. It is a godless, communist dictatorship that is rapidly building a 1984-style surveillance system. If we had kept our distance from this red menace, its gross domestic product would be no bigger than one of our poorest states. China wants to take over the world, and we are helping it achieve this goal.

Why China Loves the Dollar

The People's Republic of China has had a trade surplus with the US for decades. In 2018, its surplus with America hit a record $418 billion. China's total foreign exchange reserves stand at $3.073 trillion.

Few Americans see the harm in having a $400 billion trade deficit with a single nation. Most people would think that if the Chinese are stupid enough to take our money, we should keep sending them more.

There's actually a sinister reason China loves our dollar. This massive horde of dollar wealth by China is just an illusion. In real terms, China is actually struggling to get more dollars.

The *renminbi* is the official currency of China. I've written several stories about how China has signed numerous deals with countries to trade with them in the renminbi. All that global travel by President Xi was a huge waste of time and jet fuel.

In terms of global reserve currency, the renminbi has a share of only 1.9 percent, in fifth place, barely ahead of the Canadian dollar but miles behind the US dollar (61.7 percent) and the euro (20.7 percent). Over the past two years, the renminbi has gone nowhere as a reserve currency. In 2020, it had a minuscule share of merely 1.22 percent of international cross-border payments.

Anyone who has a basic understanding of economics knows that when you print too much currency, its value should go down. The Chinese government has somehow managed to print a massive amount of renminbi without triggering hyperinflation. Since 1952, the money supply has grown by a staggering eighteen thousand fold.

America has a huge national debt, but it is small compared to China's debt load. The US economy is roughly $20 trillion. China's is roughly $13 trillion in circulation. China's banking system is north of $50 trillion. Ours is currently at $22 trillion.

Because China is a resource-poor nation, it has to import vast amounts of raw materials. No other nation on earth has imported more goods. In the past twenty years, China has consumed more cement than America has used in the past one hundred years. Since 2004, its oil imports have increased four times. China imports 68 percent of the world's supply of iron ore.

China's massive imports have resulted in a huge dollar shortage in the Chinese banking system. That's because Chinese businesses still owe more than $2.5 trillion in dollar-denominated debts that are maturing over the next few years.

The Chinese government has been spending huge amounts of money on its military. In 2009, it spent 400 billion renminbi on its military. By the end of this year, it will spend 1,200 billion renminbi, a threefold increase in a decade.

With the Chinese economy now hopelessly addicted to Middle East oil and raw materials from Africa, some economists are starting to wonder if China will turn to the military option once its supply of dollars runs out. Hitler made a mad grab for resources before he turned to blitzkrieg to wipe out his foreign debts.

A China-explosive economic growth is the clearest indication that the kings of the East are about to move out. A decade ago, China had no ability to project military power on the international stage. In the past few years, the nation's wild spending has suddenly transformed it into a global giant. Because it only has a limited amount of time and money to maintain such a massive military force, the Tribulation hour must be very near.

And the sixth angel poured out his vial upon the great river Euphrates; and the water thereof was dried up, that the way of the kings of the east might be prepared. (Revelation 16:12)

Saying to the sixth angel which had the trumpet, Loose the four angels which are bound in the great river Euphrates. And the four angels were loosed, which were prepared for an hour, and a day, and a month, and a year, for to slay the third part of men. And the number of the army of the horsemen were two hundred thousand thousand: and I heard the number of them. (Revelation 9:14–16).

I don't think China will ever run out of dollars. If it did develop a desperate need for greenbacks, the Federal Reserve will gladly issue it a trillion-dollar swap line to tide them over. When you own the world's reserve currency, you can write a check for any amount.

There is a possibility that China hopes to crash the value of the dollar. Many investors think it would not want to see the dollar decline because of its massive treasury holdings. If you have $3.0 trillion in treasuries and $3 trillion in dollars denominated debt, a crash in the dollar world have no net financial impact on you.

China's answer to a possible decline of the dollar seems to be a return to a gold standard. The nation's officially declared holdings of 1,948 tonnes make up just 3 percent of its $3.2 trillion in foreign exchange holdings, but the real number is much larger than that.

Since 2000, China has mined roughly 6,500 tonnes. Already, that official 1,948 figure looked doubtful. Crucially, China keeps all the gold it mines; exporting domestic mine production is not allowed. Beijing's willingness to so boldly lie about its gold holdings tells me it has been very highly dependent on the yellow metal.

As well as being the world's biggest producer, China is the world's biggest importer. It is hard to get precise import figures because the nation encourages citizens to own gold. The best-guess estimate on China's total gold holdings points to a figure of 10,000–15,000 tonnes.

When America was at its economic peak in the early 1950s, our gold holdings stood at 22,000 tonnes. Once we started the welfare system and the Vietnam war, our gold holdings began to decline. The tonnage would be at zero if Nixon had not ended the exchangeability of gold in 1971. We claim to have 8,000 tonnes, but there has not been an audit in decades.

A lot of Christians have a *dislike* for gold because the Bible says people will cast it into the street near the end of the Tribulation. I think the opposite is true. There will be such *fear* of the coming judgment that people will cast their valuables into the street.

They will throw their silver into the streets, And their gold will be like refuse; Their silver and their gold will not be able to deliver them In the day of the wrath of the LORD; They will not satisfy their souls, Nor fill their stomachs, Because it became their stumbling block of iniquity. (Ezekiel 7:19)

Why So Many Global Pandemics Come from China

In all of human history, infectious diseases have been a constant threat. The small mutation in the genome of a virus or bacterium could trigger a pandemic that could sweep over the world and kill millions of people. The last major pandemic with high levels of mortality was the 1918 Spanish flu outbreak; it was estimated to be responsible for the deaths of approximately fifty to one hundred million people.

The 2009 flu pandemic was the most recent pandemic. First described in April 2009, the virus appeared to be the result of a triple assortment of bird, swine, and human flu viruses. This new strain was so different from previous viruses that it was able to breach the immune system of a vast number of people. It is estimated that 11–21 percent of the global population contracted the illness, and 151,000–579,000 died.

It's no odd coincidence that many of the world's influenza strains originate in China. When you have hundreds of millions of farmers living right next to various animals, you have a perfect breeding ground for a new deadly virus. It should come as no surprise that China just had two major viruses in its farm animal population. The African swine fever has wiped out a third of China's pig population. Another virus killed millions of ducks.

The Chinese culture is an equal, if not greater, source of new virus strains. With China being a communist nation, the first impulse is to always cover up any outbreak, which allows the contamination to spread. The Chinese fondness for eating anything that crawls on the earth adds to the risk. The coronavirus currently grabbing world headlines is said to be related to the bat and snake market trade. There are also the "wet" markets, which are popular in China, as customers like to purchase their meat "warm"—that is, recently slaughtered. In short, China is one giant Petri dish.

The Chinese government seems to have made an impressive effort to contain the coronavirus. Beijing has imposed a series of lockdown measures on major cities, which includes sixty-five million people at one time. Bans were placed on all transport links, which suspended buses, subways, and ferries. The airport and train stations were also shut down to outgoing passengers.

The coronavirus should have transformed how we deal with China. When it became clear that a deadly virus was spread in the Wuhan region, the fire doors between China and the rest of the world should have closed. I found a stat that indicated 1.01 million Chinese citizens live or work overseas. During any given year, about three hundred thousand workers will come and go between China and the rest of the world.

When the coronavirus was turning into a global pandemic, little effort was made to control its spread. President Donald Trump was seen as a racist for being one of the first to restrict traffic from Asia. Even with restrictions, the number of daily travelers, including Chinese citizens entering the US by air, was at four thousand.

I did not know that, before the pandemic, thousands of Chinese citizens were working in Italy. With the nation open to flights from China, Italy was hit hard by the coronavirus; 4.5 million people were infected, with a loss of around two hundred thousand lives.

As I am writing this, the virus has infected more than two hundred million people and killed 5.4 million. As authorities fight to contain the virus, experts warn that the death toll will almost certainly rise.

The left has done everything it can to cover up for China. People who call the virus the "Wuhan flu" or argue that it may be a bioweapon are shouted down or banned from platforms. YouTube pages are blocked for simply mentioning the COVID-19 virus.

China should be condemned for allowing this virus to bring so much pain and suffering into the world. Because someone in Wuhan wanted to have bat soup, millions of people are now dead, an untold number of businesses are wiped out, and the world has had to spend $10 trillion on stimulus packages and lockdowns.

The monetary losses are massive, but they're small when compared to the losses in our liberties. During the lockdowns, people were told when they could leave their houses, where they could go, and what they had to wear. The mandates for vaccines were most shocking. The government forced people to get a shot for something that was still under emergency-use authorization.

I think the ever-increasing threat of a global pandemic is meant to be a warning from God of worse things to come. The pale horse of pestilence is getting ready to ride. His order to ride out will not come until the Tribulation is well underway.

And I looked, and behold a pale horse: and his name that sat on him was Death, and Hell followed with him. And power was given unto them over the fourth part of the earth, to kill with sword, and with hunger, and with death, and with the beasts of the earth. (Revelation 6:8)

And great earthquakes shall be in diverse places, and famines, and pestilences; and fearful sights and great signs shall there be from heaven. (Luke 21:11)

Trade Deals from Hell

In 1979, the US and China reestablished diplomatic relations and signed a bilateral trade agreement. This instituted a rapid growth in trade between the two nations, from $4 billion (exports and imports) that year to over $560 billion in 2020.

Trade relations with China in the first two decades went well because we were receiving cheap, labor-intensive items and exporting expensive equipment that China used to modernize its economy.

It wasn't until 1990 that our trade deficit with China topped $10 billion. By 2000, it had ballooned to $83 billion.

The honeymoon ended in 2001 when China entered the World Trade Organization and began to enjoy similar access to the US market. China, in a matter of a few years, completely took over the markets for office machines, computers, and auto parts. When China started making its own heavy equipment, the deficit exploded.

President Trump tried to restore a balance by getting into a trade war with China and forcing it to agree to buy products from America. We signed a new trade deal with China, but they failed to live up to it.

Trump was simply too late to turn the tide. Walmart might as well be called the China import store. We are so heavily dependent on China for common goods that we have no leverage to force China into a better trade relationship.

In 2020, China imported $100 billion of the US goods agreed to in the deal—roughly 58 percent of the targeted $173.1 billion, according to data compiled by the Peterson Institute for International Economics. The only deal that China understands is "you send us dollars, and we will send your goods."

As I said in the previous section, China has a net balance of nearly zero dollars. It is in everyone's best interest to keep this trade charade going as long as possible. When China's credit runs out, it may come to the point that the US will ask for a $1 trillion line of credit. China may say it has the dollars to buy raw materials, but it doesn't want to upset the market by dumping its dollar holdings.

President Xi may want to go out with a flair. He could say, "Yes, we've been a bad trading partner, and I'm here to fix matters." He could send a small army of agents over to America with the simple instruction to buy anything of value: real estate, paintings, jewelry, antiques, commodities, and precious metals. Buy it all.

An American film crew was in the city of Prague in 1981 making the movie *Amadeus*, and the food table had a real pineapple on it. The locals were amazed to see a whole pineapple. I often worry that America will stumble to the point that we see things as luxuries that were once common items.

China's New Nuclear Aggression

China has been neglected in the global nuclear equation by many American policymakers, as the cold war nuclear paradigm remained centered on the Soviet Union and then Russia. The key reason for the concern is the simple fact that China has a small number of nuclear bombs. While the Soviet Union had sixteen thousand at one point, China had a few dozen. Today, its nuclear arsenal is only two hundred forty.

For a good part of the Cold War, China had zero nuclear weapons. The first nuclear weapons test conducted by the People's Republic of China was detonated on October 16, 1964, at the Lop Nur test site. It was a uranium-235 implosion fission device made from weapons-grade uranium (U-235), enriched in a gaseous diffusion plant in Lanzhou. China tested its first hydrogen bomb in 1967.

The views of Chinese Dictator Mao Tse-Tung are the primary reasons China was late in joining the nuclear club. Mao believed "the atomic bomb itself was a paper tiger." He also held the conflicting belief that nuclear weapons could be useful in warfare.

Mao thought China could withstand casualties of "100 million men or more" in a nuclear attack from America and could maintain the strength to "assert its rights until the end." He sought Soviet cooperation in 1958 for a plan to lure US troops into the heartland of China, then attack them with Soviet nuclear weapons. Nikita Khrushchev was horrified by Mao's ideas on the use of nuclear weapons.

The Soviets had promised to deliver atomic bombs to China, but they stalled on the delivery in the wake of Mao's dangerous statements. Khrushchev instead tried to assure them in September 1958 by saying, "Invaders of China are also invaders of the Soviet Union." Joint defense ministry exchanges became increasingly testy over the issue.

By 1959, it became clear to the Chinese that the Soviets were only trying to stall China's nuclear progress. In June 1960, Nikita Khrushchev decided to stop helping the Chinese with their nuclear program. Mao immediately shifted toward a policy of self-reliance.

If it weren't for help from the Soviets, it would have taken China several more years to develop its nuclear program. When the Soviets developed an intercontinental missile capable of transporting an atomic bomb, they shipped two R-2 missiles (a related model) to China in January 1958.

China believes the ultimate goal of nuclear disarmament is eliminating all nuclear weapons and that the best way of achieving this is to first constrain their use. It also claims to be worried about the threat of nuclear proliferation. China claims to have a no-first-use-of-nuclear-weapons rule, but I think one day that will be proven a lie.

After spending decades in Russia's nuclear shadow, China has become more aggressive in developing its nuclear arsenal. Just as the Soviets claimed, the development of more nuclear missiles and bombs is protection against American aggression.

Chinese military experts have recently published a report citing the strategic threat from the US as a reason China needs to increase the number of nuclear weapons—especially to increase its sea-based nuclear deterrent of intercontinental, submarine-launched ballistic missiles—to deter potential military action by US warmongers. The report said the United States' new defense budget plan to modernize its nuclear arsenal was the reason for the countermeasure.

Open-source researchers using satellite imagery were able to identify that China is building over one hundred new intercontinental ballistic missile silos out in the desert. It is concerning for the countries where those missiles will be aimed, including the United States and its allies.

If China were worried about a US first strike, it would put nuclear weapons on platforms that are hard for the Pentagon to target, like mobile missiles and submarines—not in fixed silos. This portends a dangerous shift in Chinese nuclear strategy to include the possibility of a first-strike or launch-on-warning posture against America's strategic forces.

China's ability to produce plutonium will greatly increase in the coming years. A new generation of nuclear power facilities China is developing could produce large amounts of plutonium that could be used to make nuclear weapons. China is developing fast-breeder reactors as it seeks to reduce dependence on coal. But the plants also produce plutonium that could be used to make nuclear weapons. The first fast-breeder reactor is projected to come online in 2023.

In February 2021, China published a report titled "China's Civil Nuclear Sector: Plowshares to Swords," which stated that nation has started building a second plant to reprocess spent nuclear fuel. With China building nuclear reactors faster than any other nation, it could soon be producing large qualities of plutonium.

Japan has three operational breeder reactors, and they have produced a massive stockpile of plutonium. Japan now has 45.5 tons of separated plutonium, enough to make about six thousand atomic bombs.

Japan claims the stockpile is for powering a plutonium power reactor; but for years, it has failed to build such a reactor. It may need to reach into its nuclear stockpile to produce a few atomic bombs for deterrence. The city council of Baoji in northwestern Shaanxi province recently posted this statement: "If Japan intervenes in military affairs to reunify Taiwan, I must recommend the 'exceptional theory of nuclear strikes on Japan.'"

The narrator then declares Japan "has not learned its lesson from history," which means China must "continuously using nuclear bombs until

Japan announces its unconditional surrender for the second time"—in reference to WWII.

The "exceptional theory" is the controversial view held by many Chinese officials that China's "self-defense only" use of atomic bombs doesn't apply in the case of Japan; thus, an "exception" can be made.

There is still a burning hatred in China from Japan's World War II invasion of the nation and the Nanjing Massacre. Since no city council is allowed to speak without Beijing approval, the statement is likely an official response to a remark made by Japanese Deputy Prime Minister Taro Aso.

He said in 2021 that any future Chinese invasion of Taiwan would likely be interpreted in Tokyo as a "threat to Japan's survival," allowing the government to deploy its self-defense forces for collective self-defense.

Stop, Thief

China has long-term plans for global domination. It has a very simple method for achieving this goal. It plans to steal its way to the top by hacking into vast computer networks and keeping data that cost hundreds of billions of dollars to create, which allows the Chinese to leapfrog over us.

The Chinese have been extremely effective in stealing American technology because we don't understand how they operate. Beijing leaders are very patient and thorough in how they acquire information. They will send an agent into a company and have him work for years to gain a level of trust to gain access to sensitive data. Chinese hackers don't target key data. They download everything so that it can be meticulously studied for useful information.

When Russian hackers attacked the Continental Pipeline company, all they wanted was money. The Chinese would use their access to study how the oil-pumping network operates. I'm sure they have knowledge of how our electric grid and our financial systems work.

This fixation on knowing how our infrastructure works makes China a very dangerous foe. If they ever decide to launch a cyberattack against us, they could hit us on multiple fronts. They might be able to lock up the Continental Pipeline in nine different ways or do long-lasting damage.

We have such a complex network of interconnected computer systems that you can gain access to many systems by compromising just one. This is what happened when Microsoft Exchange was hacked by China. The hack compromised tens of thousands of computers around the world and was swiftly attributed to China's Ministry of State Security.

Stealing isn't always the way for China to gain data. Chinese regulators often require American companies operating in China to share their information with other firms. When it comes to Chinese firms operating in America, Beijing doesn't want them to share information.

Chinese firms are flouting US rules requiring public companies to disclose a range of potential risks to their financial performance. It would be nice to know the company you just invested in is not technically bankrupt. Since all Chinese companies are state-controlled, I don't think we should have any of them listed on the American stock exchange.

"This is one more piece of evidence that private companies do not actually exist in the People's Republic of China—they are all under the control of the Chinese Communist Party," US Representative Michael McCaul, the top Republican on the House Foreign Affairs Committee, said in a statement.

Nothing Will Stop China's Financial Miracle

When John the Revelator wrote about an army of two hundred million, generations of people were mystified by the prediction. Since the global population was less than two hundred million, many people saw these hordes as a demonic force that would sweep over the world. Now that we have 7.7 billion people on earth and China has a population of 1.4 billion people, it is possible to outfit such a vast army.

The army had 200 million soldiers on horses. I heard them say how many there were. I saw, as God wanted to show me, the horses and the men on them. The men had pieces of iron over their chests. These were red like fire, blue like the sky, and yellow like sulphur. The heads of the horses looked like the heads of lions. Fire, smoke, and sulphur came out of their mouths. One-third of all men were killed by the fire, smoke, and sulphur that came out of their mouths. (Revelation 9:16–18, New Life Version)

As the population of China grew rapidly in the twentieth century, it finally became possible for people to see the passage as related to a physical army of that many soldiers. Even though China reached a population of 1.4 billion, making it theoretically possible for China to man such a vast army, it had the financial resources to make this possible.

During the 1990s and 2000s, an absolute miracle occurred that saw China's economy grow faster than any other nation in history. In 2005, its oil consumption was two million barrels per day. By 2019, it was five times higher.

China built more skyscrapers in 2018 than anywhere else in the world—or at any other time in history, according to data released by the Council of Tall Buildings and Urban Habitat (CTBUH). There are now over one hundred Chinese cities with a population of above one million people.

China is the only nation on earth that has managed to expand its money supply by well over 10,000 percent without triggering hyperinflation. The rules of the basic monetary model don't apply to China because it has a destiny to fulfill. At least a hundred nations have tried to copy China and have had their currency wiped out.

The Chinese government has had a few financial problems over the years. In 2020, several banks had to be bailed out by the government. In 2021, the massive real estate giant EverGrande worried global markets when it got into monetary hot water. This miracle economy keeps trucking along because demonic forces are clearly in control of events.

And I saw three unclean spirits like frogs come out of the mouth of the dragon, and out of the mouth of the beast, and out of the mouth of the false prophet. For they are the spirits of devils, working miracles, which go forth unto the kings of the earth and of the whole world, to gather them to the battle of that great day of God Almighty. (Revelation 16:13–14)

SECTION V

PLANET EARTH ON GOD'S RADAR SCREEN

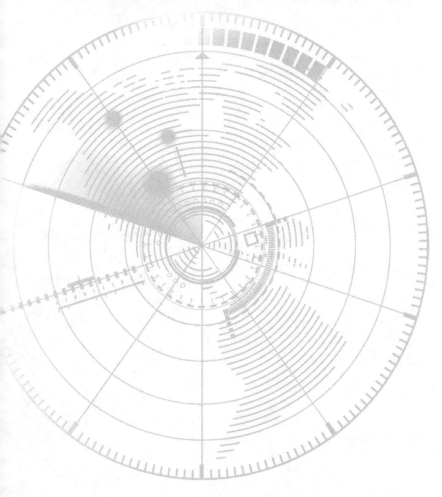

CHAPTER 16

MIDEAST MALEVOLENT MAELSTROM

By Bill Salus

WELCOME TO THE "Mideast Malevolent Maelstrom" chapter. When Terry James presented me with the privilege of authoring this chapter, I was intrigued by the title assigned to it. It represents clever alliteration, with the letter "M," and is admittedly a bit of a tongue-twister, but not as much as "Peter Piper picked a peck of pickled peppers. A peck of pickled peppers Peter Piper picked."

Moreover, I knew the word "Mideast," of course, meant the Middle East, but I wondered about the meaning of the other two "M" words that followed. These scholarly words were not an integral part of my layman's vocabulary.

As such, I considered it important, in case some of the readers are lay-persons like me, to define the inherent meaning within the title and then proceed to write the chapter. All of the following definitions are taken from Merriam-Webster's online dictionary.

- *Mid-East or Mideast*—The countries of northern Africa and southwestern Asia that are on or near the eastern edge of the Mediterranean Sea: the Near East.

- *Malevolent* —Having, showing, or arising from intense, often vicious, ill will, spite, or hatred (*that is*) productive of harm or evil (emphasis added).
- *Maelstrom*—A powerful, often violent, whirlpool sucking in objects within a given radius. Something resembling a maelstrom in turbulence, (*such as*) the *maelstrom* enveloping the country (*or*) a *maelstrom* of emotions (emphasis added).

Putting these words into perspective for this chapter, they address a manifest evil hatred that envelopes the radius of the Middle East that is violent and harmful. I have been asked to explain how the Lord will have to deal in judgment and wrath with this malevolent maelstrom in order to put down that rebellion and make all things right when Jesus Christ returns.

The Mideast Nations

In their alphabetical order, the Mideast countries include Algeria, Bahrain, *Egypt, Iran, Iraq, Israel, Jordan,* Kuwait, *Lebanon, Libya,* Morocco, Oman, Qatar, *Saudi Arabia, Syria,* Tunisia, *Turkey,* United Arab Emirates, and *Yemen*).

The *italicized countries* above are clear subjects of biblical prophecy, and some of these nations will be featured in this chapter. This is not to suggest the other Mideast nations are not identified within Bible prophecy, but if they are, they tend to be more obscure and therefore their futures are less decipherable.

In order to understand why the Lord must deal in judgment and wrath with this Mideast malevolent maelstrom, it's important to:

1. Identify God's foreign policy for the nations.
2. Evidence the breach of God's foreign policy by the nations.
3. Reveal the specific prophecies pertaining to the nations.

1. Identify God's Foreign Policy for the Nations

The preface is that God has made all the nations in the hope that these countries will seek Him, feel for Him, and ultimately find Him.

> And [*the Lord*] hath made of one blood all nations of men for to dwell on all the face of the earth, and hath determined the times before appointed, and the bounds of their habitation; That they should seek the Lord, if haply they might feel after him, and find him, though he be not far from every one of us. (Acts 17:26–27, KJV; emphasis added)[146]

God's goal is that, under His guidance, the nations will all live peacefully together throughout the earth. This is not presently happening, but in the Millennium it will be the case.

> He [*the Messiah Jesus Christ*], shall judge between the nations [*in the Millennium*], And rebuke many people; They shall beat their swords into plowshares, And their spears into pruning hooks; Nation shall not lift up sword against nation, Neither shall they learn war anymore. (Isaiah 2:4; emphasis added. Also read Isaiah 9:7 and Micah 4:3.)

Ignorance of God is no excuse for the Mideast nations to behave in breach of God's foreign policy because:
- His eternal power and Godhead has been purposely made self-evident throughout the entirety of the creation:

> For since the creation of the world His invisible *attributes* are clearly seen, being understood by the things that are made, *even* His eternal power and Godhead, so that they are without excuse. (Romans 1:20; emphasis added)

- His foreign policy was made through Abraham more than four thousand years ago and all of these Mideast nations, whether they are Muslim, Jewish, or Christian, consider Abraham to be their patriarchal father. God determined those who blessed Abraham and the great nation he would father would be blessed. On the flip side, countries that cursed Abraham and his great nation would be cursed.

Now the Lord had said to Abram: "Get out of your country, From your family And from your father's house, To a land that I will show you. I will make you a great nation;

I will bless you And make your name great; And you shall be a blessing. I will bless those who bless you, And I will curse him who curses you; And in you all the families of the earth shall be blessed." (Genesis 12:1–3)

Abraham's great nation is Israel and is traceable through Abraham's seed in Genesis 22:18, through his son Isaac in Genesis 26:1–4, and through his grandson Jacob in Genesis 28:10–14. Jacob was renamed Israel in Genesis 32:28, and he fathered the Twelve Tribes of Israel.

2. Evidence the Breach of God's Foreign Policy by the Nations

Thus far, it has been determined that the Mideast nations that do not seek after God, feel for Him, or ultimately find Him are out of sync with Him. As such, His benevolent intentions for them are denied to them and puts them at risk of God's judgment and wrath. All of the Mideast nations, apart from Israel, are predominately Muslim, which means they worship the false pagan god named Allah. Allah and the God Jehovah are not the same God.

STRIKE ONE!

Furthermore, most of these nations have a war-torn history of fighting against each other. A few examples in relatively modern history include:

- Turkey's military stronghold over most of the Mideast between 1514–1914 as the Ottoman Empire
- The Iran vs. Iraq war between 1980–1988
- The Iraqi invasion of Kuwait in 1990
- The current conflict between Saudi Arabia and Yemen

Since God's intentions, as pointed out in Isaiah 2:4 and Micah 4:3, are that a nation shall not lift up a sword against another nation, or even learn about war anymore, these warring Muslim nations are in breach of God's sovereign will.

STRIKE TWO!!

Recapping thus far, STRIKE ONE is that these nations don't seek after, feel for, find, or worship the One True God. STRIKE TWO is that they learn war, develop weapons of war, and continually go to war—all of which are actions contrary to God's will for the nations.

Lastly, the final shoe will soon drop upon these Muslim nations because of their mistreatment of Abraham's great nation of Israel. On November 29, 1947, the Mideast nations of Egypt, Iran, Iraq, Lebanon, Saudi Arabia, Syria, Turkey, and Yemen voted against the recreation of Israel as per UN Resolution 181, known as "The Partition Plan." Jordan wasn't a member of the UN at the time, or it would have likely also voted nay on the reestablishment of the Jewish State.

Adding insult to injury between May 15, 1948–March 10, 1949, the Mideast nations of Egypt, Syria, Lebanon, Iraq, Saudi Arabia, Yemen, and Jordan (then called Transjordan) went to war against the newly founded Jewish state of Israel. Then, during the Six-Day War in June of 1967, Egypt, Syria, Jordan, and Iraq, to a lesser extent, fought again against Israel. Having not yet learned their lesson, Egypt, Syria, and Jordan, to a lesser extent, arose up against Israel again in the Yom Kippur War of 1973.

After taking three severe shellackings, Egypt in 1979 and Jordan in 1994 made peace treaties with Israel. Although these treaties are still in effect, they are paper thin and the prophecies about to be revealed regarding Egypt and Jordan will evidence that they will become nonexistent.

Also, in addition to Egypt and Jordan, Syria, Saudi Arabia, Iraq, Lebanon's Hezbollah, Gaza's Hamas, and the Palestinians scattered throughout the Mideast are predicted in several unfulfilled prophecies to confederate and attack Israel in a final conflict. For these predominately Jew-hating countries and terrorist populations, this will be STRIKE THREE!!!

Ancient Arab Hatred of the Jews

As mentioned earlier, the definition of "Mideast Malevolent Maelstrom," when paired together, can mean "a manifest evil hatred that envelopes the radius of the Middle East that is violent and harmful." As this relates to the Arab states that have warred against Israel in modernity, the origin of this "evil hatred" was acknowledged long ago within the Bible.

The comparable words in Hebrew for this "evil hatred" are *olam ebah*. When paired together in Scripture, they are translated as either "ancient hatred" or "perpetual enmity." They can be interpreted as "a condition of hatred stemming back long ago in ancient times that became more violent as time went on. A hatred that will not end."

In other words, it is a cancerous evil that continues to metastasize in the Mideast throughout time like a malignant tumor that will ultimately need to be surgically removed. According to Bible prophecy, this removal will happen militarily, rather than politically. The prophecies about to be revealed will evidence that diplomacy will fail and war will ensue.

The first passage of Scripture below points out that this ancient (*olam*) hatred (*ebah*) began with the Edomites. The prophecy is specifically spoken against historic Mt. Seir, located in what is now known as southern Jordan. This is where the Edomites dwelt in former times. Throughout history, certain circumstances caused many of the Edomites to migrate into Israel. Presently, they have ethnic representation within the Palestinians of today.

Because you, [*Mount Seir*], have had an ancient [*olam*] hatred [*ebah*], and have shed *the blood of* the children of Israel by the power of the sword at the time of their calamity, when their iniquity *came to an* end, therefore, as I live," says the Lord God, "I will prepare you for blood, and blood shall pursue you; since you have not hated blood, therefore blood shall pursue you. (Ezekiel 35:5–6; emphasis added)

In the above verses, we discover the Edomites harbored the ancient hatred. In the next passage, Ezekiel informs that centuries later, when the Philistines came onto the scene, they embraced this hatred. This means the ancient hatred not only still existed, but had spread far westward from Mt. Seir (southern Jordan) to Philistia, which is where the Gaza Strip is today. Presently, this territory is home to the Hamas terrorist group.

Thus says the Lord God: "Because the Philistines dealt vengefully and took vengeance with a spiteful heart, to destroy because of the ancient [*olam*] hatred [*ebah*]," therefore thus says the Lord God: "I will stretch out My hand against the Philistines, and I will cut off the Cherethites and destroy the remnant of the seacoast. I will execute great vengeance on them with furious rebukes; and they shall know that I *am* the Lord, when I lay My vengeance upon them." (Ezekiel 25:15–17; emphasis added)

In both of these passages, we discover this age-old hatred will eventually be stopped militarily, rather than politically. In the case of the Palestinians from Mt. Seir, they will be prepared *for blood* and it *will pursue* them. Along these same lines, the Philistines, likely alluding to the Hamas, will face off with God's *vengeance*, which will be executed through *furious rebukes.*

3. Reveal the Specific Prophecies Pertaining to the Nations

Now that the Mideast nations are identified and indicted for being in breach of God's foreign policy, it's time to reveal some of their respective punishments according to Bible prophecy. You are encouraged to have your Bible open for the next section, which will mostly refer to and comment upon the prophetic passages, rather than specifically quote all of them.

We have already looked briefly at the Palestinians and Hamas, but they are the subject of additional judgment predictions.

The Philistia Prophecies

The additional Hamas judgments are provided in Zephaniah 2:4–7, Isaiah 11:14, and Psalm 83. These prophecies primarily address the cities and territories of the Philistines in historical Philistia, which generally represents modern-day Gaza. Whether or not the Hamas are the actual subject of these prophecies is unknown, but it appears likely they will still be on the scene when they find fulfillment. (Psalm 83 involves several of the Mideast nations and terrorist populations, and because of this, it will be briefly explored later in this chapter.)

The Zephaniah 2:4–7 foretellings about the Gaza area reveal the following:

1. The overall territory will be forsaken and desolated (Zephaniah 2:4).
2. The inhabitants will be sent into exile and many will be killed (Zephaniah 2:4–5).
3. The punishment will be so severe that no inhabitant will remain (Zephaniah 2:5).
4. The territory will become part of Judah (Zephaniah 2:7).
5. The land will ultimately be used to pasture and shelter folds of flocks (Zephaniah 2:6).

Isaiah's prophecy is quoted below. It addresses the Gaza and the country of Jordan.

But they [*Israeli Air Force*] shall fly down upon the shoulder of the Philistines [*likely the Hamas*] toward the west [*in the Gaza*];

Together they shall plunder the people of the East [*probably the Jordanians*]; They shall lay their hand on Edom [*southern Jordan*] and Moab [*central Jordan*]; And the people of Ammon [*northern Jordan*] shall obey them. (Isaiah 11:14; emphasis added)

The Palestinian Prophecies

The inhabitants of the Gaza are Palestinians, but the majority of the Palestinian peoples are scattered throughout much of the Mideast, with heavy concentrations in Jordan and the West Bank. A couple of additional Palestinian prophecies are found in Obadiah 1:18, Ezekiel 25, and Psalm 83.

Obadiah's prophecy below points out that the Edomite descendants within the Palestinians will cease to exist forever as a result of being conquered by the Israeli Defense Forces (IDF).

The house of Jacob [*IDF*] shall be a fire, And the house of Joseph [*IDF*] a flame; But the house of Esau [*Edomites*] shall be stubble; They [*the IDF*] shall kindle them and devour them, And no survivor shall *remain* of the house of Esau, For the Lord has spoken." (Obadiah 1:18; emphasis added)

Obadiah points out that the IDF will be like a flame of fire and the Palestinians will serve as stubble that will burn like kindling. This war theme is also quoted by the prophet Zechariah, who informs that the IDF will be like a fiery torch not only to the Palestinians, but to all of the surrounding nations that confederate with them.

In that day will I make the [*IDF*] chieftains of Judah like a pan of fire among wood, and like a flaming torch among sheaves; and they shall devour all the [*Arab*] peoples [*of the neighboring nations*] round about, on the right hand and on the left; and *they of* Jerusalem shall yet again dwell in their own place, even in Jerusalem. (Zechariah 12:6, ASV; emphasis added)

The peoples that are "round about" Israel "on the right hand and on the left" appear to be part of the Psalm 83 Arab confederacy. According to Zechariah, they will be torched by the IDF in a war that devours them. (Refer to the image under the Psalm 83 prophecy section).

In the next passage, Ezekiel declares that the IDF will become the tool used by God to execute His vengeance upon the Palestinians, especially in southern Jordan. This judgment also kills some soldiers from the neighboring nation of Saudi Arabia that will be part of the Arab confederacy that attacks Israel. These Arabs are guilty of avenging themselves on Israel.

> Thus says the Lord God: "Because of what Edom [*Palestinians*] did against the house of Judah [*Israel*] by taking vengeance, and has greatly offended by avenging itself on them," therefore thus says the Lord God: "I will also stretch out My hand against Edom, [*southern Jordan*] cut off man and beast from it, and make it desolate from Teman; Dedan [*Saudi Arabia*] shall fall [*militarily*] by the sword. I will lay My vengeance on Edom by the [*IDF*] hand of My people Israel, that they may do in Edom according to My anger and according to My fury; and they shall know My vengeance," says the Lord God. (Ezekiel 25:12–14; emphasis added)

The Toppling of Jordan Prophecies

Jordan has a fragile peace treaty with Israel, but the toppling of Jordan prophecies below point out that this treaty will ultimately be abolished. Previously identified in Isaiah 11:14, Jordan is also the subject of prophecies in Jeremiah 49:1–6, Zephaniah 2:8–9, Ezekiel 25:14, and Psalm 83. These prophecies inform that:

- Amman, formerly known as Rabbah of the Ammonites, is the capital of Jordan. It will become a desolate mound, and its neighboring villages will be burned with fire as a result of a war with Israel. Jeremiah 49:2 predicts the following,

"Therefore behold, the days are coming," says the Lord, "That I will cause to be heard an alarm of war In Rabbah of the Ammonites; It shall be a desolate mound, And her villages shall be burned with fire. Then Israel shall take possession of his inheritance," says the Lord.

- Both Jeremiah 49:6 and Zephaniah 2:8–9 foretell that Northern and Central Jordan will be plundered and by the IDF and then possessed by Israel.
- Zephaniah promises that the god of Jordan, who is Allah, will be reduced to nothing as a result of these Jordanian war prophecies.

The Lord will be awesome to them, For He will reduce to nothing all the gods of the earth; People shall worship Him, Each one from his place, Indeed all the shores of the nations. (Zephaniah 2:11)

The Terrorization of Egypt Prophecy

Presently Egypt also has a fragile peace treaty with Israel, but according to the terrorization of Egypt prophecies in Isaiah 19:1–18, it will likewise be eradicated. Isaiah predicts Egypt's judgment will happen quickly, like a swiftly moving cloud races through the sky.

The burden against Egypt. Behold, the Lord rides on a swift cloud, And will come into Egypt; The idols of Egypt will totter at His presence, And the heart of Egypt will melt in its midst. (Isaiah 19:1)

Once the Lord rides the swift cloud over Egypt, the sequence of judgment events go as follows:

1. Egypt has internal civil strife, which leads Egypt into a regional conflict (Isaiah 19:2).

2. Egypt's religious clerics falter and are overtaken by a cruel dictator (Isaiah 19:3–4).
3. Egypt experiences drought-like conditions that affect rivers (Isaiah 19:5–7).
4. Egypt's fishing and textile industries collapse and lead to an unemployment crisis, whereby "all who make wages will be troubled of soul" (Isaiah 19:8–10).
5. Egypt's political system begins to collapse (Isaiah 19:11–13).
6. Egypt's economic system begins to collapse (Isaiah 19:14–15).
7. All of the above will cause Egypt to become fearful and cowardly (Isaiah 19:16).
8. Israel will wage war with Egypt and become a terror to Egypt (Isaiah 19:17).
9. Israel will take over five cities in Egypt after the war as per Isaiah 19:18, and:
   a. The language of Canaan, which is Hebrew, will be spoken in these cities as Jews move into them.
   b. One of the five cities will be called the "City of Destruction," apparently to commemorate Israel's victory over Egypt.

The Syria Prophecies

"Israel says struck Iranian targets in Syria 200 times in last two years" (Reuters, September 4, 2018). As this headline points out, Syria does not have a peace treaty with Israel. Israel struck Syria approximately two hundred times between 2016–2018, not to mention the hundreds more missiles Israel launched into Syria since 2011, which is when the Syrian revolution started. Israel has primarily conducted these strikes to prevent the flow of weapons coming from Iran through Syria for Hezbollah's use in Lebanon.

The prophetic outlook for Syria is very grim, according to prophecies in Isaiah 17, Jeremiah 49:23–27, and Psalm 83. These Isaiah and Jeremiah prophecies declare the Syrian capital city of Damascus, considered the oldest continuously inhabited city in the world, will be destroyed. Follow the prophetic flow of events below.

1. Damascus will someday be reduced to rubble and become a "ruinous heap":

The burden against Damascus. "Behold, Damascus will cease from being a city, And it will be a ruinous heap." (Isaiah 17:1)

2. The destruction of Damascus, as well as other Syrian cities, will be caused by the IDF:

In that day his strong cities will be as a forsaken bough And an uppermost branch, Which they left because of the children of Israel; And there will be desolation. (Isaiah 17:9)

3. Damascus will be destroyed over the course of one night:

Then behold, at eventide, trouble! And before the morning, he is no more. This is the portion of those who plunder us, And the lot of those who rob us. (Isaiah 17:14)

4. The missile attack against Damascus might originate from the Mediterranean Sea, according to Jeremiah 49:23.
5. Damascus will undergo heavy civilian and soldier casualties when attacked as per Jeremiah 49:26.
6. The governmental and palatial structures will be burned at the time, says Jeremiah 49:27.

The Saudi Arabia Prophecies

Saudi Arabia appears to be the subject of four end-times prophecies. The first is revealed in Ezekiel 25:13, which states that "Dedan shall fall by the sword." Historical Dedan was located in what is presently northwest Saudi Arabia. The other three Saudi prophecies are found in Psalm 83, Jeremiah 49:8, and Ezekiel 38:13.

In Psalm 83:6, the Saudis are identified as the Ishmaelites. They enlist in the Arab confederacy of Psalm 83:4–8 that will attempt to destroy Israel. The prophet Jeremiah warns Dedan to not enlist in this Arab coalition:

Flee, *turn back, dwell in the depths*, O inhabitants of Dedan! For I will bring the calamity of Esau upon him, The time that I will punish him [alluding to his Palestinian descendants]. (Jeremiah 49:8; emphasis added)

Ezekiel 25:13 foretells that the Saudis refuse to "turn back" and "dwell in the depths." Instead, they participate in Esau's calamity and that seems to explain why "Dedan shall fall by the sword."

Although many Saudis will "fall by the sword," some will survive, according to Ezekiel 38:13. This prophecy includes Dedan along with several other countries. These nations are protesting the invasion of Israel by Russia, Turkey, Iran, and some other countries in the latter years. These Ezekiel 38 invaders are coming to possess Israel's plunder and booty.

The fact that Dedan is merely a protestor in this major prophecy seems to suggest many Saudis had previously fallen "by the sword" in Ezekiel 28:13. Perhaps they had learned their lesson about the dire consequences of invading Israel at that prior time. It's a good thing the Saudis are not among the Ezekiel 38 invaders, because they are all destroyed supernaturally by the Lord as per Ezekiel 38:19–22. (I have written extensively about the Ezekiel 38 prophecy in my book entitled *The NOW Prophecies*, which is available at Amazon.)

The Iran Prophecies

Iran is the subject of dual end-times prophecies. Iran is identified as Persia in Ezekiel 38:5, but in Jeremiah 49:34–39, this rogue nation is referred to as Elam. Jeremiah issued his Elam prophecy around 596 BC, about twenty years prior to Ezekiel's prediction about Persia. Elam hugs the Persian Gulf in western Iran.

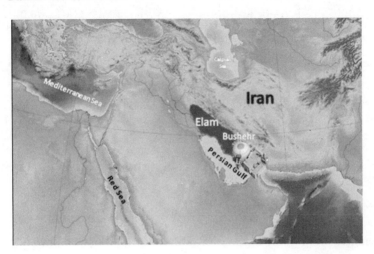

Jeremiah's prophecy seems to have nuclear implications and is summarized below.

1. The Lord becomes fiercely angry with Iran (Jeremiah 49:37).
2. The fierce anger is caused by bad leadership, whom the Lord will destroy (Jeremiah 49:38).
3. These bad leaders apparently want to launch lethal missiles somewhere, and although we are not specifically told the target location, it is probably Israel. Therefore the Lord will prevent this from happening by breaking the bow at the foremost of Iran's might (Jeremiah 49:35).
4. When the Lord breaks the bow at the chief place of Iran's might, it causes a massive disaster in Elam (Jeremiah 49:37).
5. This disaster appears to have nuclear implications, as it seemingly causes a humanitarian crisis. The prophecy predicts the indigenous population flees from Iran into the nations of the world (Jeremiah 49:36).

6. When this disaster occurs, Iran will be extremely dismayed before the onlooking eyes of its enemies (Jeremiah 49:37). Iran's enemies presently include Israel, Saudi Arabia, the UAE, and some other GCC Arab states bordering the Persian Gulf. Additionally, some of the international community is at odds with Iran about its nuclear aspirations.

7. Although the territory of Elam is highly seismic, the disaster appears to result from a military conflict (Jeremiah 49:37).

8. The Lord will ultimately establish His authority in Elam (Jeremiah 49:38). This verse says, "I will set My throne in Elam."

9. Lastly, we are told the Lord will bring back the exiles dispersed as a result of the disaster "in the latter days" (Jeremiah 49:39).

The Psalm 83 Prophecy

This three thousand-year-old imprecatory prayer, which appears to also be a prophecy, includes many of the nations and/or terrorist populations already identified in this chapter. The only exceptions are Russia, Turkey, and Iran. None of these countries are included in Psalm 83.

Since I have authored an entire book about this prophecy, I will only briefly summarize this Psalm here. (The book, for your future reference, which is also at Amazon, is entitled *Psalm 83, The Missing Prophecy Revealed, How Israel Becomes the Next Mideast Superpower.*)

Psalm 83 involves a ten-member Arab confederacy that seeks to destroy the Jewish State and banish the name of Israel forever.

They have said, "Come, and let us cut them off from being a nation, That the name of Israel may be remembered no more. For they have consulted together with one consent; They form a confederacy against You." (Psalm 83:4–5)

This coalition is identified by their ancient names in Psalm 83:6–8. The image superimposes their modern-day equivalents over their historical names and locations.

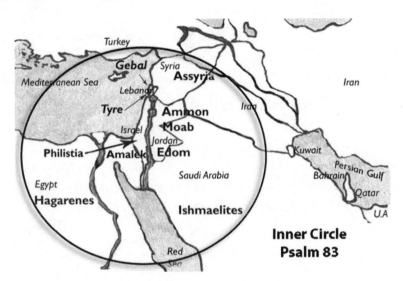

These are most of the nations that fought against Israel in the 1948 War of Independence. Some believe Psalm 83 was fulfilled at that time, but Psalm 83:9–18 points out that when the prophecy is fulfilled, these nations will never be capable of oppressing or fighting against Israel again. Presently, many of these Arabs are still oppressing Israel and opposing the existence of the Jewish State.

In the Arab-Israeli wars of 1948, 1967, and 1973, these Psalm 83 Arab nations have struck out with God on all three categories. Psalm 83 will represent the final strike.

STRIKE ONE: They didn't seek and find the One True God; rather, they sought and found the false god of Allah.

STRIKE TWO: They have not lived together in peace, but have engaged in wars.

STRIKE THREE: They have not blessed Abraham, but have cursed him by attempting to destroy his great nation of Israel.

For the reasons laid out in this chapter, it's understandable why the Lord will have to deal in judgment and wrath with this malevolent maelstrom in order to put down that rebellion and make all things right when Jesus Christ returns.

When Christ returns at His Second Coming, He will establish His Messianic Kingdom and reign on the earth for one thousand years, according to Revelation 20:4. During the Millennium, He will fulfill the promise made to Abraham and Israel will become a great nation.

Blessing I will bless you [*Abraham*], and multiplying I will multiply your descendants as the stars of the heaven and as the sand which is on the seashore; and your descendants [*Israel*] shall possess the gate of their enemies. (Genesis 22:17; emphasis added)

CHAPTER 17

TRACKING THE FINAL WORLD EMPIRE

By Alan Franklin

Thus he said, "The fourth beast shall be the fourth kingdom upon earth, which shall be diverse from all kingdoms, and shall devour the whole earth, and shall tread it down, and break it in pieces." (Daniel 7:23)[147,148]

THE WORLD'S EYES FLIT around the ever-changing trouble spots. My spotlight will shine on the European Union, the Revived Roman Empire, which the book of Daniel (9:26) shows will be the empire ruling at the end of the Church Age, and we are almost there now. Antichrist will rule from his power base in the European Union.

Students of Bible prophecy through the centuries have looked for two great events to signal that history is winding down to a conclusion. Those events, both predicted thousands of years ago, are the revival of the old Roman Empire and the restoration of the state of Israel, which occurred in May 1948 precisely as prophesied.

The incredible has happened. Both Israel and the Roman Empire are back. Most of the nation-states of Europe have banded together into the European Union, the EU, which began with the Treaty of Rome, signed in 1957 at the Vatican at the pope's invitation. It came into force in 1958.

Major prophecies in Daniel chapters 2 and 7 indicate that the revived Roman Empire will be the dominant force in the world when our Lord returns. Twenty-five hundred years ago, Daniel saw that empire in the end times. Those prophecies are being fulfilled today in Europe, where the EU's motto is "Ever Closer Union."

As we enter the final days before the Lord's return, the manufactured "COVID crisis" is being used to usher in ever-more EU-wide joint and coordinated action, in everything from vaccinations to calls for a banking union. This is predictable, for it takes a crisis to force actions that in normal times people wouldn't tolerate—like giving up their sovereignty, or what's left of it.

One EU official even said, as a major problem emerged, "Never waste a good crisis." In most major respects, Europe is already run as one nation, with common borders, laws, courts, Parliament, president, and much else.

Few people understand that the EU is a spiritual as well as a political entity. On December 8, 1955, before the EU was formed, its predecessor, the European Council, adopted what is now the EU flag—blue with a circle of twelve stars. December 8 is the Feast of the Immaculate Conception of Mary. Europe was consecrated to Mary in 1309 and the Shrine of Our Lady of Europa in Gibraltar was renovated with EU funds. Where flags fly, the Euro flag (Madonna's stars) is given the same status as national flags.

In the prayer room at Brussels Airport, gateway to the main EU "capital," stands a statue of the Madonna, surrounded by the stars of Europe. A former secretary-general of the Council of Europe, Leon Marchal, said the stars are those of "The Woman of the Apocalypse." The EU, which now has twenty-seven full member countries, has confirmed the number of stars will always stay at twelve, which indicates the stars do not represent countries.

I quote from a leaflet, "Building Europe Together," which I was given on a visit to EU headquarters in Brussels:

The European flag (is) a shared flag, blue with twelve gold stars symbolising completeness. The number will remain twelve no matter how many countries there are in the European Union.

(How odd this must strike Americans, whose flag proudly sported a new star as each fledgling state came into the union!)

The same document, issued to commemorate Europe Day, May 9, also boosts Europe's new common anthem, "Ode to Joy," the prelude to the last movement of Beethoven's Ninth Symphony. The EU document states:

> Officially the Ode to Joy, but which in this context also means the ode to freedom, to a sense of community and to peace between the countries which have decided to unite and to others which will freely decide to join them.

My wife Pat says Beethoven's Fifth would have been more appropriate. In fact, the "Ode to Joy" is more of an ode to paganism, as the lyrics, by a man called Schiller, concern the entering of the shrine of a pagan goddess and the uniting of all men in brotherhood, by the power of magic, according to Adrian Hilton in his book, *The Principality and Power of Europe.*

The EU flag is treated as the symbol of a nation-state. I had an interesting letter at a newspaper I edited. It came from a patriotic Roman Catholic man. He was complaining that the Euro flag was flying without authority all through Britain, and that this was an insult to his Madonna.

This is further confirmation that the stars have a religious symbolism, but clearly most Catholics haven't a clue what this really signals—the aim of a united, Catholic Europe dedicated to "our lady." However, a strict warning from the EU bosses—the Commissioners—bans anti-European groups from using the stars logo. Apparently the Commission fears they might write something rude across it.

The EU's twelve stars were inspired by the halo of twelve stars that appear in Catholic paintings of the Madonna.

> If by a sudden miracle a one-world government were established, the Roman Church would not have to undergo any essential change to retain its dominant position to further its global aims.

This was Malachi Martin, a former Jesuit priest and Vatican insider, writing in *The Keys of the Blood* about control of the New World Order.

I interviewed the late Count Otto von Habsburg, head of the House of Habsburg and Europe's most important lay Catholic, in the EU headquarters at Strasbourg. He aimed to revive the crown of the Holy Roman Empire. In his book, *The Social Order of Tomorrow*, he wrote:

> Now we do possess a European symbol which belongs to all nations. This is the crown of The Holy Roman Empire which embodies the tradition of Charlemagne, the ruler of a united occident.

Dr. Habsburg wanted to see Europe have an elected head of state, a man in power for life. This influence of both Charlemagne and the Habsburgs hangs heavily over the new federal Europe. Back in 1978, the leaders of France and Germany made a pilgrimage to the throne of Charlemagne at Aachen.

The then French president, Giscard d'Estaing, said, "Perhaps when we discussed monetary problems the spirit of Charlemagne brooded over us." This crown of Charlemagne, the first person to attempt to revive the Roman Empire in AD 800, is an inspiration to those who promote the breaking down of nation-states, and a Charlemagne prize has been established for those who work hardest for European unity.

One who won the Charlemagne prize is former President Bill Clinton, who in June, 2000, was the first American president to receive the Charlemagne prize for his work on promoting European unity. He received the prize at the cathedral in Aachen, Germany, where the first Holy Roman Emperor lies buried.

Clinton called for an enlargement of the EU to take in even Russia.

The truth is whatever EU propagandists proclaim. One blunder by the spin doctors of Europe was revealed when the European Commission's media service accidentally released a memo that called for "hypocrisy" and "evasion" to be used when dealing with the press. In other words, truth is what these people say it is at any given time. We live in deadly dangerous times, when truth is being stood on its head. I would apply the same attitude of total skepticism to today's censored news about COVID! I was once offered a job spin doctoring by a major political organization. "No thanks—I like the unvarnished truth."

"Blasphemy" against the EU? Not possible if it is merely a political organization. An EU court has ruled the EU can suppress criticism, and the reasons are revealing. Former EU official Bernard Connolly exposed the EU in a book, *The Rotten Heart of Europe*. He was taken to court and accused of publishing words "akin to blasphemy" against the EU. The EU has the power to suspend all rights, including the right to free speech and the right to life! (In order to "protect European values…")

Free speech, including demonstrations, is not an EU value, and their will is ruthlessly enforced. The EU was upset after Connolly said they were a threat to democracy, freedom, "and ultimately peace." Connolly was sacked for his honesty and lost his five-year battle against unfair dismissal in a ruling by the European Court of Justice on March 6, 2001. He said the court "is acting as the sinister organ of a tyranny in the making."

On a visit to Strasbourg, I was shown the French riot police, then deployed with their vehicles a few hundred yards from the EU parliament building. An EU minder recounted with glee how, when French peasant farmers were protesting at the building against the loss of their livings, they were ambushed by this ruthless force, armed with steel-tipped wooden clubs, CS (tear) gas, and every kind of modern police attack weapon.

The EU has twin capitals in Brussels, Belgium, and Strasbourg, France. In Strasbourg, a dramatic, vast illustration of the demonic heart of Europe lies in a structure known as the Tower of Eurobabel, because its centerpiece is an enormous replica of the unfinished Tower of Babel. Bab-el's original meaning was "gate to God," but Nimrod founded an idolatrous religious system in which people were expected to worship the images he set up. He also brought in a political dictatorship, and his tower was a symbol of one man's revolt and desire to make a name for himself.

If you have a powerful, one-world leader in rebellion against God, you have a formula for world dictatorship. The choice is between Bible or Babel. Even the secular press could not miss the connection between the old and new towers of Babel. A member of the European Parliament (MEP) who was there on the day Eurobabel opened and reported total chaos in the £300 million structure, commented: "If they can't run a building, should we trust them with a continent?" Nigel Farage was a MEP who said after the opening day: "We realise we are not merely entering a building, but being allowed access to the temple of a bold new empire."

There has been a unity of church and state from Babylon to the EU. Babylon was a political/civil union of earth's inhabitants. The tower was for religious purposes. This was the first example of world government and world religion joined as one. A secular journalist living in Strasbourg asked EU officials this question: "Why the Tower of Babel?" The official answer: "What they failed to complete 5,000 years ago we in Europe will finish now." Nimrod and his followers tried to build a tower to reach the heavens, but it was the counterfeit building of a counterfeit religion. In those days, stone was commonly used for buildings, but in the Tower of Babel, bricks were used—man-made objects as opposed to God-made.

The Babylonian "Queen of Heaven" was the mother/wife of Nimrod. Today, that is what Roman Catholics call Mary, mother of Jesus. The story of the rise and fall of Babylon told in Genesis chapter 1 should have been a warning to all men for all time. Nimrod's tower was intended to serve religious purposes, for it is thought to have honored deities in the heavens. Mystical Babylon is now being rebuilt in Europe, and although they don't speak each other's languages, this is not stopping those behind this incredible, evil project,

When I speak at conferences, I show pictures of the Tower of Babylon as rebuilt by the EU, and people are shocked to see its motto: "Europe: many tongues, one voice." This was on a poster issued by the European Union that shows the Tower of Babel being rebuilt by what look like robotic slave laborers, with a crane in the background.

Even more telling, especially for those like me with a background in the occult, is the fact that the stars of Europe depicted over the new Tower of Babel are shaped like inverted pentagrams, with the central point downward, as in witchcraft. Pentagrams were used symbolically in ancient Greece and Babylonia. Is spiritual Babylon dedicated to Satan?

Guess what? The demonic imagery continues. The "woman riding the beast" is a symbol of the European Union! You couldn't make this up! I have a Greek two euro coins featuring the Woman Riding the Beast motif. And outside the European Council of Ministers building in Brussels, where the EU leaders meet to decide policy, their spiritual inspiration is Sculpture 2000, a monstrous, twelve-foot bronze statue of the Woman Riding the Beast. This same image is found throughout the EU on stamps, murals and posters.

The apostate church is pictured as a prostitute riding the Beast in Revelation 17. The "mother of harlots" will ride the Beast (Antichrist system). The woman is the ecumenical, one-world religion being formed now. She is "drunk with the blood of the saints" (Christian martyrs).

In Revelation 17, John sees "the judgment of the great harlot," spiritual Babylon, which is Rome:

Then one of the seven angels who had the seven bowls came and spoke with me, saying, "Come here, I will show you the judgment of the great harlot who sits on many waters, with whom the kings of the earth committed acts of immorality, and those who dwell on the earth were made drunk with the wine of her immorality."

In classical mythology, Europa was a princess (of Phoenicia), and paintings of the woman on the Beast usually depict the abduction of Europa by the Greek god Zeus, who disguised himself as a bull. There is a famous painting by Titian, *The Rape of Europa*. Europe is indeed fast turning into the kingdom of the Beast.

I was invited to Brussels to report on a momentous occasion in the history of the European Parliament in my role as a publisher and editor. I watched the vote taken as eleven countries abandoned their own currencies to form a united Eurozone, with the euro replacing everything from the lira of Italy to the Irish pound.

They were effectively voting for the abolition of the nation-state, and it was astonishing to see with what ease countries like France and Germany gave up control of their financial and economic destinies to join in the project to create "a common European home," as the founding fathers of the European Union put it. Today you can use the euro in nineteen EU countries.

After the vote, I went to lunch with six MEPS of different political parties. We talked about the future, and I said that, as they now had one Parliament and one currency, they were in many senses effectively one country. They could not really disagree, as the EU has all the trappings of a state, even an army, the sixty-thousand-strong, rapid-reaction Eurocorps.

I then asked, "Have any of you thought about the next step?" They asked me what I meant. So I explained that, with one currency, one parliament, etc., the next big step was to have one leader, one führer, and then one Antichrist! Hitler was the last leader who tried to unify Europe under one government with one currency.

That many in Europe have been thinking on these lines for years is shown in a chilling quote from the late Paul-Henri Spaak, former Belgian prime minister and president of the Consultative Assembly of the Council of Europe. He said:

We do not want another committee. We have too many already. What we want is a man of sufficient stature to hold the allegiance of all people, and to lift us out of the economic morass in which we are sinking. Send us such a man and, be he God or the devil, we will receive him.

More recently Jack Lang, then president of the French National Assembly's foreign affairs committee, said that the EU "needs a single figure at the helm." Attacking the inertia in European foreign policy, he said Europe needed a strong central government with a single "personality" at the helm. Students of Bible prophecy will have little doubt who this "personality" will be. The present format of the EU cannot last, and it was never intended that it should.

Right from the beginning, the founders had grand globalist ambitions. The coming world leader, Antichrist—whom I believe is an adult man probably involved with the EU in some way—is waiting in the wings of the world scene for his moment of destiny. He will have Roman origins, according to Daniel 9:26–27:

> And after sixty-two weeks the Messiah be cut off, and have nothing: and the people of the prince who is to come will destroy the city and the sanctuary. And its end will come with a flood; even to the end and there will be war desolations; are determined.
>
> And he will make a firm covenant with the many for one week, (of years): but in the middle of the week he will put a stop to sacrifice and the grain offering; and on the wing of abominations will come one who makes desolate, even until a complete and that destruction.

The "he" in verse 27 is the prince who is to come—Antichrist—and the city, Jerusalem, was destroyed by the Romans in AD 70, so that will be Antichrist's nationality. The founding document of the European Union is called the Treaty of Rome. We learn from Daniel 9:27 that Antichrist will be the man who signs a seven-year peace treaty with Israel, presumably on behalf of the European super state he will then be heading. This signals the start of the seven-year Great Tribulation.

Addressing the European Policy Centre in September, 2000, Belgian Prime Minister Guy Verhofstadt described the subterfuge adopted to setup the embryonic EU:

> With the European Coal and Steel Community, the seeds were sown of the European Union of today.

It was the initial impetus to the development of a community approach, step by step forging European integration by joining, and sometimes also by abolishing, national sovereignty into a joint approach.

Turning to the next great leap forward, Verhofstadt says, "It is of the utmost importance to keep in mind a global vision of the ultimate goal of European unification. This is a good thing," he explains, because "the European Union as it is now could never be the ultimate goal."

He says the pace of integration must never slacken, lest "in the worst case countries will start to plead for the restoration of their former sovereignty." Notice that national sovereignty—independence—is referred to in the past tense. The Belgian said there must be values underpinning this vast undertaking, the largest coming-together of countries in history. But whose values? "In short, a Europe that attaches great importance to the values which result from the French Revolution." So the values of the new Europe will be those of the country that gave us the guillotine, the Reign of Terror, and blood washing through the streets of France.

The *Portman Papers* newsletter that monitored developments in the super state commented:

> Eight years before the French Revolution began in 1789 with the Declaration of The Rights of Man, the General Council of Freemasonry at Wilhelmsbad, convened by Adam Weishaupt, founder of the Illuminati, drew up the blueprint. Its evil spirit was epitomised in Maximilian Robespierre, whose technique anticipated Stalin's by 100 years.
>
> His master plan was to transform France into a Socialist state where absolute equality would prevail. But the population of France, then 25 million, was too large to carry out his ideal. A plan of systematic depopulation was then decided upon. Conceived by the Jacobins, political intellectuals who sneered at "the stupid people of France" with their "souls of mud," the Reign of

Terror claimed over a million victims. Inmates of prisons were slaughtered. Mass drownings in the dark waters of the Loire were organised, known as the Noyades of Nantes. Human heads were counted up like scores on cards. The terror was justified in the name of "democracy."

Ironically, Robespierre himself went to the guillotine, a victim of the "values" he proclaimed.

Similarly, the coming clampdown on free speech, religious freedom, and free political parties by the "Beast of Brussels" system is being justified by words like "anti-discrimination" and "charter of rights." Human rights can easily become political wrongs; rules were in force in Britain until Brexit said any group wishing to put up candidates for local or national government or the European Parliament must first be registered as a political party, which means red tape and cost.

Here's the sting. Parties would not be registered unless their "financial structure" has been approved by the EU Commission. Donations are to be regulated and overseas contributions generally forbidden. If you or your donors are not approved by the EU, you are out of business. Goodbye, Independence parties? An electoral commission rules on elections, referendums, and campaigning groups.

The police state is still taking shape in most of Europe, where French Prime Minister Emmanuel Macron recently decreed that those wise enough to refuse the so-called COVID vaccines could not go out to restaurants, public events, or even shops! This was challenged and partly halted by a court. However, the octopus is tightening its grip. The fast-expanding Euro police force, Europol, could soon be used as the enforcement arm of the EU. Even the European Parliament's own report into this little-known organization said it could turn into "a repressive monster." Even worse, Europol staff have immunity from prosecution, something that even the royal family is denied.

Countries in the EU have no means of getting out of the euro currency or getting back national powers given over to the super state. The

European Court of Justice has already judged that powers transferred to the EU cannot be returned to national governments. Far from impartial, this court has a political remit to encourage ever more centralisation of power.

Incidentally, after the people of the United Kingdom voted to leave the EU and Brexit, the UK's exit from the EU was completed in January 2020. People who reject Bible prophecy gloated over how wrong I was in saying the EU is going to produce the end-times version of the revived Roman Empire.

My response was that Brexit is in line with prophecy because it was revealed in Nebuchadnezzar's vision that the end-time empire of the Antichrist would be one of clay mixed with iron, an indication that the empire would be highly unstable.

One independent voice still within the EU is that of Viktor Orban, prime minister of Hungary for ten years who has repeatedly clashed with the EU over his anti-immigrant and other policies. He is now in big trouble for pushing through legislation that bans the "promotion" of homosexuality to minors, now part of the gender-bending agenda in nations across Europe.

After Ursula von der Leyen, the European Commission's German president, opened an investigation into this "outrage," Viktor hit back, saying, "The EU empire threatens our democracy." That puts it mildly, as there is little or no democracy in the EU puppet parliaments, where the main aim of many members is to turn up to claim their generous allowances. They cannot initiate legislation, just suggest minor amendments.

Dr. Anthony Coughlan is Ireland's leading Eurosceptic, and when a new nation is embraced by the EU octopus, he sends its leaders a postcard saying, "Welcome to the EU—the prison house of nations."

Now read our website: www.thefreepressonline.co.uk.

CHAPTER 18

WHIRLWIND OF THIRD-WORLD WICKEDNESS

By Matt Ward

How did it all go so wrong for the people of Haiti? Papa Doc Duvalier was meant to be their savior, not their tormentor. When elected president of the Republic of Haiti on October 22, 1957, Haitians at the time could have been forgiven for thinking better days were ahead for them, especially after suffering through the chronic instability and rampant corruption that had so blighted the country for decades.

With a newly elected president who had begun his career as a provincial medical doctor, touring the countryside vaccinating the poor against the widespread scourge of malaria and other tropical diseases, surely Haiti was about to turn a corner.

It had begun well. Duvalier initially campaigned to overturn the dominance of the traditional ruling elite. These were the minority, of European and African descent, men who had kept Haiti in a state of near apartheid for decades. It was a system so divided that huge swathes of the majority black population were not even allowed to enter specifically designated no-go areas of the capital. These areas were reserved exclusively for the minority ruling elite.

Hopes were high that Duvalier would bring genuine change to Haiti. His background was flawless.

Yet from the very beginning, there were ominous warning signs. In the general election of 1957, some of the regions of Haiti had returned more votes for "Papa Doc Duvalier" than there were voters eligible in those regions. People frowned, yet ultimately decided to look the other way, ignoring the uncomfortable implications that the saviour they were expecting in Duvalier might not actually be the man they were electing into high office. To many international observers, though, the implications were clear: Rampant, obvious and undisguised corruption had taken place, and Duvalier had usurped power for himself.[149]

The reality was that Duvalier was blatantly tyrannical. Worse, as his presidency wore on, he became increasingly obsessed by the occult—in particular, by voodoo. So completely captivated by voodoo did Duvalier become that he eventually came to think of himself as being the reincarnation of the voodoo deity Baron Samedi, "the lord of all cemeteries."

Worse, and quite blasphemously, Duvalier believed himself not only to be a voodoo deity, but to be personally superior even to the God of the Bible, reworking the Lord's Prayer for the people of Haiti to reflect this: "Our Doc, who art in the National Palace for life, hallowed by Thy name by present and future generations…"[150]

Within a matter of years, Duvalier's regime became one of the most repressive in all of the Western hemisphere.[151] By the end, "Papa Doc" had exiled many and had murdered any opponent he could get his hands on, with estimates that as many as sixty thousand Haitians were sent to their deaths during his presidency.[152]

Intimidation, repression, and widespread corruption became the hallmarks of Duvalier's regime—bribery as well as violence. Domestic businesses were extorted and government funds were stolen. Peasant land was given over to the militia, Duvalier's personal quasi police force. The rest, the peasants and the dispossessed, fled to newly created slums in the capital city, where they were forced to live out the rest of their days in the direst of poverty, with disease and malnutrition endemic.

But the damage Duvalier caused Haiti was not confined to his own lifetime. He left a legacy of suffering that lasts to this day. As a result of the violence, corruption, and intimidation, a mass exodus from Haiti began, with many of the most educated leaving for America, Canada, and France. This only served to greatly exacerbate the already serious lack of doctors and teachers present in Haiti, which still affects Haiti today.

Yet Duvalier is no isolated example. History is replete with men who rise to power only to turn the mechanisms of government against their own people. Men like Jozef Tiso, Khorloogiin Choibalsan, Le Duan, Ramfis Trujillo, and a plethora of others besides. Some of these men are infamous, others less so, but they are all dictators whose names in their own poverty-stricken countries have become bywords for brutality.

For the most part, we take our freedom completely for granted, yet representative government is a luxury few throughout human history have ever enjoyed. Indeed, history is rife with criminals, oppressors, and the morally reprehensible who have risen to become the unelected heads of governments—often to the terrible hurt of their own people.

In Vietnam, Le Duan, from 1960–1986, oversaw a government-backed system of purges against the South Vietnamese that resulted in as many as two million people being imprisoned,[153] and up to eight hundred thousand people fleeing Vietnam, mostly by boat.[154] Duan's failed economic centralization effort in Vietnam would also become utterly ruinous for the country for generations.

In Mongolia, from the mid-1930s until 1952, Khorloogiin Choibalsan applied the policies and methods he had witnessed in the Soviet Union under Joseph Stalin to Mongolia with utter ruthlessness. Tens of thousands of people were killed by the oppressive, dictatorial system he created as a consequence. Choibalsan became the "Stalin of the steppes."[155]

In 1966, Michel Micombero, then an army captain and minister of defense, led a counter-coup in Burundi that ended with him as prime minister. An ethnic Tutsi, Micombero wasted no time in carefully cultivating a Tutsi elite within both the army and the government, inevitably raising tensions with the country's large Hutu community.

Following a Hutu insurrection in 1972, Micombero then oversaw the organized mass killings of an estimated three hundred thousand. The simmering tensions that remained thereafter became a key cause of the subsequent civil war and genocide that took place in Burundi between the Tutsis and Hutus from 1993 until 2005.[156]

In the 1970s, Carlos Arana Osorio became the president of Guatemala and promptly "disappeared" an estimated twenty thousand people.[157]

Jorge Rafael Videla launched a coup d'état in 1976 that effectively made him the ruler of Argentina. He swiftly closed down all the courts and then began a notorious "dirty war" in which thousands upon thousands of people, all considered subversives, were either abducted or murdered. Some believe as many as thirty thousand people lost their lives.[158]

The first president of Equatorial Guinea, Francisco Macias Nguema, a kleptocrat, had himself declared leader for life in 1968, after which he killed or exiled up to one-third of the country's entire population of three hundred thousand people. He is widely recognized as one of the most brutal world dictators in all of history.[159] With a system of extensive forced labor programs, Swedish researcher Robert af Klinteberg famously described what he saw of Equatorial Guinea during Nguema's reign as "the concentration camp of Africa—a cottage industry Dachau."[160] Nguema quickly gained a reputation that led to easy comparisons with Cambodia's Pol Pot.

In Rwanda in the mid-1990s, Theodore Sindikubwabo became the head of a government that oversaw the slaughter of eight hundred thousand people. Appearing on television on April 20, 1994, Sindikubwabo was at pains "to thank and encourage" the militants carrying out the genocide. Further, he promised "he would send soldiers to help local people finish killing the Tutsi who were barricaded" in a local church.[161]

All former third-world countries suffered under the oppression of real tyranny and despotic dictatorship.

Today is no different. Modernity is full of such individuals, with men like Daniel Ortega, Nicolas Maduro, and Kim Jong-un. These, and many others like them, systematically use the apparatus of government and the power they wield to suppress and oppress their own people. These are men who often take advantage of chaos to sweep into power.

In Latin America, Venezuela's President Nicolas Maduro, first elected in 2013, has continued his term despite the fact that his presidency has now been under dispute since 2019. Millions suffer under his leadership. At this point, Maduro is reducing Venezuela to a dictatorship, and he has used every opportunity available to him to tighten his grip on the already impoverished nation. Ruling by decree since 2015, Venezuelans have seen their living standards crash, with many searching garbage dumps for food.

Maduro's administration is also actively mismanaging the economy for his own personal gain and is attempting to "crush the opposition by jailing or exiling critics, and using lethal force against anti-government protesters."[162]

Human Rights Watch and Amnesty International believe Maduro's government to be guilty of actions tantamount to "crimes against humanity,"[163] including significant extra judicial executions, as well as forced disappearances, the jailing of opposition figures, the widespread use of military courts for civilians, and the widespread torture of detainees.[164]

There is no truly independent judiciary anymore in Venezuela, and as a consequence of this, the human-rights abuses perpetrated by ruling officials and heavy-handed security forces mean they operate with almost complete impunity.[165]

Additionally, the ongoing COVID-19 pandemic is being used powerfully as a cover to punish dissent—not just in Venezuela, but in a swathe of other countries that have authoritarian leanings.

As conditions in Venezuela continue to deteriorate, the Venezuelan governmental response is to hasten and increase the militarisation of the security services so as to further repress and control their own people. Maduro is consolidating his power, and in doing so is squeezing the people until the pips squeak.

Yet Venezuela can in no way be considered as an isolated example of our modern age. If only it were so. Also, in Latin America, Nicaragua's President Daniel Ortega has pursued a ferocious crackdown on dissent and nationwide protests, with state-sanctioned violence accounting for hundreds of recorded deaths.[166]

Indeed, Daniel Ortega's Nicaragua can now be considered perhaps one of the most autocratic regimes in all of Latin America. Opposition in Nicaragua is non-existent at this point,[167] and any independent voices that do light a spark of opposition are ruthlessly supressed. The United Nations High Commissioner for Human Rights in Geneva has openly referred to many of the deaths caused by Ortega's violent crackdowns on descent as "unlawful killings."[168]

In Honduras, President Juan Orlando Hernández has overseen widespread systematic corruption and developed a blatantly authoritarianism regime. He has been accused of widespread electoral fraud[169] as well as extensive human rights violations.[170] State security forces continue to forcefully repress any and all opposition to the government, just as in Nicaragua and Venezuela.[171]

North Korea, on the Korean peninsula, is a country that perhaps stands alone in modernity. It is the most reclusive of all countries in the world today. If one wants to catch a glimpse of a people who are truly oppressed, look no further than North Korea. Ruled exclusively by Kim Jong-un, who exercises total power over all government apparatus and policy, its people are amongst the most impoverished on earth. It is a government that tolerates no dissent and is well known for its inhumane brutality.

Indeed, so harsh is the North Korean government that the United Nations Inquiry Report into North Korea concluded the following in 2013: "The gravity, scale and nature of these violations reveal a state that does not have any parallel in the contemporary world."[172]

Since then, things have only gotten worse. Basic rights in North Korea are routinely denied, including the freedoms of association, expression, and religion. Official government opposition, in any form, does not exist. Forced labor as well as unpaid labor is commonplace, with its weary citizens forcibly co-opted into building works and other government programs entirely without pay or rights.[173]

To maintain control, the people are systematically stripped of any potential for power through brutal repression, harsh indoctrination, and isolation. Freedom of religion is non-existent in this officially atheist state.

North Koreans are not permitted to leave the country without their government's express permission, nor can they talk to any foreigners within the country. North Koreans are isolated digitally, with no Internet connection to the outside world. Televisions and radios are pre-set to government-sanctioned channels, and foreign broadcast signals are jammed. North Korean people cannot make any international phone calls.[174]

In North Korea, poverty is enforced so as to keep the people down with mass starvation a regular occurrence.[175] It is no exaggeration to say that life in North Korea, for all but the very few at the top of the ruling elite, is a true living hell.

It is clear from these few examples, and many others besides, that human rights are increasingly just a meaningless byword for many, especially in the countries of the former third world.

Multitudes today live under the burden of tyranny. Yet, strangely, many of these millions also vigorously cheer on the same dictators who so cruelly and systematically oppress them. But they are cheering out of fear. Fear of what might be if anybody were to suspect them of disloyalty. Fear of being denounced. Fear of the knock on the door in the middle of the night. Fear of the "re-education" centers that nobody ever returns from. These are people who genuinely fear for their own lives and the lives of their families and loved ones.

So, they cheer, by the millions, and they wave flags, and they bring lying tears to their eyes—crocodile tears brought on by fear, not love. Tears that they hope show loyalty. Only ever in private do they express their real thoughts and fears, and only ever to those closest to them…to wives, mothers, or fathers. Never ever in public. So, they cheer.

This is the daily reality for a huge number of people today, and on the face of it such an experience would seem to be a long way from our own. Yet too often are we guilty of taking our own liberty and freedoms entirely for granted. Freedom, though, is a fragile thing indeed; it needs to be tended and cared for. Freedom needs to be jealously guarded.

As Christians today living in these last days of the end times, we need to be astute. It is in examining some of the nations of the former third world, where life is hardest and repression most severe, that we get a glimpse of the world that will shortly come to be on a global scale. We get to glance at the conditions that will exist not just nationally, but on an international level in the final world kingdom spoken of so extensively in both the Old and New Testaments.

Crucially, if we are shrewd, we can also get a glimpse of the spiritual forces at work in such regimes, which are also hard at work right now in our own nation as the end of this age fast approaches. We can glimpse something of their motivation, of their spiritual stratagems, even perhaps of the modus operandi that will be used by the Man of Sin himself in establishing this final kingdom of man.

There are critical lessons for us all to learn here. Many of these countries, like Venezuela or Nicaragua, are not really that different from our own. Many of these nations were also once firmly established in the democratic tradition, just like our own. But something happened to them, something that turned freedom-loving peoples and nations into some of the harshest regimes on earth today, into dictatorships with subjugated peoples, breaking under the huge weight of oppression. The difference between these countries and our own is, shockingly, not that great.

It is a sobering truth indeed that at some point in the near future, all nations will fall to the same kind of tyranny we see around us in the world today. The final world ruler, the Man of Sin, will have the obedience of the entire world, and that includes the United States of America:

All the inhabitants of the world will worship the beast. (Revelation 13:8)

Understanding how this climactic situation is being orchestrated satanically at the highest possible spiritual level, and how it will come about in America and Europe, still ostensibly freedom-loving nations, is absolutely imperative if we are to maintain an impactful and effective witness—especially as we see the shadow of these events begin to fall across our own collective horizons.

We should all of us be under no illusion: There is a satanic battle plan. This current world system and almost everything in it is Satan's domain, and he is very much orchestrating what happens within it:

> For our struggle is not against flesh and blood, but against the rulers, against the authorities, against the powers of this dark world and against the spiritual forces of evil in the heavenly realms. (Ephesians 6:12)

This plan is being followed scrupulously, and when we look at some of the regimes that exist today, we get a very real glimpse at the madness and violence of the orchestrating evil that lies behind it. These regimes are a microcosm of what will soon be on a global scale in the final world empire. That final empire is this world's immediate destiny.

We will witness the same scenes of mass public adoration for a "beloved leader" in the streets of America as we see today in the plazas of Pyongyang for Kim Jong-un. Just like in Pyongyang, the people of that near future time will also be living in abject fear—fear of the regime, fear of a government apparatus that at any moment could be turned against them. It will be a time so fraught, when people trust each other so little, that Jesus said of that time:

> Brother will betray brother to death, and a father his child; children will rebel against their parents and have them put to death. (Matthew 10:21)

In all this, Satan is really only interested in one thing. In fact, he has only every been interested in one thing, and that is keeping individuals away from Jesus Christ. It is his—his entire kingdom's—primary war aim against this world, both corporately on a nation-state level, and individually within our own lives.

Despite the many types of political systems that exist all over the world—from democracy to dictatorship, authoritarianism to totalitarianism, communist systems to those led by a monarchical system of government—in reality, there are only two competing world systems. In fact, only two realms have ever existed in world history: the realm of God and His Son, Jesus Christ, and the realm of Satan. Absolutely everything and everybody falls into one of these two realms, even if people don't believe, and even if they don't care.

> We know that we are of God, and that the whole world lies in the power of the evil one. (1 John 5:19)

We belong to the heavenly realm in Jesus Christ, a fact that should comfort us all of our lives, especially as the days visibly darken all around us. We are not a part of this world; this is why we will face opposition while we're in it:

> If you were of the world, the world would love its own; but because you are not of the world, but I chose you out of the world, because of this the world hates you. (John 15:19)

We are indeed "aliens and strangers" here on this earth (1 Peter 2:11). Paul even goes so far as to tell us plainly that "our citizenship is in Heaven" (Philippians 3:20), not on earth.

While this is our individual reality, conversely, the whole world belongs to Satan. Everything in it is his. It's politics, education, all its multiple religious systems, the global financial system, all of its entertainments, and every single nation-state. Anybody who does not today know Jesus Christ as Savior is in the realm of Satan, including those most dear to us who are not yet saved.

The Bible refers to Satan in surprisingly authoritative terms. Jesus Himself referred to Satan as the "ruler of this world" (John 16:11). In Ephesians, the writer describes those who choose not to follow Jesus as walking "according to the course of this world, according to the prince of the air, the spirit who now works in the sons of disobedience" (2:2). Satan is even referred to as being "the god of this age" (1 Corinthians 4:4).

This world system, because it is dominated by Satan, hates God. There is no middle ground; there are no shades of grey at all. Yet Satan, powerful though he is, is limited on this earth. God has placed strict constraints on what he and his minions can do in our own physical realm. Though I suspect Satan would simply annihilate mankind if he could, God prevents him from doing so. Therefore, Satan must use other means to achieve his diabolical ends.

It is mainly through people that Satan seeks to accomplish his nefarious goals. It is through individuals open to his influence that he advances his own kingdom, and oftentimes he does this by simply engendering rebellion against God.

Dictatorships and regimes of the kind we can see all around us in the world today, over time, often come to encapsulate such rebellion. Examine firmly entrenched regimes, of the kind previously referenced, and you will usually find widespread, often state-sponsored opposition to the true gospel of Jesus Christ, either in the form of false religion, a perversion of it, or in some form of humanist-based philosophy, like socialism or communism. All are pathways away from God.

Many such regimes also subtly teach that mankind doesn't actually need God, that man himself is in fact capable of becoming God, especially through adherence to some form of "revolution," where a perfect utopian society, like a return to a quasi-Garden of Eden, can be accomplished at some distant future point. It is, of course, a lie.

Satan was a liar from the beginning (John 8:44), and is himself the father of lies. The world system we live in today is based on a complicated and very intricate web of lies:

When he lies, he speaks his native language, for he is a liar and the father of lies. (John 8:44)

Often in such societies, the true gospel, that salvation is to be found in Jesus Christ alone (Acts 4:2, Romans 4:5–6), is gradually removed. Once a society gets to the point that Jesus and God have been removed entirely from the public consciousness, the masses are then left wide open to real satanic deceit and control. It is in this context that we should view the culture war occurring in our own society so as to allow for real satanic deceit to take place right here at home.

In such regimes, we also regularly witness the near-slavish adherence to a "dear leader," like with the Kims of North Korea, or in the adherence to the ideals of "the revolution," often on pain of death, as in Cuba.[176]

A game of spiritual smoke and mirrors thus begins to take place, with the replacement of the True Messiah and true salvation with some form of False Messiah-like figurehead or false salvation, designed to keep both the masses and the individual as far away from Jesus Christ and the gospel as possible.

Unfortunately, it works. Multitudes throughout history, and today, are living and have lived with no real knowledge of Jesus Christ or the salvation found in Him alone.

This is why such regimes are microcosms of the final world kingdom, when a one-world kingdom will be ruled by the most brutal dictator the world has ever seen. It is a glimpse of the future right here in the present.

Just like the Man of Sin, many current world leaders over time come to take on an almost pseudo-Messianic guise amongst their followers, and sometimes amongst their people more widely, too. History gives us a plethora of such examples, from Nicolae Ceausescu of Romania to Papa Doc Duvalier of Haiti, and the three successive generations of Kims from North Korea who all displayed pseudo-messianic qualities, as did the late Muamar Gaddafi of Libya, the self-styled "king of kings" of Africa.

We see it in Equatorial Guinea, one of the most repressive regimes in the world, with its leader Teadoro Obiang Nguema Mbasog. We see it in Sudan, with President Abdalla Hamdock. Tajikistan's President Emomali Raymond certainly has pseudo-Messianic traits, as does Turkmenistan's Gurbanguly Berdimuhamedow. It is an anti-God madness that is, at its core, satanically orchestrated and driven.

Each of these world leaders is a mere prototype of the Man of Sin who is yet to come. Unfortunately, they will all pale into complete insignificance next to his messianic madness, a man who will demand that the whole world worships him as the Messiah.

> All inhabitants of the earth will worship the beast. (Revelation 13:8)

It is in such circumstances that we see people forced into the most extreme public displays of loyalty, either affection or grief, because the pride of their dictator demands it in order to validate their own particular "God complex." It is the oldest of all sins, inspired by the father of lies himself, who was judged for such a sin by God:

> You said in your heart, "I will ascend to the heavens; I will raise my throne above the stars of God; I will sit enthroned on the mount of assembly, on the utmost heights of Mount Zaphon." (Isaiah 14:13)

Every dictator throughout history, and many people who clearly manifest such traits in our own time, are essentially following the same satanically inspired modus operandi, to varying degrees. They are overthrowing the authority that belongs to God, both within their own lives and as leaders in their nations.

But it is a fallacy, as there is no security apart from God, even though our own society teaches more and more that the opposite is in fact true. It will reach its inevitable zenith very soon when the words of Psalm 2 become this world's reality:

Why do the nations conspire and the peoples plot in vain? The kings of the earth rise up and the ruler's band together against the LORD and against his anointed, saying, "Let us break their chains and throw off their shackles. (Psalm 2:1–3)

All who reject Jesus, like in many of the examples listed above, over time come to replace God with something else, whether that be a false religion or adherence to a set of ideals, like communism. The natural outcome of this over time is a people who become utterly lost and devoid of hope. This is the outcome Satan wants.

Each country in the world today is in an obvious and steep decline. Multiple events are now beginning to spin out of control, cascading and merging. Satan's endgame is in sight and humanity itself is clearly approaching some kind of a watershed moment.

The church, which should be one of the main barriers to this decline in our own society, is increasingly directionless and silent. God says through the prophet Hosea, "my people are destroyed for lack of knowledge" (Hosea 4:6). Never has this been quite as much the case as it is today, with an unprecedented and enormous fall in biblical literacy. True faith, even in the church, is more diluted now than it has ever been. Even the church itself now sits on the cusp of serious satanic deceit.

That deceit pervades everything at this point: our government, our children's classrooms, our courts, our workplaces, our churches, and even our own families. At the highest levels of government, deceit—and often outright lies—encapsulates every policy, every initiative, every school program, every press conference or briefing. We take it almost for granted these days that our elected officials, up to the president himself, lie and are not to be trusted.

A new day is clearly coming, but it will be a dark day, one that will give rise to a kingdom our generation has been warned about in the Bible for thousands of years. Even in our own free society, which too many people take entirely too much for granted, democracy is now being used as a tool to undermine freedom itself, to legitimize and augment the authority of

men and governments that are increasingly authoritarian in their decisions and policies. It will not be long until "democracy" is also being used
as a justification for brutal domestic repression. Many would say that it
already is being used in just this way.

Our government at home has clear authoritarian leanings. It is
attempting to benefit from the appearance of democracy while undermining it at every point and trampling on basic and fundamental freedoms.
The same thing happened in Haiti, in Venezuela, in Nicaragua, and in
a host of other countries. Now it is happening in the United States of
America.

The relentless gains into our culture and our freedoms will culminate
in the establishment of a final global dictatorship that will only end with
the personal return of Jesus Christ. It will be a time so harsh that it will
be completely without equal in human history, so horrific that Jesus states
that:

If the time had not been made short, no life would have been
saved. (Matthew 24:22)

Yet most people today are already so deluded that they are going to
welcome this tyranny with wide open arms.

No other society has been undermined as quickly as our own. This is
why our personal ministries on earth, with our families, coworkers, and
friends, is so vitally important. Our mandate today is the same as our
Lord's two thousand years ago: "To seek and save that which was lost"
(Luke 19:10) by helping lead people to a knowledge of Jesus, thereby "sav-
ing others by snatching them from the fire" (Jude 1:23).

As Jesus commanded Paul on the Damascus road, so he commands us
today "to open their eyes and turn them from darkness to light, and from
the power of Satan to God" (Acts 26:18) This commission has never been
as prescient or urgent as it is right now.

At some point, every democratic nation will walk down the path
towards dictatorship. Ours is no exception. It is merely a question of

where we currently stand on that road. Unfortunately, I strongly suspect that we are much farther along that well-trodden path than many would dare to believe.

Keep looking up.

When these things begin to take place, stand up and lift up your heads, because your redemption is drawing near. (Luke 21:28)

CHAPTER 19

NORTH AMERICA'S ANTI-GOD ANTAGONISM

By Tim Moore

I will make you a great nation, and I will bless you, and make your name great; and so you shall be a blessing; and I will bless those who bless you, and the one who curses you I will curse. And in you all the families of the earth will be blessed. (Genesis 12:2–3)[177]

IN THE LONG LINE OF NATIONS that have arisen upon the earth and faded back into the dust of history, only one has persevered from antiquity: Israel.

The nation that sprang from Abraham, Isaac, and Jacob was named after that final patriarch. Its heritage mirrored that of Jacob himself; throughout its own long history it has also wrestled with God and with men and has prevailed (Genesis 32:28). But God's promise was not just for the children of Israel. As He proclaimed to Abram, His blessing would also flow through Abraham's chosen offspring toward those who would bless them.

Few nations would realize the direct benefit of that promise—receiving a blessing for consciously blessing Israel, but all the nations of the earth would receive a blessing indirectly through Israel, for God's revelation flowed to and through the Jews. They recorded His Holy Word. They transcribed His omniscient prophecies. They provided the lineage for His Anointed Messiah. And they constituted the first members of the Church. In all those ways and more, God has indeed poured out a blessing through the Jewish people.

Yet, Israel strayed grievously from God—largely even rejecting His Messiah. In relatively recent human history, one nation emerged that sought to live up to the principles outlined in the Bible. Founded with intentional purpose by Christians, it has been a beacon of opportunity for Jews and Gentiles alike. And, although its own track record has been inconsistent (as with all nations—and individuals too, for that matter), it has endeavored to bless the reestablished state of Israel more than any other nation. That nation, of course, is the United States of America.

Early Promise and Manifest Blessings

When Christian Pilgrims first began to venture to the New World, they likened America to the Promised Land. It offered a place where they would be free to practice their religion and live according to biblical principles. As US Supreme Court Chief Justice Earl Warren observed to *Time* magazine in 1957, "No one can read the history of our country without realizing that the Good Book and the spirit of the Savior have from the beginning been our guiding geniuses…. Whether we look to the first Charter of Virginia…or to the Charter of New England…the same objective is present…a Christian land governed by Christian principles."[178]

This is not to say that America was a righteous nation in an ontological sense—meaning in the essence of its being. But it was a righteous nation when compared to others steeped in paganism or embroiled in international intrigue or religious strife. This principle was established with men like Noah—who was declared righteous by God, not because he was perfectly sin-free but because he was dedicated to the Lord and determined to obey him. Compared with his contemporaries, Noah was indeed righteous.

Similarly, America is not without fault or blemish. For example, our nation was tragically wrong with regard to slavery and fought a bloody

Civil War to eradicate that scourge. In his second inaugural address in 1865, President Abraham Lincoln recognized the recompense for that particular failing. He said:

> If God wills that [the war] continue, until all the wealth piled by the bond-men's two hundred and fifty years of unrequited toil shall be sunk, and until every drop of blood drawn with the lash, shall be paid by another drawn by the sword, as was said three thousand years ago, so still it must be said "the judgments of the Lord, are true and righteous altogether.

Then, citing an abiding faith in the God who established and blessed our foundling nation, Lincoln concluded:

> With malice toward none; with charity for all; with firmness in the right, as God gives us to see the right, let us strive on to finish the work we are in; to bind up the nation's wounds; to care for him who shall have borne the battle, and for his widow, and his orphan—to do all which may achieve and cherish a just, and a lasting peace, among ourselves, and with all nations.

That such a sentiment could be expressed by the nation's chief executive during a national calamity demonstrates the depth of Christian identity unique to America. Our founders expressed the same recognition in their writings. Thus, in the nation's Declaration of Independence, Thomas Jefferson could write:

> We hold these truths to be self-evident, that all men are created equal, that they are endowed by their Creator with certain inalienable rights, that among these are life, liberty and the pursuit of happiness.

The men who crafted our constitutional order also knew that an imposed adherence to a particular denomination or doctrine in the name of religion would stifle true liberty (as Sharia law is doing today in Islamist countries). But they universally recognized the virtue of the Christian faith and commended citizens to maintain that central pillar of national identity.

George Washington said:

Of all the dispositions and habits which lead to political prosperity, religion and morality are indispensable supports…in vain would that man claim the tribute of patriotism who should labor to subvert these great pillars of human happiness.

And he did not mean generic religion or pagan observance; by his living testimony he meant the Christian religion.

President Dwight D. Eisenhower cited the testimony of a "wise philosopher who came to this country" and recognized the key to America's greatness from its very founding:

Not until I went into the churches of America and heard her pulpits flame with righteousness did I understand the secret of her genius and power. America is great because she is good, and if America ever ceases to be good, she will cease to be great.

America may have declared its independence from England in 1776, but it shamelessly affirmed its dependence on God. Each new state added to the union reiterated that realization in its own constitution. All fifty, including those added in the middle of the twentieth century, cited gratitude to Almighty God as the source of civil and material blessing.

For more than one hundred years, our unofficial national hymn has been "America the Beautiful." Offering both an observation and a prayer, it unashamedly declares, "America! America! God shed His grace on thee, and crown thy good with brotherhood from sea to shining sea." [179]

Even with our foundation of biblical ideology and Christian religion, America has not always lived up to the great aspirations of our founding documents or the lofty ideals we espoused. But Katherine Lee Bates' hymn testifies to the undeserved blessing God has poured out on this land. Because our founders purposed to establish a city on a hill and pursue Christian principles, God indeed blessed America. This great truth was once taught in schools, esteemed on college campuses and universities (most of which were originally founded to train up Christian preachers and missionaries), celebrated by our elected leaders, and respected by our grateful citizens.

A Conduit of Blessing

God's intent for Israel was that it would be a conduit of blessing. Similarly, when America came into its own as a great power, it served as a conduit of blessing for others.

In the nineteenth century, America—along with Great Britain—sent more missionaries around the world than any other nation. America's cup of blessing was beginning to overflow into the lives of individuals and nations around the world.[180]

As a matter of national policy, however, with a few pointed exceptions, America was reluctant to become entangled in foreign affairs. By the early twentieth century, it seemed determined to remain isolated in the world.

World War I—known then as the Great War—changed all that. America was drawn into the conflagration in Europe and sent troops "over there" to make the world safe for democracy. America's presence finally tipped the scales in favor of the Allied forces. As a result of that Allied victory, Great Britain came into possession of the portion of the Middle East that included Palestine (a term handed down from the Romans that described the land, not a particular people). In 1917, thankful for the contribution of Jewish scientist Chaim Weisman and others, British Foreign Secretary Lord Balfour issued his famous proclamation committing Great Britain to support "the establishment in Palestine of a national home for the Jewish people."[181]

Following the First World War, misguided Allied policies led to the

Second World War. Although that is not the focus of this chapter, suffice it to say that miscalculation and indecision allowed Adolf Hitler to rise to power in a resurgent Nazi Germany. The cataclysm he unleashed would present an existential threat to the Jewish population of Europe and draw America once again into a conflict with global ramifications. By the end of 1945, Europe was exhausted and devastated, the world was geopolitically separated into two bipolar camps, and the stage was set for the prophecy of Ezekiel 37 to finally come to pass.

America emerged from World War II stronger than ever before. It was unscathed at home, and its economy was ready to burst forth. That is why America quickly became the key player in rebuilding war-torn parts of the world that did not fall into Soviet domination. It is also why the entire twentieth century would later be known as the "American Century."

As vital as America became to the world—as a beacon of hope and a proponent of right and justice—its greatest moment would come shortly after World War II. For one singular moment, America's light shone on a dark corner of the world where God was making something new once again.

Next Year in Jerusalem

In the aftermath of World War II, the civilized world recoiled in horror at the atrocities perpetrated by the Nazi regime in Germany. Untold millions had been killed in the war instigated by Hitler. The Allied nations were unified in their outrage over the Holocaust. Consumed with anti-Semitic hatred, Hitler and the Nazi machine had sought to obliterate the Jews throughout Europe. For one brief moment, the victors were also unified in their sympathy for the Jews.

World War II changed Jewish attitudes as well. Although pogroms and persecution had been perpetrated since the time of Christ, the Holocaust represented, as stated earlier, an existential threat to the Jewish people. Many Jews who lived through that period decided to never again rely on the good graces of a host Gentile nation for their safety and preservation. They determined to establish their own state.

Thus, out of great tragedy God worked a modern miracle. Jewish people were motivated to move out of the European countries where they had been relatively comfortable (despite recurring persecution) for many generations. They turned their weary gaze toward the land they recalled at every Passover Seder: Eretz Israel. Once a casual wish, "Next year in Jerusalem" became a unifying vision of a hope and a future (Jeremiah 29:11).

As Jews began to stream toward the Promised Land, Great Britain handled its post-War "Palestine problem" very poorly. Under pressure from oil-rich nations to the east, British politicians reneged on the promise made in the Balfour Declaration to the Jewish people. At one point, England resorted to interring Jews in concentration camps in Cyprus rather than allow them to emigrate to Palestine. Eventually, the British government decided to wash its hands of the whole matter and declared a hard exit date of midnight, May 14, 1948. Intermittent skirmishes with Arab *fedayeen* (guerrillas) turned into pitched battles as the Jews in Palestine fought for their land and their lives.

That period of alternating heartbreak, near disaster, and miraculous deliverance is worthy of serval books. Suffice it to say that on May 14, 1948, the dry bones described in Ezekiel 37 stood up. As David Ben Gurion read the Israeli Declaration of Independence, the vision Theodor Herzl had communicated at the end of the nineteenth century finally came to pass in the sliver of land west of the Jordan River.

I Will Bless Those Who Bless You

The question of the hour on the afternoon of May 14, 1948, was how long the new Jewish nation would last. American military and diplomatic advisors warned President Harry Truman that a state of Israel could not survive. Between intermingled Arab guerrillas and massed Arab armies surrounding the militarily indefensible Jewish nation, they considered it likely that the Jews in Israel would be annihilated in a horrific bloodbath.

But against all counsel, President Harry Truman officially recognized the fledgling nation moments after David Ben Gurion read the Declaration of Independence—assuring Israel of America's solidarity from the moment it was born.

The United States got much wrong over the following years, but President Truman's decision to bless Israel paid dividends that are beyond measure. The United States became the lead superpower of the world. In spite of fits and starts, it was a force for good throughout the world. One could argue that America's ascendency to prominence and blessing came on the heels of that providential moment in 1948.

Wars and Rumors of Wars

Over the next fifty years, Israel was beset by hostile neighbors to the north, east, and south. In addition to ongoing skirmishes with Palestinians close at hand (in the last half of the twentieth century, that term came to mean the Arab peoples living in and around Israel), it also fought major wars in 1956, 1967, 1973, 1982, and 2006. Every war represented a possible war of annihilation to Israel, because the stated Arab goal was the destruction of the Jewish State.

In each of those situations, Israel was more or less supported by a rotating cast of quiet allies. In 1956, Britain and France actually encouraged Israel to attack Egypt, hoping to regain control over the Suez Canal. In 1967, Israel stood relatively alone, as Western nations were reluctant to light a match in the Middle East that might lead to war with the Soviet Union. In each war, however, the United States provided some degree of intelligence and political support.

By the late 1960s, Israel had become fully aligned with the United States. The Yom Kippur War of 1973 marks a bittersweet moment in US-Israel relations. Reluctant to endorse Israel's desire to strike first as it had in 1967, and facing its own headache in Vietnam, American leaders advised Israel to stand down and wait to be attacked first. National Security Advisor and Secretary of State Henry Kissinger inferred to Israeli Prime Minister Golda Meir that if she attacked first, the United States would not send a single bullet to help Israel.[182] Meir clearly understood that threat. In a classified post-war inquiry, she was asked why Israel had not launched a preemptive strike. She said, "I can say with 100 percent [certainty]" that the airlift of American arms and supplies would not have been delivered.[183]

The unprovoked Arab attack on Yom Kippur—the holiest day on the Jewish calendar—resulted in the most desperate battle for survival Israel has ever faced. The United States did come to Israel's support, flying in massive quantities of ammunition and replenishing destroyed equipment in what was known as Operation Nickle Grass.[184] Some American fighter aircraft and tanks were delivered and sent immediately into battle with the paint of their new Star of David insignia still wet. Arab outrage at America's support for Israel provoked the OPEC oil embargo that led to gas shortages throughout the US.

Some of the best examples of US support were based on covert action. When Israel determined to liberate the Jews from Ethiopia and Sudan, the American CIA stepped in to help with Operations Moses, Joshua, and Solomon. US pressure also ensured the eventual opening for Russian Jews to escape persecution in the Soviet Union. And, in recent years, American intelligence operatives partnered with Israel to launch a cyberattack that crippled Iran's nuclear program for a season.[185]

Still, over the years, American support for Israel has been fickle at best. With alternating American presidential administrations, Israel often found itself the victim of American pressure instead of the benefactor. Beginning with the Carter administration and continuing to this day, America has regularly pressured Israel to pursue a policy of "land for peace." The deluded idea is that if Israel gives land to its enemies, they will finally live side by side with the Jews in peace.

The fixation of one American president after another to solve this problem through negotiation also ignores Palestinian intransigence. The PLO (Palestinian Liberation Organization) charter, which remains in effect, pledges eternal animosity toward Israel. Both Hamas and the Palestinian Authority remain officially committed to regaining all the land "from the river to the sea" (meaning from the Jordan River in the east to the Mediterranean Sea to the west), demonstrating the foolishness of appeasement.[186]

History bears this out. When President Bill Clinton hosted Palestinian Authority President Yassar Arafat and Israeli Prime Minister Ehud Barak at Camp David in 2000, he pressured the Israelis to yield on practically every point. Yet even when offered virtually everything the Palestinians claimed to want, Arafat refused to accept peace. Clinton's scheme to secure a legacy for himself at the expense of Israel ended in failure.

Abba Eban, Israel's legendary diplomat, once observed, "The Arabs never miss an opportunity to miss an opportunity."[187] Tragically, adding insult to injury as he shunned the opportunity for peace, Arafat subsequently unleashed the Second Intifada on Israel, leading to the death of one thousand Israelis and three thousand Palestinians.

Ignorant of the biblical principle at stake, most American presidents have ignored God's promise that anyone who endeavors to divide the land of Israel will come under His omnipotent curse.[188]

I Will Curse Those Who Curse You

Bill Koenig of World News Daily has documented the ramifications of America's foolhardy actions relative to Israel. Every time we have leaned on Israel to give up land, stop building apartments for its growing population, undermine its own security, or kowtow to Palestinian terrorists, God has delivered a dose of judgment. The curse of Genesis 12:3b is still very much in effect.

Here are some of the many examples of natural and economic disasters Koenig cites in his book:[189]

1991—President George H. W. Bush pressured Israel to relinquish land. Almost immediately, a "perfect storm" with hundred-foot waves hit the US East Coast (damaging the Bush family home in Kennebunkport, Maine).

1993—President Clinton's secretary of state announced a new peace initiative that would apply pressure to Israel. Within days, another "storm of the century" again battered the East Coast.

2000—President Clinton spent four days urging Israel to relinquish some of its covenant land. During those same four days, the US NASDAQ market experienced an unprecedented collapse.

2001—President George W. Bush worked for seventeen days on "the most comprehensive plan and message ever to be offered about Israel's covenant land by an American President." That work was completed on September 10; on September 11, Islamic terrorists attacked the United States at the World Trade Center and the Pentagon.

Koenig lists scores of catastrophes that have hit the US immediately following a faithless and unbiblical action relative to Israel. In a subsequent book, he documented how President Barack Obama "worked tirelessly to disrupt the friendship" between the United States and Israel. From 2017 to 2020, President Trump proved to be a reliable friend to Israel, but President Joe Biden is once again working to undermine that friendship.[190]

Things to Come

Do our leaders have eyes to see and ears to hear? Will the United States be a reliable ally to Israel going forward?

Eventually, America will come against Israel like every other nation of the world. God's prophetic Word declares it will happen in the end times.[191] America's final act of faithlessness will happen during the Tribulation.

In the meantime, it appears that America will continue to be a fickle friend to Israel. When we elect a God-fearing leader, policies will lean toward strong support of Israel. When we elect a godless leader who doesn't care what God has declared through His Holy Word, the United States will abandon Israel and elevate their mortal enemies.

And, when our national leaders pressure Israel to restrain itself in the face of existential threats or to trade its covenant land with those who seek its destruction, they call down the wrath of God on our own nation. Oh, that they would heed His warning given through the prophet Isaiah (28:14–16) to those who lord over the inhabitants of Jerusalem:

> Therefore, hear the word of the LORD, you scoffers,
> Who rule this people who are in Jerusalem,
> Because you have said, "We have made a covenant with death,
> And with Sheol we have made a pact.
> The gushing flood will not reach us when it passes by,
> Because we have made falsehood our refuge and we have con-
>   cealed ourselves with deception."
> Therefore thus says the Lord GOD:
> "Behold, I am laying a stone in Zion, a tested stone,
> A precious cornerstone for the foundation, firmly placed.
> The one who believes in it will not be disturbed."

Paul rightly identified Jesus Christ as that "stone of stumbling and block of offense" and declared, "He who believes in Him will not be disappointed" (Romans 9:33).

In addition to ignoring God's Word regarding Israel, our nation seems determined to offend God. Sadly, it's not only our leaders who have forgotten the God who has shed His grace on us.

A Generation Arose Who Did Not Know God

To this point, I've focused on America's special relationship with Israel. At a critical moment in the establishment of the modern state of Israel, the United States was its first champion. In the years since, America has been a usually helpful but frustratingly fickle ally.

And there is another sad dynamic at work in our nation. Twenty-first-century America demonstrates the biblical principle that to whom much is given, much is expected (Luke 12:48). Our nation has been the beneficiary and conduit of so much of God's blessing, but it has turned its back on the God who blessed us—with calamitous results.

The twentieth century, the "American Century," represented a period of unprecedented American influence and affluence. Yet as the next century dawned, the United States seemed adrift. Awash in prosperity, America followed the sad trajectory of ancient Israel:

> There arose another generation after [their fathers] who did not know the LORD, nor yet the work which He had done for [them]. (Judges 2:10)

The seeds of humanism and hubris sown by philosophers like John Dewey and Charles Darwin produced a cancer of rebellion and ungodliness that is still metastasizing.

I could spend many pages citing examples of America's falling away from God. As David Reagan has documented, our downfall began to accelerate with the cultural revolution of the 1960s.[192] For example:

- America spends more money each year gambling than we do on food.
- America has murdered over sixty million babies since 1973 and the Democratic Party now celebrates the ungodly scourge of abortion.
- Our culture and leaders actively promote the perversion of homosexuality and gender dysphoria—willfully undermining the God-ordained covenant of marriage.
- Although we constitute only 5 percent of the world's population, we consume over 50 percent of all the illegal drugs produced in the world.
- The US is the world's leading producer and consumer of pornography.
- Through our immoral, violent, and blasphemous TV programs and movies, we have become the moral polluter of planet earth.

Having rejected Almighty God and His law as the basis for our society, we have unleashed wave after wave of immorality and violence. And, adding insult to injury, the church in America is apathetic to rising apostasy. America has not only turned its back on God, it is shaking its fist and flipping its finger at the Almighty.

I could go on and on recounting a sordid demonstration of our abject rebellion. Instead, I'd like to invite you to prayerfully recollect the mounting evidence you have witnessed with your own eyes. Can there be any doubt that America has rejected God and is committing national suicide?

Oh, How the Mighty Have Fallen

Hearing of Saul and Jonathan's demise at the hand of the Philistines, David wrote a dirge for the man he called the Lord's anointed and his beloved friend. He sang:

O daughters of Israel, weep over Saul, who clothed you luxuriously in scarlet, who put ornaments of gold on your apparel. How the mighty have fallen in the midst of the battle! Jonathan is slain on your high places. (2 Samuel 1:25–26)

That Saul's death could come as such a blow to David is a testament to his faithfulness. But Saul's fall from grace had been pronounced long before by Samuel:

You have rejected the word of the LORD, and the LORD has rejected you from being king over Israel. (1 Samuel 15:26)

Despite once being filled with the Holy Spirit, Saul's eventual removal from the throne was inevitable. Dismissal of the Word of God and disobedience to Him always leads to tragically predictable consequences.

Similarly, America was once filled with people committed to godliness or at least to demonstrating a practical respect for the ordinances of God.

Harry Truman cited his childhood Sunday school Bible lessons as the reason he disregarded the counsel of his advisors and foreign policy experts.[193] He wanted to honor God's Word and bless His chosen people.

But as America has strayed grievously—flaunting its sinfulness and gleefully encouraging others toward sin—God has rejected us as well.

You Ought to Know Better

When I was a child, my parents held me to a higher standard of behavior than my peers. They would tell me, "You know better."

Peter makes clear that individuals who "have escaped the defilements of the world by the knowledge of the Lord and Savior Jesus Christ [and are] again entangled in them and are overcome, the last state has become worse for them than the first" (2 Peter 2:18–21). The same principle surely applies to nations once proclaiming themselves "Christian." Our Father in Heaven also expects that those who know better should reflect the discernment that comes with knowledge. Some nations are not built on Judeo-Christian principles. Their people could legitimately claim ignorance of the revealed Word of God. America cannot make such a claim. Indeed, our leaders still pay lip service to God and invoke His continued blessing on our land even as they ignore His laws and insult His character.

For several generations, America has fallen into the pit described by Alexandr Solzhenitzyn: We have forgotten God. Not unlike the militantly atheistic Soviet Union, many of our cultural leaders reject any possibility that we are accountable to a Holy God. How else to explain their headlong rush to undermine every truth revealed in Scripture.

America ought to have known better.

In his letter to the Roman Christians, Paul speaks of those who ought to know better but instead heap insult upon injury. In Romans 1, he outlined the inevitable outpouring of judgment that follows the progressive debasement of people who turn away from God.

Then he wrote:

Although they know the ordinance of God, that those who practice such things are worthy of death, they not only do the same, but also give hearty approval to those who practice them. (Romans 1:32)

What is the consequence of such willful disobedience? Paul was unequivocable:

The wrath of God is revealed from heaven against all ungodliness and unrighteousness of men who suppress the truth in unrighteousness. (Romans 1:18)

Where Are We, and Where Are We Headed?

In a book about trajectories, it is appropriate that we consider where we've been, where we are, and where we're going.

From its founding, America aspired to be a nation set apart. Our founders oriented our nation and established our laws with reverence for God. They recognized that He was the source of all blessing and endeavored—albeit imperfectly—to live accordingly.

God indeed shed His grace on the United States, enabling us to become a conduit of blessing to the new nation of Israel in 1948 and beyond. We achieved our greatest stature as a nation immediately following President Truman's decision to bless Israel.

Since then, we have strayed grievously. The state of our union is so bad that it must offend our Holy God for us to claim to be a Christian nation. Not only do we avidly practice every type of abomination—from the murder of the unborn to the celebration of sexual perversion to the insistence on dividing the Land of Israel—we insist that other nations join us in these ungodly activities.

Our trajectory started strong. Like the fins of an arrow in flight, built-in mechanisms of introspection and correction offered hope that we would achieve a more perfect union. For many years, America did strive to be the beacon of Christian hope our founders envisioned.

But along the way we have gone astray. And we have not merely forgotten God, we are thumbing our nose, shaking our fist, and flipping our finger toward Him. For that reason, we are destined for judgment. God will not be mocked. Just as a single man will reap what he sows, so will a nation of men and women (Galatians 6:7). We have sown the wind and will soon reap the whirlwind (Hosea 8:7).

Even in Wrath, God Remembers Mercy

Soon and very soon, God will unleash judgment on the world. At some point, He will pour out His wrath on America. When that occurs, the United States will fade from the world scene—just as other mighty nations and empires have in the past. It may happen when least expected and at breathtaking speed—as when the Taliban humiliated the United States during its withdrawal from Afghanistan in the summer of 2021.

Along with David Reagan, I think our nation has passed the point of no return. Like Israel and Judah in the Old Testament, our wound is incurable.[194] There is no hope for America.

Habakkuk delivered a similar message of judgment and doom to his people. He was shocked when God revealed His intention to judge His chosen people by a nation that was far more evil. The prophet prayed, "In wrath remember mercy" (Habakkuk 3:2). Thankfully, our merciful God has provided a pathway to salvation. That is because our God is a God of hope.

While hope for America is fading, the same is not true for individuals. Every person reading this book needs to know that hope springs eternal—in the person of our Blessed Hope, Jesus Christ.

What is your trajectory? What is your eternal destination?

Do not rely on your status as a citizen of America or any other worldly nation. While you still have breath, you can call on the Lord Jesus Christ and be saved from the wrath to come. Become a citizen of Heaven and join me in eagerly waiting for our great God and Savior, our soon-returning King, the Lord Jesus Christ (Philippians 3:20–21).

CONCLUSION

CALMING THE TRIBULATION STORM

By Terry James

THE END OF THE JOURNEY has been determined by the prophetic Architect of Heaven. The course is unalterable. Mankind moves ever more swiftly through the waters of history in trajectory toward a destination both catastrophic and magnificent.

The waters of everyday life mankind sails today seem to most people who are, because of moment-by-moment concerns, like a smooth, glassy lake rather than choppy oceanic waters portending an approaching storm. Like those aboard the *Titanic* in 1912, there is no recognition of the gargantuan iceberg ahead.

Like those passengers headed into the cold, dark night of that time, today's passengers aboard Spaceship Earth leave it to the captains of government to keep the ride smooth and uneventful. Those at the helm, however, like the captain of the Titanic, have no idea of the prophetic storm ahead—because they have no communications with the Lord of creation. They haven't and won't listen to the heavenly forecast that tells of the oncoming monster that is far more deadly than the iceberg Titanic approached that fateful night in the North Atlantic.

These rulers who steer the ships of state feel supremely confident that they have the ability—and the right—to negotiate the waters through which they take the nations, whether the waters are calm or stormy.

The globalists elite who believe they alone have the right to chart earth's future don't know, nor do they want to know, the True Master of history's potentially disastrous sea, the One who spread His hands out on the small boat that day on Galilee and said the words to which the very elements of creation instantaneously responded: "Peace…be still."

Those who want to chart the course of human history have no wish to navigate the unknown with the help of deity. The psalmist points to the captains of world power and their self-appointed command posts at the helm of the earth's future.

> The kings of the earth set themselves, and the rulers take counsel together, against the LORD, and against his anointed, saying, Let us break their bands asunder, and cast away their cords from us. (Psalm 2:2–3)[195]

To Christians familiar with God's prophetic weather forecast, the circumstances could not be more different from those viewed by the passengers compliantly under the globalists-elite, would-be masters—those sailing what they believe to be a calm sea as usual. The signals of the approaching Tribulation storm couldn't be clearer. The choppy waters are becoming billowing waves that portend ominous things to come.

To these believers, Jesus said, "And what I say unto you I say unto all, Watch" (Mark 13:37).

For what are believers through the ages to "watch"? Jesus laid out the signs of the end-times turbulence.

> And as he sat upon the mount of Olives over against the temple, Peter and James and John and Andrew asked him privately, Tell us, when shall these things be? and what shall be the sign when all these things shall be fulfilled? And Jesus answering them began to

say, Take heed lest any man deceive you: For many shall come in my name, saying, I am Christ; and shall deceive many. And when ye shall hear of wars and rumours of wars, be ye not troubled: for such things must needs be; but the end shall not be yet. For nation shall rise against nation, and kingdom against kingdom: and there shall be earthquakes in divers places, and there shall be famines and troubles: these are the beginnings of sorrows. (Mark 13:3–8)

Jesus' words according to other Gospel accounts of the Olivet Discourse include "there shall be distress among nations with perplexity." All of this the Lord likened to labor pains experienced by a woman leading to the time of a birth of her child. The contractions, He indicated, would manifest as convulsions, as if the earth was experiencing swelling upheavals that forewarned the coming of profound occurrence.

Most every believer in Jesus Christ who views Bible prophecy from the pre-Tribulation, premillennial standpoint, and who earnestly "watches" the prophetic weather warnings taking place across the world, clearly sees the end-times storm raging on the prophetic horizon. They see the *trajectory* of that most destructive storm of history. They understand the course into that tumultuous sea on which all of humanity is set. Lost mankind is inevitably—and soon—to collide with the time Jesus described.

For then shall be great tribulation, such as was not since the beginning of the world to this time, no, nor ever shall be. (Matthew 24:21)

The authors of *TRAJECTORY: Tracking the Approaching Tribulation Storm,* have expertly reported on the coming end-times turbulence. They have determined to cover for the reader the most vital signs that indicate we are indeed in the time nearing that seven-year period of unprecedented trouble prophesied by the Lord Jesus Christ.

We consider here, in brief, two signals we believe show the trajectory the peoples of the earth are on at the very end of this dispensation of Grace (the Church Age).

TRAJECTORY Indicator 1: Israel

It is essential to be alert to Satan's sleight-of-hand in diverting attention from what's really going on, like in the old shell game called thimblerig.

The pea is placed under the one of three shells and the player is invited to guess which one the pea is under after the shells are shuffled. The shuffling increases in speed, and soon the human eye can't follow the movement to keep up with the shell concealing the pea.

In most cases, the player ends up the loser after betting on being able to pick the correct shell.

Like in the matter of globalist activity, where Satan and the demonic and human minions hide their true efforts to bring in their changed world order (with distractions of such activities as those of the cancel culture), the evil one diverts attention from things involving the number-one sign of these end times. He, for example, foments revolution within the United States and others of the Western world.

All the while, the nation Israel and the entire Middle East region are being rearranged, setting the stage for the great, end-times play that will see the triumphant return of Christ.

The devil, in his sin delusion, believes he is orchestrating the demise of God's chosen people. But it is the Lord who is the master director. His omniscient hand has already written the prophetic script that will soon unfold.

So wise observers should keep their eye—their spiritual senses—on what's happening that involves Israel. We must do this despite all of the other troubling distractions that otherwise plague us.

And there is more than enough going on in Israel and vicinity to keep us transfixed.

An example is that the COVID-19 pandemic, as it is designated, has brought the entire world to focus on the tiny Jewish state. Based upon how the virus fear now seems to pulsate intensely from Israel, it is good to question if that prophecy-centered nation is being prepped by external forces for the time of Tribulation.

It takes neither a scholar in Bible prophecy nor a scholar of Middle Eastern history to understand that dynamics in the region are building toward war. Those who would be governors of world geopolitics, such as the elite of the UN, fear the region to be the ignition point for a future conflict that will explode into full-blown nuclear conflagration.

We know from God's prophetic Word that Israel is destined both to suffer a time of great trouble and, ultimately, a thousand years of glory as the head of all nations. This turmoil and eventual emergence into great victory involves threats and pressures from surrounding nations that hate that Jewish State.

While Bible prophecy outlines and even details to some extent how all of this eventuates, the moment-by-moment, day-by-day developments are not always clear in regard to how all will unfold. Those pressures mentioned take the form of many points of shaping and influencing God's *chosen* as the nation interacts among nation states of the region and world.

One such point of pressure is being used at present by Satan to cause God's *chosen people* to be seen as prototype for how he intends to manipulate and control the world's population when allowed to foment his final moments of evil.

Bible prophecy writers have looked a number of times at how COVID-19 has been wielded as a powerful tool with which to bludgeon the entire populations of the planet into submission. This globalist-generated biological weapon, I believe, was planned and is being used to establish a worldwide mindset of being willing to submit to authoritarian rule.

In this sense, Israel is being somehow *prepped* to serve Satan's purpose for the coming Tribulation holocaust.

We see story after story of COVID-19 being used to lock down cities, and now entire nations. Australia, for example, has become almost again the prison colony it once was. The rulers in some parts—South Wales, for example—have become despotic in their evil demands. First they seized all private weapons they could force the Aussies to give up, and now they go house to house to demand vaccine proof. Those not compliant go to something called "wellness camps" or some such designation.

But, regardless from where the stories of lockdowns, etc., come, it is more and more the tiny Jewish State that is being put in the world spotlight—all with the complicity of Israel's own growingly despotic leadership. The nation leads the world in people vaccinated to protect against COVID apparently, yet incongruent facts have emerged. The following report frames developments.

Just a few months ago, the mainstream media praised Israel for its "pandemic-ending" vaccination campaign. With over 40 percent of the population "fully vaccinated" in the first quarter of 2021, Israel was well on its way to stopping community spread and clearing out its hospitals.

The nation of Israel imposed some of the strictest lockdowns during that time, violating the Nuremberg Code and segregating the unvaccinated from public life. Israel bought up the Pfizer/BioNTech mRNA covid vaccine and began issuing mandatory Green Pass "vaccine passports" as a requirement for citizens to enter public spaces. By August, Israel had intimidated and coerced its population into having one of the highest vaccination rates in the world, with 78 percent of people 12 years of age and older classified as "fully vaccinated."

The world was reassured that this rate of vaccination was more than enough to ensure individual and "herd immunity." However, infection rates have skyrocketed across the country since then, and Israel is now logging the world's highest infection rates, with nearly 650 new cases daily per million people. At times, hospitalizations for the "fully vaccinated" have reached upwards of 95 percent.[196]

The nation is now again under draconian lockdown.

A fascinating question has been proposed by some Bible prophecy observers. They ponder whether Israel is in probably the most dictatorial-type lockdown of any nation on earth, keeping its citizens from leaving en masse for some divine purpose.

Perhaps, they conjecture, it is because some action by the Lord or an evil entity is pending. The severe sequestration keeping Israeli citizens more or less in lockdown is maybe to protect or benefit them in some way from imminent something or the other.

We know the following is always true, no matter what the facts are surrounding that which seems to be *prepping* Israel for what is to come.

Behold, he that keepeth Israel shall neither slumber nor sleep. (Psalm 121:4)

Israel's God *is* God. He is aware of the trajectory His *chosen people* and all of mankind are on while moving ever nearer the apocalyptic storm. He has forewarned the signals of that coming terrible tempest to look for throughout His prophetic Word.

One such signal became clear with the fall of Afghanistan to the Taliban in September of 2021 and the formation of the terrorist government.

Immediately, the most prominent nations in prophecy were invited to participate in that formational activity. Russia, Turkey, and Iran were welcomed by the Taliban as coalition partners in taking over Afghanistan, which is comprised of geographical territory that, like Iran, made up the ancient Persian Empire.

The end of America's years-long military occupation created a monumental power vacuum. The power players for the windup of human history this side of Christ's Second Advent immediately filled that void.

The Gog-Magog forces scheduled to storm over the mountains of Israel toward Jerusalem seem now set firmly in place for prophetic fulfillment. Additionally, China—considered by prophecy students to be the king of *the kings of the east*—joined in the organizational partnership.

The most powerful entity of the oriental world, that nation is likely the leader of *the kings of the east* of Revelation chapters 9 and 16, and now seems securely in its place for fulfilling its destruction of a third of earth's population.

TRAJECTORY Indicator 2: Beast's Tower Arising

Mankind's trajectory, like in Nimrod's time following the world system-destroying Flood of Noah's day, is again on track to take the planet into a time of devastating turbulence. The tumult allows—even invites—dictatorships to arise. The globalists are in unrelenting determination. They want to reconstruct a geopolitical system of New World Order. They are, in effect, rebuilding the tower God came down to destroy.

> And the LORD came down to see the city and the tower, which the children of men builded. And the LORD said, Behold, the people is one, and they have all one language; and this they begin to do: and now nothing will be restrained from them, which they have imagined to do. Go to, let us go down, and there confound their language, that they may not understand one another's speech. So the LORD scattered them abroad from thence upon the face of all the earth: and they left off to build the city. (Genesis 11:5–8)

Bringing up the Beast and the Tower

Planet earth is undergoing a "reset" of observable dimension, as the term "reset" is used by secular pundits. "Stage-setting" is the term we biblical prophecy watchers use to describe the things taking place at a phenomenal pace. In both cases—secular and biblical—the "reset" or "stage-setting" has undeniably accelerated to quantum speed since the American presidential election of 2016.

Secular observers see the dynamic changes taking place as ideological transformation that occurs cyclically—like seasonal weather patterns that can bring great, destructive storms. From the biblical view, the changes are heading in one direction, and for a singular purpose. Movement at such a swift pace is being employed by evil's master strategist to bring to the world stage his final and most terrible tyrant of human history.

It's more than interesting, I notice, that those coming from the secular standpoint more and more use the word "beast" to describe this rise of powers in opposition to traditional Western cultural, societal, political, and religious norms. To my thinking, this is yet another proof that God's Word is truth. Even those who would no doubt gag at the thought that they were validating anything from the Bible can't help contributing to the outcomes foretold thousands of years ago.

I recently received an email containing an interesting article related to this. My thanks to Nancy, who apparently reads my commentaries on raptureready.com and terryjamesprophecyline.com.

The writer of the article Nancy sent seems to have no biblical knowledge as he gets into things going on in the "reset." While his words would be considered conspiracy-laden by those in most news media, the author—despite not knowing Bible prophecy, as far as I can tell—lays out well what is likely behind the scenes in Lucifer bringing the beast to power.

Again, it's the writer's use of the word "beast" that is most interesting. He makes no reference throughout his article to the beast of Revelation 13, yet that beast is the very entity to which he unwittingly is referring.

Here is the beginning of the article. I highly recommend that, if possible, you read the entire piece.

Imagine, you are living in a world that you are told is a democracy—and you may even believe it—but in fact your life and fate is in the hands of a few ultra-rich, ultra-powerful and ultra-inhuman oligarchs. They may be called Deep State, or simply the Beast, or anything else obscure or untraceable—it doesn't matter. They are less than the 0.0001%.

For lack of a better expression, let's call them for now "obscure individuals."

These obscure individuals who pretend running our world have never been elected. We don't need to name them. You will figure out who they are, and why they are famous, and some of them totally invisible. They have created structures, or organisms without any legal format. They are fully out of international legality. They are a forefront for the Beast. Maybe there are several competing Beasts. But they have the same objective: A New or One World Order (NWO, or OWO).

These obscure individuals are running, for example, the World Economic Forum (WEF—representing Big Industry, Big Finance, and Big Fame), the Group of 7—G7, the Group of 20—G20 (the leaders of the economically" strongest" nations). There are also some lesser entities, called the Bilderberg Society, the Council on Foreign Relations (CFR), Chatham House, and more.

The members of all of them are overlapping. Even this expanded forefront combined represents less than 0.001%. They all have superimposed themselves over sovereign national elected and constitutional governments, and over THE multinational world body, the United Nations, the UN....

Co-opted or created by the Beast(s) are also, the European Union, the Bretton Woods Organizations, World Bank and IMF, as well as the World Trade Organization (WTO)—and—make no mistake—the International Criminal Court (ICC) in The Hague. It has no teeth. Just to make sure the law is always on the side of the lawless.

In fact, they have co-opted the UN to do their bidding.[197]

As addressed in books and columns before, many are already falling under the delusion being foisted by those whom this secular-oriented author calls "beasts." Koening further relates:

The supremacy of these obscure unelected individuals becomes ever more exposed. We, the people consider it "normal" that they call the shots, not what we call—or once were proud of calling—

our sovereign nations and sovereignty elected governments. They have become a herd of obedient sheep. The Beast has gradually and quietly taken over. We haven't noticed. It's the salami tactic: You cut off slice by tiny slice and when the salami is gone, you realize that you have nothing left, that your freedom, your civil and human rights are gone. By then it's too late. Case in point is the US Patriot Act. It was prepared way before 9/11. Once 9/11 "happened," the Patriot Legislation was whizzed through Congress in no time—for the people's future protection—people called for it for fear—and—bingo, the Patriot Act took about 90% of the American population's freedom and civil rights away. For good.

We have become enslaved to the Beast. The Beast calls the shots on boom or bust of our economies, on who should be shackled by debt, when and where a pandemic should break out, and on the conditions of surviving the pandemic, for example, social confinement. And to top it all off—the instruments the Beast uses, very cleverly, are a tiny-tiny invisible enemy, called a virus, and a huge but also invisible monster, called FEAR. That keeps us off the street, off reunions with our friends, and off our social entertainment, theatre, sports, or a picnic in the park.[198]

Every indicator appearing on our minute-by-minute headline news today validates the end-times trajectory of this judgment-bound world system of rebellion. It's becoming clearer by the moment *how* the Beast of Revelation 13 will have little trouble ascending the steps of the neo Tower of Babel platform that Satan's globalist minions are at present in overdrive preparing for when the Church leaves this world.

To the reader of *TRAJECTORY: Tracking the Aproaching Tribulation Storm*, we urge you to seek the only Shelter from that approaching end-times tempest. His name is *Jesus Christ*. There is no other Way to escape God's wrath against sin. Jesus has died, was buried, and resurrected from the grave to save all who will but reach out to accept the grace gift of salvation.

Jesus says to the human spiritual heart: "Peace...be still." You can have that *peace that passes all understanding.*

Here is God's formula for clinging to Jesus, God's eternal life preserver.

That if thou shalt confess with thy mouth the Lord Jesus, and shalt believe in thine heart that God hath raised him from the dead, thou shalt be saved. For with the heart man believeth unto righteousness; and with the mouth confession is made unto salvation. (Romans 10:9–10)

ABOUT THE AUTHORS

Terry James is author, general editor, and/or coauthor of more than thirty books on Bible prophecy and geopolitics, hundreds of thousands of which have been sold worldwide. He has also written fiction and nonfiction books on a number of other topics.

James is a frequent lecturer on the study of end-time phenomena and interviews often with national and international media on topics involving world issues and events as they relate to Bible prophecy. He is partner with Todd Strandberg and general editor in the www.raptureready.com website, which has for several years been rated as the number-one Bible prophecy website on the Internet. The website has more than twenty-five thousand articles and much more material for those who visit the site.

A member of the Pre-Trib Research Center founded by Dr. Tim LaHaye, James speaks often at prophecy conferences. His personal blog is terryjamesprophecyline.com. He lives with his wife, Margaret, near Little Rock, Arkansas.

Jonathan C. Brentner is an author, blogger, Bible teacher, and retired financial analyst. Through his writing, he reaches thousands each month with his perspectives on biblical prophecy through his website at www.jonathanbrentner.com.

Jonathan has a BA in biblical studies from John Brown University along with an MDiv degree from Talbot Theological Seminary. He was a pastor for six years before pursuing an MBA degree at the University of Iowa, which led to a lengthy career as a financial analyst at a large corporation. He retired in 2016 to devote his time to writing.

Jonathan and his wife Ruth reside in Roscoe, Illinois. Together they have five children and a dozen grandchildren scattered about in Wisconsin, Iowa, Texas, and Illinois.

Daymond Duck, by God's grace, is a graduate of the University of Tennessee in Knoxville, the founder and president of Prophecy Plus Ministries, the best-selling author of a shelf full of books (three have been published in foreign languages), a member of the prestigious Pre-Trib Study Group, a conference speaker, and a writer for raptureready.com. He is a retired United Methodist pastor, has made more than three hundred television appearances, and has been a member of the Baptist church in his hometown since 2006. He can be contacted at duck_daymond@yahoo.com

With a BA in journalism, **Jim Fletcher** has spent many years as a book editor in the Christian publishing industry. Since 2007, he has been a freelance writer and editor, authoring several books and writing columns and op-eds. A frequent visitor to Israel, Jim has cultivated rich contacts over the years, and loves to teach Bible prophecy as an evangelism tool. He lives in a pastoral setting in the Ozark Mountains of northwest Arkansas.

Alan Franklin is a journalist, writer, and speaker with a great fascination for the unfolding of world events in the light of prophecy, especially as we near the end of the end times. He has interviewed many thousands of people from Count Otto von Habsburg to Prince

Andrew and politicians including Prime Ministers Margaret Thatcher and John Major.

Alan has working for all the main UK media outlets including radio and TV networks as well as editing and publishing many titles, covering everything from regional news to health and business. He and his journalist wife Pat run a website: thefreepressonline.co.uk

 **Pete Garcia** is a writer, speaker, and teacher of Bible prophecy and apologetics. He is also an aviator and a twenty-two-year Army veteran, with numerous deployments to the Middle East, as well as numerous overseas tours to both Europe and Asia. He holds a BA degree in international relations, with a focus in Russian and military history. Pete began his writing career with *The Omega Letter* (2011–2018) and has since branched out to create his own website, www.rev310.com. To date, he has written over four hundred articles published on numerous websites and platforms. Pete is happily married and a father to five wonderful children. Most importantly, he is a believer in our Lord Jesus Christ.

 Evangelist and author **Mike Gendron**, a 1992 graduate of Dallas Theological Seminary, is a frequent speaker at international Bible conferences and teaches the students and faculty at The Master's Seminary, The Master's Academy International, Dallas Theological Seminary, Moody Bible Institute, and Tyndale Theological Seminary. He has done seminars at hundreds of churches throughout the world and has appeared as a guest on many radio and TV programs, including the History Channel. He has also written monthly articles for the *Ankerberg Theological Journal* since 1998.

Mike is director and founder of Proclaiming the Gospel Ministry, a thirty-year-old evangelistic outreach to those who are lost in religion. The ministry conducts short-term missions, trips, and evangelistic seminars in

churches throughout the world. It has over thirty thousand subscribers in fifty states and forty foreign countries.

A devout Roman Catholic for over thirty-four years, Mike was saved by God's amazing grace when he began reading the Bible for the first time in 1981. Upon completion of a master's degree at Dallas Theological Seminary, he served as pastor of evangelism and outreach at a Bible church in Dallas for three years and founded Proclaiming the Gospel Ministry. He is married to Jane, his co-laborer in the ministry.

Wilfred J. Hahn has worked on the front lines of global money for a period spanning five decades. His executive roles have included chief investment officer managing billions of roving capital around the world, a research director for a major Wall Street firm, chairman of a large offshore mutual fund company, and an associate editor with respected international economist Dr Kurt Richebächer. Uniquely, he is versed in Scripture and eschatological perspectives as well as economic and financial theory. He is sought out for his reasoned views with respect to Christian eschatological perspectives and global political economic developments.

Wilfred has authored hundreds of articles and produced some forty books and booklets. Earlier books, *The Endtime Money Snare: How to Live Free* (2001) and *Global Financial Apocalypse Prophesied: Preserving True Riches in an Age of Deception and Trouble* (2009) served as insightful forewarnings.

An avid student of prophecy, long-time television and radio personality, author of dozens of best-selling books and publisher of many others, **Thomas R. Horn** serves as the chief executive officer of SkyWatchTV, Defender Publishing, and whole-foods supplements retailer Eden's Essentials.

Thomas J. Hughes is the founder of Hope for our Times and lead pastor of 412 Church in San Jacinto. He has been teaching Bible prophecy for over thirty years and has a unique gift for helping people understand what the Bible calls the "last days." Tom shares weekly prophecy updates on the Hope for our Times website and YouTube channel. He regularly appears on a variety of TV, radio, and Internet programs, including World News Briefing on HisChannel. Tom lives in Southern California with his wife and two children.

Nathan Jones serves as the Internet evangelist for Lamb & Lion Ministries. He can be found co-hosting the ministry's television program *Christ in Prophecy*, growing and developing the web ministry at christin-prophecy.org, authoring books such as *12 Faith Journeys of the Minor Prophets*, blogging daily on the Christ in Prophecy Journal, discussing current events on the Christ in Prophecy Facebook group, producing video Q&As such as *The Inbox*, being interviewed on radio programs, speaking at conferences and churches, and answering Bible-related questions sent in from all over the world.

A life-long student of the Bible and an ordained minister, Nathan graduated from Cairn University with a bachelor's in Bible, attended Southern Baptist Theological Seminary, and received his master's in management and leadership at Liberty University.

Jeff Kinley is a former pastor who has authored over thirty books. He travels the country and internationally speaking about Bible prophecy. Jeff's weekly *Vintage Truth* podcast is heard in over sixty countries worldwide. His website is jeffkinley.com.

Tim Moore, chief executive officer and senior evangelist for Lamb & Lion Ministries, hosts Lamb & Lion's weekly television program *Christ in Prophecy*, publishes the bimonthly *Lamplighter* magazine, and leads pilgrimages to Israel. He also travels extensively to share the message that Jesus Christ is coming soon.

A graduate of the United States Air Force Academy, Tim served for thirty-four years in the Air Force on active duty, in the Kentucky Air National Guard, and in the Air Force Reserve as an instructor pilot. Colonel Moore flew multiple missions in Iraq and Afghanistan. For thirteen years, served in the Kentucky legislature as a state representative, where he was an outspoken voice for godly principles—championing life, traditional marriage, and government that reflects Christian principles and is limited to its appropriate sphere.

Tim and his wife Amy have four children and four grandchildren.

Dr. David Reagan is founder of Lamb & Lion Ministries (www.lamblion.com), an interdenominational, evangelical ministry devoted to proclaiming the soon return of Jesus. He holds graduate degrees in international relations and, before entering the ministry, Dr. Reagan had an extensive twenty-year career in higher education. He served both as a professor and an administrator at several colleges and universities.

A life-long Bible student, teacher, and preacher, Dr. Reagan is the author of many religious essays published in a wide variety of journals and magazines, and he has written eighteen books, all related to Bible prophecy. Dr. Reagan has conducted prophecy conferences all over the world, and he has led more than forty-five pilgrimages to Israel that focus on the prophetic significance of the sites visited.

A lifelong Texan, Dr. Reagan lives in a suburb of Dallas with his wife, Ann, of fifty-nine years.

Gary W. Ritter is a lay pastor, Bible teacher, and pro-lific author. His Whirlwind Series comprises three end-times books: *Sow the Wind, Reap the Whirlwind,* and *There Is a Time.* These books are contained in the collected volume of the Whirlwind Omnibus. Gary has written many other Christian thrillers that will challenge you, including *The Minion Protocols* in conjunction with Terry James. You can learn about Gary's books and blog writings at his website: www.GaryRitter.com. You can also watch Gary's video Prophecy Updates on Rumble at his Awaken Bible Prophecy channel: https://rumble.com/c/c-783217.

Bill Salus, the founder of Prophecy Depot Ministries, is a bestselling author, researcher, conference speaker, and media personality. He has appeared on Fox TV and major Christian television programs, including TBN's *Praise the Lord,* Daystar's *Marcus and Joni, Sid Roth, Jim Bakker, Jewish Voice,* Prophecy Watchers, and more. His articles have been published world-wide over the Internet on sites like Rapture Ready, World Net Daily, and the Christian Post.

Bill is an expert at explaining the prophetic relevance of current Middle East and world events. Readers appreciate his unique insights, and sensible, rather than sensational, approach to understanding the Bible. He allows prophecy to speak for itself, rather than modernizing it into newspaper exegesis.

Several of Bill's books became instant bestsellers in Bible prophecy on Amazon, including *Psalm 83: The Missing Prophecy Revealed, How Israel Becomes the Next Mideast Superpower; Nuclear Showdown in Iran; Revealing the prophecy of Elam; The NOW Prophecies; The NEXT Prophecies; The Apocalypse Revelations Novel;* and *Isralestine, The Ancient Blueprints of the Future Middle East.*

Shortly after becoming a Christian in 1992, writing became a daily discipline for Bill. It has become Bill's personal challenge to demonstrate the love of God through prophecy to each reader.

The discovery of prophecy as a gift rather than a threat is what most characterizes Bill's work. People all over the world are learning through his steadfast efforts, that prophecy is not just for the scholarly, but also for every common man, woman, and child. He may be reached at at prophecydepotministries@gmail.com or by visiting his website, www.prophecydepot.com.

Todd Strandberg is the founder of www.raptureready.com, the most highly visited prophecy website on the Internet. He is a partner in the site with Terry James. The site has been written about in practically every major news outlet in the nation and around the n 1987 when few websites existed, Rapture Ready now commands the attention of a quarter million visitors per month, with more than thirteen million hits registered during most thirty-day periods.

Strandberg is president of Rapture Ready and coauthor of *Are You Rapture Ready?* (Penguin/Dutton). He has written hundreds of major articles for the site, which have been distributed in major publications and websites around the nation and the world. He writes a highly read column under the site's "Nearing Midnight" section. Strandberg created "The Rapture Index"—a Dow Jones-like system of prophetic indicators—which continues to draw the attention of most major news outlets.

Matt Ward has been studying Bible prophecy for over thirty years. He writes regularly about Bible prophecy, and how this relates to world events today. He currently lives in the UK with his wife and two young children, and teaches history.

NOTES

1. Unless otherwise noted, all Scripture quoted in this chapter is from the New American Standard Bible.

2. Dr. David R. Reagan, "The Prophecy of the Week of Millenniums," *Lamplighter*, January–February 2021, p. 5.

3. Ibid., pp. 3–7.

4. Unless otherwise noted, all Scripture quoted in this chapter is from the New American Standard Bible.

5. Dr. David R. Reagan, "50 Reasons Why We Are Living in the End Times," *Lamplighter*, January–February, 2008, p. 3.

6. Gianluca Alimonti and Luigi Mariani, "On the Exponential Increase of Natural Disasters in the 20th Century," www.scienceclimatenergie.be/ontheexponentialincreaseofnaturaldisastersinthe20thcentury.

7. Dr. David R. Reagan, *God's Plan for the Ages*, "The Outpouring of the Holy Spirit," chapter 35, 2nd edition (McKinney, TX: Lamb & Lion Ministries, 2020) pp. 294–295.

8. Dr. David R. Reagan, *Living on Borrowed Time: The Imminent Return of Jesus*, 2nd edition (McKinney, TX: Lamb & Lion Ministries, 2015).

9. Dr. David R. Reagan, *The Man of Lawlessness: The Antichrist in the Tribulation* (McKinney, TX: Lamb & Lion Ministries, 2012).

10. Dr. David R. Reagan, "The Exponential Curve: Is It a Sign That Jesus Is Returning Soon?" *Prophecy Insights*, 2018.

11. Dr. David R. Reagan, *Israel in Bible Prophecy: Past, Present & Future* (McKinney, TX: Lamb & Lion Ministries, 2017).

12. Dr. David R. Reagan, "The Revival of the Hebrew Language," *Lamplighter*, March–April, 2014, pp. 3–9.

13. Dr. David R. Reagan, "Israel in Bible Prophecy: The Resurgence of the Military," *Lamplighter*, July–August 2013, pp. 3–9.

14. Dr. David R. Reagan, "Jewish Preparations for the Messiah," *Lamplighter*, May–June, 2021, pp. 3–7.

15. Dr. David R. Reagan, *Living on Borrowed Time,* pp. 76–78.

16. Unless otherwise noted, all Scripture quoted in this chapter is from the King James Version.

17. Daymond Duck, "Deception and Confusion—Watching Bible Prophecy Unfold," September 6, 2020.

18. Pete Garcia, "Even the Elect—Part I: Deception," https://rev310. com/2019/09.

19. Entropy is defined as a law of physics recognizing a gradual and inevitable decline into disorder.

20. Social critics from Supreme Court nominee Robert Bork ("Slouching Toward Gomorrah") to hard-rock musician Ozzie Osbourne ("Crazy Train") have written about the dangerous trends.

21. https://christinprophecy.org/ sermons/a-nation-begging-for-destruction-part-2/.

22. https://www.youtube.com/watch?v=ArOQF4kadHA.

23. Unless otherwise noted, all Scripture quoted in this chapter is from the New American Standard Bible.

24. https://www.theguardian.com/us-news/2015/jul/25/barack-obama-african-states-abandon-anti-gay-discrimination and https://www.reuters.com/article/ us-obama-africa-gay/obama-in-kenya-says-gays-need-equality-draws-african-criticism-idUSKCN0PZ0MZ20150725.

25. https://www.hrw.org/news/2020/10/19/submission-human-rights-watch-un-special-rapporteur-right-privacy# and https://www.ohchr.org/en/ professionalinterest/pages/crc.aspx.

26. *Paul Kengor, The Devil and Karl Marx: Communism's Long March of Death, Deception and Infiltration* (Gastonia, NC: TAN Books, 2020).

27. John 10:10.

28. https://www.heritage.org/progressivism/commentary/ the-agenda-black-lives-matter-far-different-the-slogan.

29. https://abcnews.go.com/US/start-black-lives-matter-lgbtq-lives/story?id=71320450.

30. https://www.npr.org/2021/06/07/1003872848/the-complicated-history-behind-blms-solidarity-with-the-pro-palestinian-movement.

31. https://dailycaller.com/2021/08/20/air-force-academy-training-black-lives-matter/.

32. https://www.washingtonpost.com/wp-srv/style/longterm/books/chap1/comingracewar.htm.

33. https://www.militarytimes.com/news/pentagon-congress/2021/08/25/china-blasts-us-over-afghanistan-pullout-describes-effective-talks-with-taliban/.

34. https://www.blueletterbible.org/lexicon/g1484/kjv/tr/0-1/.

35. "The Second Coming" – a poem by William Butler Yeats, in the Public Domain.

36. R. Albert Mohler, Jr., *We Cannot be Silent* (Nashville, TN: Thomas Nelson, 2015); and Erwin Lutzer, *We Will Not Be Silenced* (Eugene, OR: Harvest House, 2020).

37. Unless otherwise noted, all Scripture quoted in this chapter is from the King Jamves Version.

38. Harry Lear, "Open Letter to President Trump," They Fly Blog. January 29, 2018. Accessed March 29, 2021. https://theyflyblog.com/2018/02/15/.

39. https://www.sciencedirect.com/science/article/pii/S0019103516307643.

40. https://www.youtube.com/watch?v=xaW4Ol3_M1o.

41. Sue Bradley, "The Fourth Turning: The Protocols and the Gray Champion," *The Sue Bradley Archives.* Last accessed May 25, 2013, http://suebradleyarchives.com/have-we-entered-the-fourth-turning/.

42. Ibid.

43. Ibid.

44. Ibid.

45. Ibid.

46. https://www.foxnews.com/media/aoc-commission-truth-rein-in-media-slammed-unamerican.

47. Wikipedia, Shangri-La.

48. Unless otherwise noted, all Scripture quotations in this chapter are from the New King James Version.

49. "What is the meaning of pestilence in the Bible?" https://www. gotquestions.org/pestilence-in-the-Bible.html.

50. John MacArthur, The MacArthur New Testament Commentary— Revelation 21–11 (Chicago: Moody Press, 1999), p. 184.

51. Quote from the WEF website: https://www.weforum.org/focus/ the-great-reset.

52. Article on the LifeNews Website: "John Kerry: Biden Presidency Would Advance Globalist 'Great Reset' with 'Speed'" at: https://www.lifesitenews.com/news/ john-kerry-biden-presidency-would-advance-globalist-great-reset-with-speed.

53. https://www.modernatx.com/mrna-technology/ mrna-platform-enabling-drug-discovery-development.

54. Veronika Kyrylenko, "COVID-19 Vaccine Manufacturers Make a Fortune, Produce Nine New Billionaires," May 22, 2021 on the New American website at: https://thenewamerican.com/covid-19-vaccine-manufacturers-make-a-fortune-produce-nine-new-billionaires/.

55. Taken from the Alliance For Human Research Protection website: https:// ahrp.org/1961-aldous-huxleys-eerie-prediction-at-tavistock-group-california-medical-school/ I also found this quote on several other websites with varying agendas; it is valid

56. Dr. Carrie Madej video from April 19, 2021, https://thenewamerican.com/ covid-shots-dna-transhumanism-with-dr-madej-2/ In this excellent video, she goes into great detail regard the threat of transhumanism.

57. Fourth Industrial Revolution page: https://www.weforum.org/focus/ fourth-industrial-revolution.

58. Sarwant Singh, "Transhumanism and the Future of Humanity: 7 Ways the World Will Change by 2030," November 20, 2017, Forbes website: https://www.forbes.com/sites/sarwantsingh/2017/11/20/transhumanism-and-the-future-of-humanity-seven-ways-the-world-will-change-by-2030/?sh=35b71a4d7d79.

59. Ibid.

60. Tyer Durden, "FDA Reportedly Planning For COVID Vaccine Booster Shot Approval By September," August 6, 2021, ZeroHedge Website: https://www.zerohedge.com/political/white-house-defies-who-plans-start-doling-out-booster-shots.

61. Ethan Huff, "Dr. Richard Fleming Warns That Fauci, NIH Have Already Developed the NEXT Bioweapon to Be Released with HIV-like Capabilities That Suppress Human Immunity," August 13, 2021, Natural News website: https://www.naturalnews.com/2021-08-13-richard-fleming-fauci-nih-bioweapon-hiv-immunity.html.

62. WO2020060606 – CRYPTOCURRENCY SYSTEM USING BODY ACTIVITY DATA, https://patentscope2.wipo.int/search/en/detail.jsf?docId=WO2020060606&tab=PCTBIBLIO.

63. Peggy Johnson, "Partnering for a Path to Digital Identity," January 22, 2018, Official Microsoft Blog: https://blogs.microsoft.com/blog/2018/01/22/partnering-for-a-path-to-digital-identity/.

64. "Bill Gates Will Use Microchip Implants to Fight Coronavirus," March 19, 2020, Biohackinfo News, https://biohackinfo.com/news-bill-gates-id2020-vaccine-implant-covid-19-digital-certificates/.

65. Unless otherwise noted, all Scripture quoted in this chapter is from the new King James Version.

66. *The Bible Exposition Commentary.* (Chariot Victor Publishing, an imprint of Cook Communication Ministries: 1980). All rights reserved. Used by permission.

67. "Tucker Carlson, "Mocking Transgender and Abortion Advocates, Says Men Have Babies Too," Daniel Villarreal, *Newsweek*, September 2, 2021.

68. *Deaths of Despair and the Future of Capitalism* by Anne Case and Angus Deaton, Princeton University Press, 2020.

69. Unless otherwise noted, all Scripture quotations in this chapter are taken from the English Standard Verson.

70. Unless otherwise noted, all Scripture quotations in this chapter are taken from the King James Version.

71. Unless otherwise noted, all Scripture quotations in this chapter are from New King James Version.

72. Excerpted from an article by Leonard E. Read entitled "How to Advance Liberty," which appeared in a lecture recorded on March 10, 1965, as Album No. 12 in the Foundation for Economic Education's Long Playing Seminar Library.

73. Charles R. Kesler, *America's Cold Civil War,* October 2018, Volume 47, Number 10.

74. From the engravings found on the Georgia Guidestones in Elbert County, Georgia.

75. Mark Steyn, *America Alone: The End of the World*, Ch. 5, p. 98.

76. Charles Caldwell Ryrie and Frank E. Gaebelein, *Dispensationalism Today* (**Chicago: Moody Press, 1978**).

77. Unless otherwise noted, all Scripture quotations in this chapter are from the New American Standard Version.

78. https://thegiantcompany.ie.

79. Unless otherwise noted, all Scripture quotations in this chapter are from the New American Standard Bible.

80. http://www.zephaniah.eu/The%20Roman%20Catholic%20Church%20by%20D%20M%20Lloyd-Jones.pdf.

81. Manfred Barthel, "The Jesuits: History and Legend of the Society of Jesus (New York, 1984), Adolf Hitler, p. 266.

82. https://christian.net/pub/resources/text/wittenberg/concord/web/smc-02d.html.

83. http://www.logosresourcepages.org/History/geneva_bible.htm.

84. https://comingintheclouds.org/christian-resources/discipleship/endtimes/charles-spurgeons-view-of-the-bibles-antichrist/.

85. https://www.gty.org/library/sermons-library/66-60/the-destruction-of-the-final-world-religion-part-2.

86. Religion News Service, May 22, 2013.

87. https://www.patheos.com/blogs/deaconsbench/2013/05/pope-francis-the-lord-has-redeemed-all-of-us-even-atheists/.

88. https://www.cnsnews.com/blog/michael-w-chapman/pope-francis-there-no-hell\.

89. https://www.vatican.va/content/john-paul-ii/en/encyclicals/documents/hf_jp-ii_enc_25051995_ut-unum-sint.html.

90. Unless otherwise noted, all Scripture quoted in this chapter is from the New International Version.

91. Ron Rhodes, *Northern Storm Rising* (Eugene, OR: Harvest House, 2008), 13.

92. Unless otherwise noted, all Scripture quoted in this chapter is from the New King James Version.

93. John F. Walvoord & Roy B. Zuck (Eds.), *The Bible Knowledge Commentary: Old Testament* (Wheaton, IL: Scripture Press Publications Inc., 1985), 1225.

94. Kyle M. Yates, *Preaching from the Prophets* (Nashville, TN: Broadman Press, 1942), 179.

95. Gaalyah Cornfeld, *Archaeology of the Bible: Book By Book* (London, England: Adam and Charles Black, 1977), 179.

96. W. MacKintosh MacKay, *The Goodly Fellowship of the Prophets* (New York, NY: Richard R. Smith, 1929), 181.

97. Tent C. Butler, (Ed.), *Holman Bible Dictionary* (Nashville, TN: Holman Bible Publishers, 1991), 565.

98. William P. Barker, *Everyone in the Bible* (Old Tappan, NJ: Fleming H. Revell, 1966), 115.

99. Stephen M. Miller, *The Complete Guide to Bible Prophecy* (Uhrichville, OH: Barbour, 2010), 128.

100. *New Catholic Edition of the Holy Bible* (New York, NY: Catholic Book, 1957), 997.

101. Edwin M. Yamauchi, *Foes from the Northern Frontier* (Grand Rapids, MI: Baker Book House, 1982), 64–109.

102. Mark Hitchcock, *The Coming Islamic Invasion of Israel* (Sisters, OR: Multnomah, 2002), 31–32.

103. Tim LaHaye & Ed Hindson (Eds.), *The Popular Encyclopedia of Bible Prophecy* (Eugene, OR: Harvest House, 2004), 119–120.

104. John. B. Taylor, *Ezekiel: An Introduction and Commentary* (Downers Grove, IL: Inter-Varsity Press, 1969), 244–245.

105. Frank E. Gaebelein (Ed.), *The Expositor's Bible Commentary* (Vol 6) (Grand Rapids, MI: Zondervan, 1986), 930.

106. Josephus, *The Works of Josephus.* "Antiquities 1.6.1." (Peabody, MA: Hendrickson, 1987), 36.

107. John Phillips, *Exploring the Future: A Comprehensive Guide to Bible Prophecy* 3rd ed. (Grand Rapids, IL: Kregel, 2003), 327.

108. Midrash Rabbah 37:1.

109. Alfred Edersheim, *Old Testament Bible History* (Grand Rapids, MI: Eerdmans, 1975), i.59.

110. Taylor, 244–245.

111. Henry M. Morris, *The Genesis Record: A Scientific and Devotional Commentary on the Book of Beginnings* (Grand Rapids, MI: Baker, 1976), 247.

112. LaHaye & Hindson.

113. Midrash Rabbah 37:1.

114. Marshall W. Best, *Through the Prophet's Eye* (Enumclaw, WA: WinePress, 2000), 146.

115. Ibid., 144.

116. Charles F. Pfeiffer, *Baker Bible Atlas* (Grand Rapids, MI: Baker, 1961), 40.

117. David Jeremiah, *Is This the End?* (Nashville, TN: W Publishing, 2016), 210.

118. Spiros Zodhiates, *Hebrew-Greek Key Word Study Bible* (Chattanooga, TN: AMG, 2008), 1133, 1960.

119. G. A. Cook, *A Critical and Exegetical Commentary on the Book of Ezekiel* (Edinburgh, Scotland: T&T Clark, 1936), 408–409.

120. John F. Walvoord, *The Nations in Prophecy* (Grand Rapids, IL: Zondervan, 1978), 108.

121. H. W. F. Gesenius, *Gesenius' Hebrew-Chalde Lexicon* (Grand Rapids, IL: Eerdmans, 1957), 752.

122. Clyde E. Billington Jr., "The Rosh People in History and Prophecy (Part Two and Three)." *Michigan Theological Journal* 3:2, (Fall 1992): 172.

123. Thomas Ice, "Ezekiel 38 and 39, Pt 4" *Pre-Trib Perspectives* vol. VIII, no. 44 (April 2007): 6.

124. Billington, 49.

125. "Vital Statistics: Latest Population Statistics for Israel (2020)," *Jewish Virtual Library*, accessed October 1, 2020, https://www.jewishvirtuallibrary. org/latest-population-statistics-for-israel.

126. Mark Hitchcock, *The End: A Complete Overview of Bible Prophecy and the End of Days* (Wheaton, IL: Tyndale House, 2012), 310.

127. Luke Baker, "Israel Asks Itself the $150 Billion Question," *Reuters*, (May 25, 2011), https://www.reuters.com/article/2011/05/25/ us-economy-israel-steinitz-idUSTRE74O38R20110525.

128. Taylor, 247–248.

129. Charles Lee Feinberg, *The Prophecy of Ezekiel: The Glory of the Lord* (Chicago, IL: Moody, 1969), 219.

130. Robert G. Clouse, *The Meaning of the Millennium: Four Views* (Downers Grove, IL: InterVarsity, 1977), 7–9.

131. David L. Cooper, *When God's Armies Meet the Almighty* (Los Angeles, CA: Biblical Research Society, 1940), 80–81.

132. Ed Hindson & Thomas Ice, *Charting the Bible Chronologically: A Visual Guide to God's Unfolding Plan* (Eugene, OR: Harvest House, 2016), 120.

133. Arnold G. Fruchtenbaum, *The Footsteps of the Messiah: A Study of the Sequence of Prophetic Events* (San Antonio, TX: Ariel Ministries, 2004), 109.

134. J. Dwight. Pentecost, *Things to Come: A Study in Biblical Eschatology* (Grand Rapids, MI: Zondervan, 1958), 354.

135. Charles C. Ryrie, *Basic Theology* (Wheaton, IL: Scripture Press, 1986), 477.

136. Louis Bauman, *Russian Events in the Light of Bible Prophecy* (Philadelphia, PA: Balkiston, 1942), 174–175.

137. Rhodes, 189.

138. Henry H. Halley, *Halley's Bible Handbook* (Grand Rapids, MI: Zondervan, 1965), 334.

139. George W. Knight & Rayburn W. Ray, *The Illustrated Everyday Bible Companion* (Uhrichsville, OH: Barbour, 2005), 512.

140. Frank E. Gaebelein, 932.

141. Jeremiah, 223.

142. Mark Hitchcock, *101 Answers to Questions About the Book of Revelation* (Eugene, OR: Harvest House, 2012), 223–224.

143. Gilbert, Martin. *Israel: A History* (pp. 191–192). RosettaBooks. Kindle Edition.

144. Unless otherwise noted, all Scripture quotations in this chapter are from the King James Version.

145. By the way, I recommend studying the article on this subject by Mark Hitchcock at the Pre-Trib website: https://pre-trib.org/articles/dr-mark-hitchcock/message/the-battle-of-gog-and-magog/read.

146. Unless otherwise noted, as in this instance, Scripture quotations in this chapter are taken from the New King James Version.

147. Unless otherwise noted, all Scripture quotations in this chapter are taken from the King James Version.

148. The fourth kingdom is the Roman Empire, which has been revived in the European Union. It is the start of the one-world government, which "shall devour the whole earth."

149. https://www.france24.com/en/live-news/20210420-50-years-after-papa-doc-haiti-democracy-still-work-in-progress.

150. https://www.irishtimes.com/news/meetings-with-remarkable-tyrants-1.348264.

151. https://en.wikipedia.org/wiki/Fran%C3%A7ois_Duvalier#Repression.

152. https://progressive.org/latest/memories-duvalier-massacre-50-years-later-danticat-130425/.

153. https://reaction.la/repression.htm.

154. https://www.independent.co.uk/news/uk/home-news/refugee-crisis-son-vietnamese-boat-people-shares-story-how-britain-treated-asylum-seekers-1980s-10493316.html.

155. https://engelsbergideas.com/portraits/khorloogiin-choibalsan-stalin-of-the-steppe/.

156. https://www.sciencespo.fr/mass-violence-war-massacre-resistance/en/document/burundi-killings-1972.html.

157. https://economictimes.indiatimes.com/people/hitler-is-not-the-only-one-tyrant-leaders-around-the-world/tyrant-timeline/slideshow/55999098.cms.

158. https://www.bbc.co.uk/news/world-latin-america-22578356.

159. https://pantheon.world/profile/person/
Francisco_Mac%C3%ADas_Nguema/.

160. https://sites.tufts.edu/atrocityendings/2015/08/07/equatorial-guinea/.

161. https://www.hrw.org/reports/pdfs/r/rwanda/rwanda94d.pdf.

162. https://www.nytimes.com/2019/03/08/world/americas/venezuela-blackout-power.html.

163. https://www.hrw.org/world-report/2021/country-chapters/venezuela.

164. https://www.amnesty.org/en/location/americas/south-america/venezuela/report-venezuela/.

165. https://www.opendemocracy.net/en/opensecurity/
heavy-hand-on-venezuelas-streets/.

166. https://www.bbc.co.uk/news/world-latin-america-57594114.

167. https://www.elobservador.com.uy/nota/
nicaragua-una-democracia-con-practicamente-un-solo-partido-2016620500.

168. .https://www.ohchr.org/EN/NewsEvents/Pages/DisplayNews.
aspx?NewsID=22980&LangID=E.

169. https://www.nbcnews.com/news/latino/
honduras-tense-time-elections-put-democracy-through-test-n827426.

170. https://www.hrw.org/world-report/2018/country-chapters/honduras.

171. https://www.americamagazine.org/politics-society/2018/02/13/
crisis-legitimacy-continues-honduras.

172. https://www.ohchr.org/en/hrbodies/hrc/coidprk/pages/
commissioninquiryonhrindprk.aspx.

173. https://www.hrw.org/world-report/2020/country-chapters/
north-korea#392b43.

174. https://www.libertyinnorthkorea.org/learn-nk-challenges?utm_
medium=cpc&utm_source=google&utm_campaign=zOldR
ightsInNorthKorea&gclid=EAIaIQobChMI0tO_3NXx8gI
Vjt_tCh3f0ArtEAAYASAAEgKEd_D_BwE.

175. https://www.amnesty.org.uk/un-report-exposes-north-korea-
human-rights-abuses?utm_source=google&utm_medium=grant&utm_
campaign=BRD_AWA_GEN_dynamic-search-ads&utm_content=).

176. https://www.hrw.org/news/2016/11/26/
cuba-fidel-castros-record-repression.

177. Unless otherwise noted, all Scripture quoted in this chapter is from the
New American Standard Bible.

178. https://christinprophecy.org/articles/what-america-desperately-needs/.

179. "America the Beautiful," Katherine Lee Bates.

180. https://www.reuters.com/article/us-missionary-massachusetts/
in-200-year-tradition-most-christian-missionaries-are-american-
idUSTRE81J0ZD20120220.

181. https://balfourproject.org/bp/wp-content/uploads/2016/12/extract.pdf.

182. https://nsarchive2.gwu.edu/NSAEBB/NSAEBB98/#doc18.

183. https://www.timesofisrael.com/
golda-meir-my-heart-was-drawn-to-a-preemptive-strike-but-i-was-scared/.

184. https://www.airforcemag.com/article/1298nickel/.

185. https://www.wired.com/2014/11/countdown-to-zero-day-stuxnet/.

186. https://avalon.law.yale.edu/20th_century/plocov.asp and https://www.
ajc.org/translatehate/From-the-River-to-the-Sea.

187. https://www.foi.org/2016/05/19/
palestinians-never-miss-an-opportunity-to-miss-an-opportunity/.

188. Joel 3:2.

189. William Koenig, *Eye to Eye: Facing the Consequences of Dividing Israel*
(Christian Publications), 2017.

190. https://www.washingtonpost.com/politics/biden-israel-
relations/2021/04/17/5d97dd58-9d31-11eb-b7a8-014b14aeb9e4_story.html.

191. Zechariah 14:2 and Joel 3:2.

192. https://christinprophecy.org/articles/the-decay-of-society/.

193. Michael Oren, *Power, Faith, and Fantasy* (New York, NY, Norton), p.
476; cited by Bill Koenig in *Revealed: Obama's Legacy* (Christian Publications),
2016, pp. 65–66.

194. Jeremiah 30:12 and Micah 1:9. Bibliography also includes: John
McTernan and Bill Koenig, *Israel The Blessing or the Curse* (Hearthstone
Publishers), 2001.

195. Unless otherwise noted, all Scripture quoted in this chapter is from the King James Version.

196. Lance D. Johnson, "Israel Now Has More COVID Infections Per Capita Than Any Country in the World, Even as "Booster Shots" Are Being Widely Administered There," CitizenFreePress, September 2, 2021).

197. Peter Koening, "The Deep State," The Global Reset—Unplugged. July 24, 2020, https://www.globalresearch.ca/global-reset-unplugged/5716178).

198. Ibid.